Charles Henry Pearson

National Life And Character

A Forecast

Charles Henry Pearson

National Life And Character
A Forecast

ISBN/EAN: 9783744724388

Printed in Europe, USA, Canada, Australia, Japan

Cover: Foto ©Thomas Meinert / pixelio.de

More available books at **www.hansebooks.com**

NATIONAL LIFE AND CHARACTER

A FORECAST

BY

CHARLES H. PEARSON

HON. LL.D. ST. ANDREWS, LATE FELLOW OF ORIEL COLLEGE, OXFORD
AND SOMETIME MINISTER OF EDUCATION IN VICTORIA
AUTHOR OF 'A HISTORY OF ENGLAND IN THE EARLY AND MIDDLE AGES'; AND OF
'HISTORICAL MAPS OF ENGLAND'

'Dir wird gewiss einmal bei deiner Gottähnlichkeit bange'

London
MACMILLAN AND CO.
AND NEW YORK
1893

All rights reserved

CONTENTS

	PAGE
INTRODUCTION	1

CHAPTER I
THE UNCHANGEABLE LIMITS OF THE HIGHER RACES   29

CHAPTER II
THE STATIONARY ORDER IN SOCIETY   86

CHAPTER III
SOME DANGERS OF POLITICAL DEVELOPMENT   134

CHAPTER IV
SOME ADVANTAGES OF AN ENHANCED NATIONAL FEELING   180

CHAPTER V
THE DECLINE OF THE FAMILY   227

CHAPTER VI
THE DECAY OF CHARACTER   259

APPENDIX A   345
APPENDIX B   347
INDEX   349

NATIONAL LIFE AND CHARACTER

INTRODUCTION

The greatest statesmen have constantly failed to predict the immediate future.—Yet there have been many successful prophecies of distant and great events.—In other words, we are fairly successful in ascertaining a general law of progress, but cannot define exactly how or when it will be worked out.—The statesman, moreover, prefers dealing with the immediate future, which he can influence, to taking precautions against great changes, which are most likely inevitable.— For instance, the transportation of an inferior race, like the negroes of the United States, to a country where they would be harmless, is too vast, and of too uncertain benefit, to be readily attempted.— Again, the tendency to increase the powers of the State, and invite its interposition, is so strong that it would be difficult to check it.— Still, we may reduce the dimensions of a danger, which we clearly see, though we cannot avert it.—This book was first suggested by the observation, that America was filling up.—Later study has added the conviction, that the higher races can only live in the Temperate Zone.—If, however, emigration, which is the rough substitute for the organisation of labour, becomes impossible, the tendency to State Socialism, which is already strongly marked in certain British colonies, will become more and more powerful.—Moreover, the tendency to entrust the State with wider functions has long been adopted in Continental policy, and is being acclimatised in England. —This inquiry does not assume that State Socialism will be pushed to its furthest development, but only that some of its simplest applications will become law.—Kings may easily put themselves at the head of a movement for State Socialism, but personal rank and transmitted wealth are likely to be viewed with jealousy in the new order.—The change from one form of political life to another is not likely to be so momentous as the effects of the general change on character.—The world may gain something to balance what it loses, even in the direction of individualism; but (present conditions of growth continuing) it cannot gain much.—Perhaps, the best it can hope will be a general low level of content, and an exaltation of the patriotic sentiment.

EVER since men have committed their thoughts to record, it has been a common-place, exulted in or deplored, according to the temperament of the moralist, that it is impossible to predict the future. History abounds in memorable instances of the rash forecasts made by men, whose genius and experience entitled their opinions to the highest respect. Lord Shelburne was one of the ablest of English statesmen; and he predicted that, whenever the independence of America should be granted, "the sun of England would set, and her glories be eclipsed for ever."[1] Lord Shelburne was fated to be the instrument of negotiating the peace by which American independence was recognised; and he lived till the year when the battle of Trafalgar established England in the position of the only maritime power. Burke, in the language of his greatest eulogist, "had in the highest degree that noble faculty, whereby man is able to live in the past and in the future, in the distant and in the unreal."[2] He was ripe in years and experience of men when the French Revolution broke out, and his counsels contributed largely to the part which England took in opposing the French Republic. Yet Burke so entirely misconceived the nature of the changes that were passing under his very eyes, that in 1793 he was most concerned, lest France should be partitioned, like Poland, between a confederacy of hos-

---

[1] Mahon's *History of England*, vol. vii. p. 204. Compare "Fox on the King's Speech," December 5, 1782. Lord George Germain used very similar language in the debate of December 12, 1781.—Wraxall's *Historical Memoirs*, vol. iii. p. 289.

[2] Macaulay's "Essay on Warren Hastings," pp. 642, 643.

tile powers.[1] Burke's distinguished contemporary, Fox, parted from him on the question, how the conduct of France ought to be judged; and where Burke was absolutely wrong, it might be supposed that Fox would be at least relatively right. He told Parliament in 1803, that he had opposed war with France, because of its tendency "to effect the total destruction of the influence of this country on the Continent."[2] In the day of her greatest humiliation, France was never in danger of being partitioned; and the longer the war lasted, the greater was the increase of English influence on the Continent. The most eminent of the Parliamentary generation that succeeded to Burke and Fox, Mr. Canning, was fascinated by the prospects of the South American colonies, anticipated that they would grow up as the United States had grown, and being challenged for his support of them, declared that he had "called a new world into existence to redress the balance of the old"[3] (1826). We who live two generations later, are painfully aware that the South American "new world" has produced little but civil wars, national bankruptcies, paper constitutions, and examples of declining civilisation. The Duke of Wellington was deservedly trusted by a large portion of his countrymen for his sound common-sense in matters political; and his reputation was not confined to England. He told a friend in 1832 that "few people will be sanguine enough to imagine that we shall ever again

---

[1] "Remarks on the Policy of the Allies."—Burke's *Works*, vol. iii. p. 447. Burke had said in the House, as early as February 9, 1790, that he considered France as "not politically existing," and as "expunged out of the system of Europe."

[2] Fox's "Speech on the Mediation of Russia," May 27, 1803.

[3] Canning's "Speech on the Connection of England and Portugal," December 12, 1826.

be as prosperous as we have been."[1] Whether we measure prosperity by wealth, by empire, or by general content, it can scarcely be doubted that the England of 1892 may challenge comparison with the country, as it was at any time, which the Duke of Wellington is likely to have had in his mind. Thirty years ago, a great quarrel broke out between the Northern and Southern States of the American Union. Sir G. Cornewall Lewis, whose sympathies did not mislead him, for they were with the North, declared in 1861 that "their true policy was to negotiate with the South, and recognise the Secession"; and Mr. Gladstone in 1863 said, that the Southern President had made an army, had made a navy, and, more than that, had made a nation.[2] We now know, that the North was certain from the first to win, if it was only true to itself; and that though Mr. Davis created an army, he was powerless to do more. These mistaken forecasts by eminent statesmen were habitually in accord with public opinion; and the general estimate of what is about to happen is as likely as not to be curiously unwise. The English Press, with very few exceptions, was as wrong in its judgment of the American war as Mr. Gladstone; and English society for ten or twelve years at least believed that Louis Napoleon had founded a dynasty. Even when the war of 1870 broke out, though a few military experts were alive to the efficiency of the Prussian organisation, the general opinion was that France would win in the early part of the campaign; and every map of the seat of war, published in London, was a map of the Rhine Provinces, and of North

[1] Raikes's *Journal*, vol. i. p. 68.
[2] Sir G. Cornewall Lewis's *Letters*, p. 395. M'Carthy's *History of Our Own Times*, vol. ii. pp. 138, 139.

Germany. Every map was accordingly useless after a few days.

It would not, however, be difficult to produce instances where remote and generally unexpected changes have been prophesied with considerable accuracy. As early as 1748, "reasoning men in New York foresaw and announced that the conquest of Canada, by relieving the Northern colonies from danger, would hasten their emancipation." "We have caught them at last," said Choiseul, when it was definitely agreed that Canada should be surrendered (1763); and in fact little more than twenty years elapsed before the English flag ceased to wave over the States England had colonised.[1] Lord Chesterfield, as early as 1753, declared that "all the symptoms which I have ever met with in history, previous to great changes and revolutions in governments, now exist and daily increase in France."[2] "We are approaching the state of crisis, and the age of revolution," wrote Rousseau in 1762. "I think it impossible that the great monarchies of Europe have still long to last; all have had their moment of splendour, and every state which achieves this is ready to wane."[3] Goldsmith in the same year declared that "the French are imperceptibly vindicating themselves into freedom"; and prophesied that the country would gain its liberties,

---

[1] Bancroft's *History of the United States*, vol. iv. pp. 460, 461. "The necessary result of such measures" (the annexation of Canada and Florida), "perfectly foreseen at the time, was pointed out by Dr. Tucker, Dean of Gloucester, as well as by others."—Wraxall's *Historical Memoirs*, vol. ii. p. 78.

[2] Chesterfield's *Letters to his Son*.

[3] Emile, livre iii. p. 218. Some years later, Rousseau in his letters expressed the opinion, that the Seven Years' War would have broken up the French Monarchy, if it had not been for Choiseul.—Martin: *Histoire de France*, tome xvi. p. 98. M. Schérer has noticed several minor predictions of the Revolution.—*Littérature Contemporaine*, p. 346.

"if they have but three weak monarchs more successively on the throne." It needed, as we now know, a good deal less than the "three weak monarchs." Goldsmith, who seems instinctively to have apprehended the conditions of change in Europe, predicted also with perfect accuracy that Sweden was hastening on to despotism; that the German Empire was on the eve of dissolution; and that Holland was only awaiting the advent of a foreign conqueror.[1] The first of these prophecies was fulfilled in ten years; the second in 1806; and the third in 1794. The American statesman, Hamilton, of whom Talleyrand said that he had "divined Europe," seems to have prophesied the concentration of commerce in London and New York as the great emporia of the world with remarkable sagacity.[2] Arthur Young's predictions of the results that France would derive from the Revolution—temporary distress from its violence, and permanent well-being from its reforms—were as wise as Burke's were unfortunate.[3] De Tocqueville foretold, thirty years before the event, that the Southern States were the one part of the American Union in which disruption was likely to be attempted;[4] Sir G. Cornewall Lewis recognised in 1856 that the outrage on Mr. Sumner was the first blow in a civil war;[5] and Victor Hugo appreciated the importance of John Brown's execution by comparing it

---

[1] Goldsmith's *Citizen of the World*, Letter 55.

[2] Talleyrand's *Memoirs*, vol. i. p. 185. Hamilton predicted that London would absorb Amsterdam, that Cadiz would be supplanted by an American port, and that Marseilles would lose the trade of the Levant.—Ticknor's *Memoirs*, vol. i. p. 16.

[3] "The advantages derived to the nation are of the very first importance. On the other hand, the extensive and unnecessary ruin—all these are great deductions from public felicity."—Arthur Young *On the Revolution in France*, pp. 343, 344.

[4] *Democracy in America*, chap. xviii. p. 434.

[5] *Letters of Sir G. C. Lewis*, p. 315.

to the Crucifixion.¹ Heine, the most French in feeling of Germans, predicted that if France came to war with an united German people, she would be overborne.²

It will be observed that the most conspicuous instances of strikingly false prophecies are taken from the utterances of statesmen of the highest rank; while those predictions that have been verified belong as often as not to publicists, or to statesmen, like De Tocqueville, whose philosophy to some extent disqualified them for active politics. The reason, however, is probably not to be sought in any special fitness of abstract politicians for making forecasts of the future; but in the fact that statesmen are constantly tempted to make predictions of immediate interest, whereas the power of divination among men seems rather to concern itself with general laws. Accordingly, the same man has often been markedly right in his speculations about the distant future, and curiously wrong in predicting the possibilities of the next few years. Napoleon's alleged prophecy, that all Europe would end by being Republican or Cossack, seems more probable now than when it was first given to the world;³ but his expectation that

---

[1] In a drawing, which was engraved, and sold in London at the time; and which represented John Brown on the Cross.

[2] "You" (the French) "have more to fear from liberated" (*i.e.* united) "Germany, than from the whole Holy Alliance, together with all the Croats and Cossacks.—Heine, *Zur Geschichte der Religion und Philosophie in Deutschland*, S. 269.

[3] The part of the prophecy that relates to Russia seems the best proved. "You are in the flower of your age, and may expect to live thirty-five years longer. I think you will see, that the Russians will either invade and take India; or enter Europe with 400,000 Cossacks, and 200,000 real Russians."—O'Meara's *Napoleon at St. Helena*, vol. i. p. 104. "The Continent is now in the most perilous situation, being continually exposed to the risk of being overrun by Cossacks and Tartars."—*Life, Exile, and Conversations of the Emperor Napoleon*, by Count de Las-Cases, part vi. p. 2.

Wellington would make himself despotic in England, because he was too great to remain a private person, failed because it was founded on French analogies, and on supposed conditions that were not true of either Wellington or his nation. De Tocqueville's general law, that "among European governments of our time the power of governments is increasing, although the persons who govern are less stable," is receiving additional illustration every year; but De Tocqueville's "unquestionable statement," that, if any portion of the American Union seriously desired to separate itself from the other States, these would not be able, nor indeed would they attempt to prevent it, was absolutely disproved on countless battlefields within a generation.[1] Beyond this it may be observed, that any attempt to fix the date at which a prophecy will be fulfilled is especially hazardous. The break-up of the Turkish Empire has been foretold for centuries. From Peter the Great downwards, every sovereign of Russia has speculated upon it; and several of these have arranged treaties of partition with other sovereigns equally convinced. Time after time these combinations have been foiled, or only partially successful; and though no one seriously doubts that the term of Turkish rule in Europe is rapidly approaching its completion, few would venture to declare when the result will be brought about. The high courage of the race, the interests of the Western Powers, and a general aversion to great change are retarding causes, which constantly prove to be stronger than was anticipated.

Leaving out of sight the fact, that certain statesmen of great sagacity are able to calculate on what will

---

[1] De Tocqueville's *Democracy in America*, book iv. chap. vi. and book i. chap. xviii. p. 420.

happen within a few hours or days,[1] and are trusted
and valued accordingly, it seems justifiable to say that
in a certain broad and vague way the tendency of the
times may be and constantly is appreciated, so that we
are landed in the apparent paradox of knowing better
what is remote than what is so near that it may seem
to be within every one's ken. Accordingly political
prophecies are for the most part little regarded. The
statesman of a modern parliament is not working for
results fifty years hence, but for the day's need; and
would be apt to distrust himself if he attempted anything more. Perhaps there are cases when we see that
a more calculating policy would have been the wiser.
If England had granted Catholic Emancipation fifty
years before she did; if the American Congress had
bought up and expatriated the slaves while they were
still a mere handful; if France had followed Talleyrand's policy, and confined herself to such acquisitions
as awakened no violent resentments;[2] if Russian administrations under Nicholas I. had been determinately
liberal, instead of absolutist, each particular country
would have gained, and the civilised world would have
been the better for rancours and miseries averted. It
is idle, however, to discuss what might have been; and
almost equally so to discuss what might be under conditions never likely to be realised. The distant future
of a country is so unimportant by the side of its immediate needs to the men in possession, that even if
they were reasonably certain that a particular evil

[1] For an instance of Talleyrand's sagacity in this line see his
directions to the Duke of Orleans, which placed that prince on the
throne.—Bulwer's *Historic Characters*, pp. 221, 222.

[2] *Memoirs of Talleyrand*, vol. ii. part vii. pp. 97-100. Madame de
Rémusat in her *Memoirs*, vol. ii. p. 399, quotes Talleyrand as saying:
"To keep the Czar shut up at home by creating the natural barrier
which Poland offers, ought to have been the Emperor's design."

ought to be guarded against at an immediate sacrifice, they would rarely be possessed of the moral force required for the effort. As a matter of fact, however, only a few persons can feel reasonably certain as to the future, because only a few busy themselves with distant speculations. Among these many will perhaps believe that the manifest destiny of the human race cannot be mitigated — much less averted — by any sacrifice or statesmanship.

One or two simple instances will explain why men should be indisposed to work for a distant object. The increase of the coloured population in the Southern States of the American Union has for some time past been the cause of very great alarm. It seems as if a portion of that magnificent country was destined to be handed over to a race who are incapable of being citizens in the highest sense of the word. The most reasonable proposal yet made for meeting this particular danger has been to remove the blacks in a body, and plant them again in Central Africa. To carry out this proposal, however, in an equitable and humane way, would mean an expenditure of many hundred millions; a sum so vast that only the United States could compass it; and that even the United States might well demur to the cost. It is easy to suppose, however, that a body of Southern statesmen, keenly interested in this particular subject, might sketch the outlines of a feasible plan, and force it upon the attention of the community. Is it not also reasonable to assume that they would be met with very strong opposition? The Northern and Western States have only a remote interest in clearing the country of the negro. Some persons believe that the negro is a valuable element in the community, and others that he is at least indispensable for certain kinds of labour. The results of the last census would be appealed to, to show that the coloured race is not increasing at any disproportionate rate; and it would be argued, that in proportion as he was civilised, would his increase be slower still. The impossibility of transporting 8,000,000 of human beings across the Atlantic, and establishing them in new homes, would be pleaded. The probabilities are that a scheme for doing effectually, what it is now almost too late to do at all, would be debated, and voted down into the establishment of a new Liberia; and would have no more noticeable effect than to make the fortunes of a few contractors.

Again, let us assume a statesman to be convinced that the present tendency to an increase of State action is perilous to individual liberty, and to the development of character. What power would such a man have of giving effect to his views in Europe or in Australia? The State has come in almost everywhere to protect the masses against employers and landlords, or to organise the forces of the community for general purposes. State Education was first systematised on something like its present lines in Prussia, because Prussia, being relatively a weak power, saw the importance of making every citizen as efficient as possible. England and France, Austria and Italy have followed in the steps of Prussia, because they dared not do otherwise. Meanwhile, costless education has recommended itself as a boon to parents; and workmen look favourably upon the school attendance that diminishes the competition of child-labour. A statesman who should try to revert to the old order, because he considered the uniform routine of our State Schools destructive of originality, would soon find that he had to contend with very powerful interests. So, again, with State limitations to labour. Whether the theory of unlimited competition be true of ancient times or not, it is certain that the influence of Adam Smith and the circumstances of their time determined the wealthy classes of England for three generations to hold as an undoubted article of faith, that the law ought not to interpose between employer and man. From the day the first Reform Bill was passed, this theory was doomed in England. Philanthropists first interfered to protect women and children; after a time the Trades Unions secured the legal recognition of their activity; and at present it is only a question, how far labour can be regulated by law, and how far it is best to leave the task of restraining it to powerful associations. It is easy to see that we are tending to a state of things we did not altogether anticipate, and to some results that are not absolutely desirable. It is difficult to see that we could retrace a single step if we went back sixty years. Most of the liberal changes of the century have been nothing more than acts of justice; but almost all have been unavoidable. Religious tolerance; the mitigation of the penal laws; the recognition of the labourer's right to associate; the diffusion of education; the extension of the suffrage, were measures eminently defensible in themselves. To have withheld education would have been to weaken the country in the scale of nations; to have denied the other reforms would have been to provoke revolution.

If we assume, then, that there is a limited power of forecasting the general trend of human progress, it does not follow that this power can be of any real use in influencing events. The English coal-measures will be exhausted, whether we foresee it or not, and no generation will stay its hand from using them in order to cheapen fires for the next. Great cities will continue to grow, if population goes on increasing, though all the statesmanship in the world should be in favour of spreading population. Whether a skiff borne along the rapids of the St. Lawrence is wisely or badly steered makes the difference of life or death to its occupants, but does not affect its destination. It must descend the stream. The object of this book is to indicate in a very general way the direction towards which we are drifting in political and social life. It is not assumed, that any human sagacity can avert the fatality of our acts for centuries past, or of our characters, as we inherit or have fashioned them. If it be true, for instance, as these pages attempt to show, that the lower races are increasing upon the higher, and will some day confine them to a portion of the Temperate Zone, the result will have been the work of our own hands; and yet we cannot change our principles of action. We are bound, wherever we go, to establish peace and order; to make roads, and open up rivers to commerce; to familiarise other nations with a self-government which will one day make them independent of ourselves. We cannot even allow them to remain weak by destroying one another; and interest and humanity constrain us to interpose when there is a Tae-Ping rebellion in China, and when Africa is desolated by Arab slave-dealers. Nevertheless, if we cannot change manifest destiny, we may at least adapt ourselves to it, and make it endurable. We may circumscribe the growth of China, though we cannot altogether arrest it; and if we cannot hope that Europeans will ever people Africa, we may at least so work that European ideas shall one day be paramount from the Red Sea to the Atlantic. Again, it might conceivably be of use if European statesmen could understand that the wars which carry desolation into civilised countries, are allowing the lower races time to recruit their numbers and strength. Two centuries hence it may be matter of serious concern to the world if Russia has been displaced by China on the Amoor, if France has not been able to colonise North Africa, or if England is not holding India. For civilised men there can be only one fatherland, and whatever extends the influence of those races that have taken their faith from Palestine, their laws of beauty from Greece, and their civil law from Rome, ought to be matter of rejoicing to Russian, German, Anglo-Saxon, and Frenchman alike.

The first chapter of this book is practically an expansion, on a very large scale, of an article which I published in the *Contemporary Review* of 1868.[1] Travel in the United States had convinced me that that great country was filling up more rapidly than was supposed in England, and would cease within measurable time to offer any great inducements to a large immigration. I predicted that "the Americans will begin to be cramped for land by the time their population numbers 20,000,000 more"; that is, by the time it reached 60,000,000. I admitted that the arrest of immigration would be "very gradual," and I pointed out that some temporary relief might be given by the opening up of Manitoba, and by the development of Southern States like Texas, or by the purchase of new territory from Mexico. Substantially these calculations have been verified, though I was wrong in

---

[1] "On the Land Question in the United States."—*Contemporary Review*, November 1868.

several minor points. The States have not increased in population as rapidly as was expected: the Chinese, on whom I had calculated as possible settlers, have been deterred by public feeling from coming over in any number; and though the British immigrants are now relatively fewer than they were,[1] this falling off has been compensated by a great increase in the number of immigrants from countries with a lower standard of comfort; from Italy, Norway, Bohemia, and Russia. Beyond this there was a period of great prosperity in England between 1870 and 1879, when tens of thousands found employment who in any ordinary year would have gone across the Atlantic. On the whole, these influences appear to have balanced one another; and the result is, that while immigrants are still anxious to pour in, there is a disinclination to receive them; and the American Congress has passed two rather stringent Acts (1885 and 1891) to limit immigration to fit persons, and to forbid the wholesale bringing over of workmen by employers.[2] Moreover, the emigrants who now go over are attracted by high rates of labour rather than by cheap rates of land. The best part of the country has been taken up.

Twenty years' residence under the Southern Cross has forced me to consider a new side of this particular

[1] In the decade 1851 to 1860 the emigration from Great Britain to the States was 1,257,000 (Mulhall's *Statistics*). In the last decade it has been 1,462,000 (*Statesman's Year-Book*). The British population of the first period was twenty per cent smaller than that of the second; while the American population of the second period offered fifty per cent more chance of employment.

[2] "Already signs are not wanting to show, that stringent as are its provisions, and drastic as are its regulations" (the Act of 1891), "a certain section of American opinion is beginning to demand something more stringent and more drastic still."—Wilkins on "Immigration in the United States," *Nineteenth Century Review*, October 1891, p. 593. Bryce's comment must be remembered: "Such laws are of course difficult of enforcement."—*American Commonwealth*, vol. iii. p. 674.

question: whether the capacity of European races to form new homes for themselves is not narrowly limited by climate, and by the circumstances of prior population. Australia is an unexampled instance of a great continent that has been left for the first civilised people that found it to take and occupy. The natives have died out as we approached; there have been no complications with foreign powers; and the climate of the South is magnificent. Nevertheless, it is still a question whether the white race can ever be so acclimatised as to live and labour in the Northern parts; and it seems certain that neither Englishman nor German can ever colonise New Guinea. The fear of Chinese immigration which the Australian democracy cherishes, and which Englishmen at home find it hard to understand, is, in fact, the instinct of self-preservation, quickened by experience. We know that coloured and white labour cannot exist side by side; we are well aware that China can swamp us with a single year's surplus of population; and we know that if national existence is sacrificed to the working of a few mines and sugar plantations, it is not the Englishman in Australia alone, but the whole civilised world, that will be the losers. Transform the Northern half of our continent into a Natal with thirteen out of fourteen belonging to an inferior race, and the Southern half will speedily approximate to the condition of a Cape Colony, where the whites are indeed a masterful minority, but still only as one in four. We are guarding the last part of the world, in which the higher races can live and increase freely, for the higher civilisation. We are denying the yellow race nothing but what it can find in the home of its birth, or in countries like the Indian Archipelago, where the white man can never live except as an exotic.

If, however, the white race is precluded by natural laws from colonising on a large scale anywhere except in the Temperate Zone, it seems certain that the condition of old countries will be powerfully modified. The eager and impetuous element that has hitherto found an outlet in new communities, will be pent up in the overpeopled countries of Europe. Either the growth of population will be arrested, as in France, or the State will have to concern itself, much more actively than English economists will like, with the organisation of labour. Now the history of the English colonies in Australia and New Zealand is particularly instructive, because it shows what the English race naturally attempts when it is freed from the limitations of English tradition. The settlers of Victoria, and to a great extent of the other colonies, have been men who carried with them the English theory of government: to circumscribe the action of the State as much as possible; to free commerce and production from all legal restrictions; and to leave every man to shift for himself, with the faintest possible regard for those who fell by the way. Often against their own will the colonists have ended by a system of State centralisation that rivals whatever is attempted in the most bureaucratic countries of the Continent. The State employees are an important element of the population; the State builds railways, founds and maintains schools, tries to regulate the wages and hours of labour, protects native industry, settles the population on the land, and is beginning to organise systems of State insurance.[1] Planted in Africa, the Englishman so adapts himself

[1] It will be understood, that these statements are not equally applicable to every colony. New South Wales is only beginning to protect native industry, and New Zealand is the only colony that has experimented with State insurance.

to the circumstances of the real population, the indigenous negro, that the black man finds his sufficient paradise under the British flag, in Natal or at the Cape, rather than in Liberia. Planted in Australia, the Englishman, to whom St. Simon and Fourier are names of derision, if they are even names, is rapidly creating a State Socialism, which succeeds because it is all-embracing and able to compel obedience, and which surpasses its continental State models because it has been developed by the community for their own needs, and not by State departments for administrative purposes. Of course, it does not follow that even a race so highly gifted with political intelligence as the British is necessarily right in what it builds up. It may be that the brain and hand are more feeble than they were in the old time. Nevertheless, it is surely safe to say, that political experiments which half a dozen self-governing British communities are instinctively adopting, deserve attention as an indication of what we may expect in the future.

It may seem rash to anticipate that the State everywhere will be entrusted with larger and more intricate functions because there is a tendency in this direction in some of the more important British dependencies. Let it be remembered, however, that every continental State—even those of Germanic origin—has worked for centuries upon these lines, and that in England itself the first entrenchments of the *laissez-faire* system have been forced. The State in England has bought telegraphs, and reserved the right to monopolise telephones; lends money for draining purposes, and has lent it for the construction of roads; regulates the hours of labour in factories; forbids women and children to work under certain conditions; and assists skilled workmen to obtain a mastery of their trade.[1] There is every indication that the so-called "labour party" will be stronger in future parliaments than it is (1891), and will force the State more and more into what is known as the organisation of industry. Nothing has been assumed as possible or probable in this book except what is already done in some civilised and prosperous part of the world, or what is being worked up to by some powerful party. The so-called nationalisation of land, though not an actual fact, is being approached in a great many countries. Victoria has reserved a great part of its land from sale, in order to try the experiment of State landlordism. New Zealand is considering the policy of buying back the land it has alienated; and meanwhile is proposing to tax large properties on a graduated scale that may incline owners to break them up. South Australia is discussing the same problem. The proposals in England to buy out the Irish landlords, and sell again to a small yeomanry, are steps in the direction of land nationalisation, though the object is to create new freeholds. For a time, at least, the State will be a landlord on a large scale, and in many cases may end by having the land left on its hands. It is not perhaps probable that any uniform system of landownership will prevail over all the world, however much institutions may tend to become iden-

---

[1] Mr. Rae's comment on this matter is instructive: "Professor Sidgwick declares the Irish and Scotch Land Acts, which provide for the judicial determination of a fair rent, to be the most distinctively socialistic measures which the English legislature has yet passed; but in reality these Land Acts are not a bit more socialistic than the laws which fix a fair price for railway rates and fares," etc.—Rae's *Contemporary Socialism*, p. 428. Compare Bryce's statement: "The new democracies of America are just as eager for State interference as the democracy of England," etc.—*The American Commonwealth*, vol. iii. p. 272.

tical. France, for instance, may consider that she gets all the good she desires from her system of compulsory subdivision, and may shrink from the costly and complicated operation of buying back small parcels of land, which it would be very difficult to administer. Even in English-speaking countries, the preference for indefeasible property, which seems innate in human nature, has acquired such strength by use that many communities may desire not to go counter to it. In that case they may attain very nearly the same results as are aimed at in State landlordism by a progressive land-tax, which will make it impossible to build up big estates, and by taxing unimproved land as heavily as improved. The essential of State Socialism in these matters is not so much that the State should keep the title-deeds of the land, as that no land should be monopolised by private persons for speculative purposes, or to give political power, or as a mere instrument of luxury.

As it has been an object in this inquiry to consider only what it is possible to achieve by a slight extension of existing machinery, the question whether the State can ever control distribution by becoming the owner of large stores, or production by taking agriculture or mining or manufactures into its own hands, has not been discussed. The assumption has been that certain departments of labour will for a long time at least be left open to private enterprise. It is proper to notice, however, that there are numerous instances of mines being worked by the State, and that where a mine can be worked without loss, or at the smallest possible, but would not return a profit sufficient to reward a speculator, it would seem eminently in accordance with the principles of State Socialism that Government should develop it. So, again, where the mineral produced is one necessary, so to speak, to national existence, like the coal of England or the salt of Wieliczka. Tobacco is a State monopoly in some parts of Europe, and alcoholic drinks in others. In Java and Egypt the State has at times been a considerable employer of agricultural labour, and still farms land of its own on a reduced scale. It is therefore possible to conceive a community which, following only actual precedents, should be the sole employer and the sole proprietor within its own boundaries. It has seemed, however, unwise and unnecessary to suppose that this extreme result will be attained generally, or even often: unwise, because it is very rare to see a theory of any kind logically carried out; and unnecessary, because if twenty per cent of any given population were in the State service, their hours of work and their wages would practically be the standard of the whole community. In Victoria at this time something like eight per cent of the adult male population is in Government employ.[1] Assume the Government to run steamers, as it has often been urged to do, to buy up the various gas-works, to start works, such as it must some day have for the manufacture of ordnance, to take irrigation into its own hands, and to supply medical aid through salaried employees, and it is easy to see how the eight per cent might swell to twenty per cent. Neither does it much matter for

[1] Mr. Hayter in his *Victorian Year-Book* for 1890 reckons the adult males at about 320,000 between the ages of 18 and 60. The persons regularly employed by the Government were at the same time 24,816, and those temporarily employed during 1889 numbered 5799. If we deduct 2200 for female teachers, 1000 for temporary clerical employees, who are only engaged for short periods, and 450 for female post-office clerks and telegraph operators, the residue will pretty nearly represent eight per cent. This number must, however, be regarded as an extreme estimate, only true of a prosperous year.

practical purposes whether the State in all cases undertakes work of this kind itself, or leaves it to be performed by some other public body, amenable to the popular vote. The State in Victoria, for instance, has handed over some important functions, occupying hundreds of employees, to the Melbourne Harbour Trust; but that body is almost as directly under the control of Parliament as any Government department. Again, it is quite conceivable that the conduct of gas-works, trams, and water-works may often be left to municipalities; but these in a democracy are controlled by the industrial vote. The working men of Victoria attach great importance—and I believe rightly so—to the comparatively high standard of comfort which the State maintains for all its servants. It is felt that, sooner or later, the ideal recognised by the State will be the measure for all; partly because otherwise the best men will all seek employment under the State, and partly because there will be an invincible reluctance to accept less than the largest employer gives. If this is to some extent the case already, the result is bound to be far greater when the State's sphere of action is doubled or trebled.

It used to be made a reproach to the English Liberals that they were always agitating for reforms connected with the machinery of government—manhood suffrage, the ballot, or the abolition of the House of Peers—and never appeared to have any use for the power they had already wrested from the aristocracy. A review of what has been done during the last sixty years will perhaps show that this accusation is not borne out by facts. The reforms made have been so great as practically to remodel English society. The penal code has been changed from one of great barbarity into one that is reasonable and humane;[1] the game laws have been made fairly tolerable; the poor-law system has been remodelled with great intelligence, though not very sympathetically; popular education has been introduced; the landlord's protective duty on food has been abolished; trades unionism has been legalised; nonconformity has been freed from its shackles; and Parliament has familiarised itself more and more with the idea of interposing between employer and employed, between landlord and tenant. If it should appear that the complement of these changes—the complete organisation of labour, and State insurance against want—can only be attained under a democratic form of government, then we may, I think, expect a republic to be established everywhere. On the other hand, it seems more than conceivable that wise sovereigns, or wise aristocracies, if they believe these changes to be inevitable, and on the whole good, will determine to guide the popular movement instead of opposing it. Wherever this is done, experience indicates that the working classes will look first to their real wants, and will acquiesce in any form of government that satisfies these. Therefore it has not appeared necessary for the purposes of this argument to consider whether thrones will be overturned or aristocracies abolished. The chances perhaps are that the world will adopt the republican form of polity more and

[1] The recent publication of Sir Robert Peel's early *Letters* by Mr. Charles Parker shows that in 1828 he was preparing to resign office if George IV. refused to sign the death-warrant of a young man who had been guilty of forgery under circumstances of peculiar temptation (Peel's *Letters*, p. 317). Indeed, so strong had the old law been, that Blackstone boasts: "There is hardly a case possible to be conceived, wherein forgery . . . is not made a capital crime."—*Commentaries*, book iv. chap. xvii. The penalty of death for forgery was, however, abolished in 1832; that is, as soon as the House of Commons was converted to the necessity of reform; and in 1833 one of the first acts of the reformed Parliament was to appoint a Commission for revising the whole Criminal Code.

more, because there are many instructive examples that it is not easy to replace a dynasty that has once been dispossessed. On the other hand, if there should be a succession of such exceptionally able and patriotic sovereigns as several European countries have enjoyed during the last fifty years, and if these should identify themselves with popular movements, it is open to believe that kings may hold their own for centuries to come. None the less, there does seem to be a natural antagonism between aristocracies of privilege or wealth and an industrial society. It is difficult to conceive that a hereditary House of Lords will long be maintained in England; and though the millionaire may be a feature of all time, the example of the United States shows that he may be deprived of political power. Personal rank and transmitted wealth accordingly seem a little less likely to maintain themselves than the centralisation of State absolutism in one hereditary monarch. Even titles, however, will perhaps be modified and transformed rather than absolutely effaced. Nothing is more remarkable in human nature than its determination to retain old forms while it invests them with a new life. Christianity took its temples, its statues, its sacred days from Paganism; Protestantism mostly copied the old Church; and the most noticeable form of anti-Christian worship has been a servile parody of Catholicism. Humanity, as it were, outgrows its vestments; but it does not cast them off and go naked; it patches them and drapes them about itself in new folds.

What therefore we are most concerned with is not the limitation of the higher races of man to a small part of earth; not the evolution of a new form of society— an autocratic and all-pervading State, instead of a State that gave free scope to individual ascendency—but the question, what man himself will become under these changed conditions of political life, and under the influence of other changes that seem inevitable. If towns are to predominate over the country; if the State is largely to supplant the churches in the direction of life, and parents in the bringing up of the family; if the new conditions of intellectual work are unfavourable to originality; if, in a word, the man seems to dwindle as the union of men grows in strength and importance, the result cannot be without interest for those who are on the brink of this future. To some it will perhaps seem that the expectation of great changes for the better in the constitution of political society is unreasonably sanguine; and that the industrial classes, when they come to the full consciousness of their power in any part of the world, are certain to attempt impracticable experiments or violent changes which will throw the world back. It has been no part of this argument to consider such possible contingencies. Here and there no doubt blunders will be made, and ignorant tribunes of the people will try their hands again at some of the old failures: unlimited issues of State paper; violent confiscations; or the appointment of State officials generally by the ballot. We are bound, however, to assume that what is unreasonable will perish of itself, and that what is reasonable will by degrees prevail. Moreover, the experience of the last century ought to guard us against a repetition of the worst blunders of the past. On the whole, it is surely correct to say that the relations of rich and poor are incomparably more healthy now than they were a hundred years ago in all matters that are regulated by law. It would be grossly unfair to charge the excesses of the Reign of Terror in France upon the

French people; they were the work of a few fanatics, and of a great many recruits from the criminal classes. So far, however, as they were tacitly justified by the public at the time of their perpetration, it was because absolute power in the State and privilege in districts had been so intolerably abused that the people scarcely considered themselves secure unless the representatives of the old order were exterminated. At present the State is everywhere regarded as the protector from whom the people have most to hope. The popular impulse is not to set the action of government aside, but to awaken it to what is conceived of as a healthier activity; and this belief in the omnipotence of law is a great guarantee for order and peaceable change; though it may of course be that the man who cries to the State to help him, when he ought to help himself, will gradually suffer paralysis of strength and will.

The tendency of the age is to be hopeful, and it may be admitted that a great deal in the past history of the world encourages us not to despair of the future of humanity. The best types of any given high race are demonstrably stronger, taller, healthier than their ancestors two hundred or a thousand years ago; enjoy better laws and many more comforts; are more humane, better educated, and have a larger inheritance of transmitted thought. That the pariah class in our great cities is in the lowest abyss of misery may be conceded; and it is probable that the working class generally has now and again had glimpses of a better life than it enjoys; but the whole tendency of modern reforms is to improve the condition of the masses. The argument developed in these pages supposes that there will actually be change for the better. What is assumed also is that the gradual decay of faith, the diminished importance of family life, and the loss of original power, as genius is deprived of its noblest fields, will be serious offsets to the material development of life; and that even physical conditions will be worse, as cities grow upon the world, and as the field of adventure in unsettled regions is closed. There is room for cheerful prognostication in this direction also. Mr. Morris has conceived a charming vision of an England in which great cities shall have been exchanged for country homesteads with an occasional street, and in which brain work shall be gradually discarded for manual labour. To attain all these results, however, Mr. Morris is compelled to imagine a great upheaval of society; and his conclusions appear to indicate that two-thirds of the population must have perished or left the country, the other third remaining stationary. Such a dream of the future differs essentially from that of the following pages, which only professes to consider what is likely to happen if we go on for two hundred years more as we have gone on for the last three-quarters of a century.

To the writer of these pages, what really seems most hopeful in the outlook for the future is the prospect that violent upheavals of society will be less and less attempted as the State appears to be the best expression of the wishes of the majority; and that some falling off in the energy and acquisitiveness, which are fostered by individualism, will be compensated by the growth of what we may call patriotism, as each man identifies himself more and more with the needs and aspirations of his fellow-countrymen. That men generally should look up to the State to take the lead in industrial undertakings is probably undesirable, and is perhaps never likely to occur. Whatever administrations may do, they can hardly monopolise more than a small portion of the field of human enterprise. Meanwhile, it is surely in the interests of all that the poorest man in the country should feel that he owes inestimable blessings to the political order under which he lives: not only protection from foreign enemies, but equality before the law, the certainty of employment in bad times, education for his children, security for the purity of his household life, and a fair chance of rising out of the ranks if he possesses the requisite ability. If this ideal has not been absolutely attained in the civilised countries of the world, it is not because the best statesmen of all times have not been habitually working towards it, but because individualism has meant privilege—privilege for rank, for wealth, and for influence—and because the outworks of individualism have been guarded accordingly. More and more as we approach the stationary state—as there are no countries to receive immigrants; as war is more and more dreaded for its chances, or recoiled from for its barbarity; as commerce and invention are restricted because there are no new regions to open up—will the old outlets for discontent or unsatisfied ambition be closed. What are now the governing classes will have to arrange reasonable compromises, by which the condition of the poor is made endurable. It may be that there will be less enthusiasm in those days, because there will be less hope; but it may be assumed that there will be less misery, more resignation, and it may even be more content. Life in itself is an inexhaustible delight to all but a few; and the conditions of life will be more tolerable, though the sky above may be more gray.

CHAPTER I

THE UNCHANGEABLE LIMITS OF THE HIGHER RACES

There is a general belief that the higher races are bound to gain more and more upon the lower.—North America, the Argentine Confederation, and Australia furnish the grounds of this belief.—The races exterminated have not been industrial races.—The character of a race determines its vitality more than climate.—Chinamen, Hindoos, and negroes cannot be exterminated.—The Cape Colony is not predominantly white, though settled under the most favourable conditions.—Natal is already not a white man's colony, and is bound to pass more and more into the hands of the coloured race.—Much more are the parts of Africa north of Natal bound to remain negro. —Were the whole emigration of Europe turned into Africa, it could not build up a white people there. The negro would increase faster. —Practically, too, there will always be parts where the white man cannot live. Malaysia is uninhabitable by the white man, as a colonist, building up families.—Central Asia is likely to be peopled chiefly from China.—The Aryan race can only make small gains in Europe, and in the Temperate Zone districts of Asia, Africa, America, and Australasia.—China is a serious competitor for empire; even in Tonquin and Burmah.—Chinese colonisation of the Straits Settlements shows what the race is capable of.—The Chinese are bound to people, and probably to rule Borneo.—There is a possibility of Chinese expansion to the North and West.—It is conceivable that the Hindoo race may spread over Beloochistan and Southern Persia. —Great parts of Southern and Central America cannot be peopled by the white race.—The autochthonous races are gradually growing upon the descendants of the Spaniards, and will absorb them and possess the country.—These Indians are showing themselves capable of self-government.—If the Indians do not supersede men of European descent, negroes or Chinamen will.—Only the parts of America from which Indians have already been driven are fitted to be the homes of the white race.—Brazil will pass more and more into the hands of the negroes, as certain of the United States are believed to be passing.—The most fertile and populous parts of the earth are therefore the inalienable freehold of the inferior races, though the higher races may contribute, and be needed in the first instance, to organise and develop them.—The development of a race within the limits of a country—India or China—is no impediment to its expansion abroad.—Emigration abroad will often stimulate the growth of a population at home.—The increase of population in Europe has been retarded for eighteen centuries by misgovernment and internal wars.—The general law is that the lower race increases faster than the higher.—The English aristocracy is favoured by a great many circumstances that would seem calculated to promote increase.—Its families are constantly dying out.—The French and the negroes of the United States furnish characteristic instances of slow and rapid growth.—England is an apparent but not a real exception to the rule that a race with a high standard of comfort increases slowly.—The condition of the Jews in Russia has been one of inferiority, but not of intolerable hardship.—Having a strong motive to make money, and no temptation to spend it freely, they have increased so rapidly as to become a danger to the Empire.—The increased humanity of war is telling in favour of the weaker races.—So are sanitation, and the increased means of transport afforded by railways.—Therefore, when we are swamped in certain parts of the world by the black and yellow races, we shall know that it has been inevitable.

It seems to be generally assumed that the higher races of men, or those which are held to have attained the highest forms of civilisation, are everywhere triumphing over the lower. North America is almost occupied by men of European ancestry, and in South America the European element has received notable accessions in Brazil and the Argentine Republic. Australasia is British; Central Asia is being Russianised; and the Turk is being driven out of Europe, where his heritage is bound to fall to some race that has assimilated modern ideas better than the Ottoman. In Africa the North-west is passing under French influence, and has received a leaven of French or Spanish colonists. Egypt is practically part of Europe; South Africa is English or Dutch; and it seems scarcely questionable that England and Germany will divide Central Africa. We are perpetually assured that countries which till now were assumed to be unfitted for European colonists, will really allow them to multiply and prosper if they will only comply with such reasonable conditions as the climate exacts. Central and Southern America, the regions of the Congo, of the African Lakes, and of Matabele and Mashonaland, Northern Australia and Borneo, are among the parts which have been recommended for European colonisation at various times; and it is not uncommon to hear those who know India declare that the Hill districts offer great opportunities for European settlement. No one, of course, assumes that the Aryan race—to use a convenient term—can stamp out or starve out all their rivals on the face of the earth. It is self-evident that the Chinese, the Japanese, the Hindoos, if we may apply this general term to the various natives of India, and the African negro, are too numerous and sturdy to be extirpated. It is against the fashion of modern humanity to wish that they should suffer decrease or oppression. What is assumed is that the first three of these races will remain stationary within their present limits, while the negro will contribute an industrial population to the states which England and Germany will build up along the Congo or the Zambesi. The white man in these parts of the world is to be the planter, the mine-owner, the manufacturer, the merchant, and the leading employee under all these, contributing energy and capital to the new countries, while the negro is to be the field-hand, the common miner, and the factory operative. Here and there, in exceptional districts, the white man will predominate in numbers, but everywhere he will govern and direct in virtue of a higher intelligence and more resolute will.

If we ask on what these calculations are based, we shall probably be referred to the experience of the past in America and Australia. In Canada and the United States the red man is little more than a memory. The

Carib has practically disappeared from the West India Islands. In the Argentine Confederation the Indians are a powerless minority, and the number of European immigrants to that country and to South Brazil seems likely to increase year by year. In Australasia, and in the islands of the Pacific, where Europeans have settled, or where they trade much, the Maori, the Kanaka, and the Papuan are dying out. We cannot close our eyes to the fact that certain weak races—even when, like the Kanaka, they possess some very high qualities—seem to wither away at mere contact with the European. Modern legislation tries to protect them; missionaries endeavour to seclude them from fatal influences; but the good as well as the bad in civilisation tells mischievously for a time upon unaccustomed constitutions. The mere wearing of clothes, as savages do it without changing them, and the disuse of artificial tribal restrictions on the inter-marriages of relations, are believed, by some of those who know the Australian aboriginal best, to be almost as much responsible for his decay as the diseases of European origin that scourge immorality.

It will be noticed that these evanescent races—different as they are in many respects—have two features in common, that they have never been very powerful numerically, and that they have never been able to settle down in any steady way to industry. The Kanakas (among whom we may include the Maories) were of course limited by area. They could not do much in the small islands they peopled. The best of them, however, have conciliated the respect of Europeans rather as soldiers and politicians than by any aptitude they have displayed for regular work. Had Chinamen or Japanese descended upon New Zealand instead of the Maories, those islands would long ago have been covered with a population of several millions, such as no modern European power would have attempted to displace. We may say even more certainly of the Red Indians, that if they had chosen to learn agriculture from the first European settlers, they would soon have been numerous enough to bar all progress to the West. The Indians of Mexico, of Central America, and of Peru, who had attained to this level were not exterminated, though they were treated for generations with the most atrocious cruelty. At this moment pure or half-caste Indians predominate in all the Spanish colonies that lie to the north of Chili, and their predominance is becoming more marked every year. Without wishing to deny or depreciate the fine qualities of a race that has produced such men as Juarez and Mejia, and the heroes who fought at Humaita, we may surely say that the Indians whom Cortez and Pizarro conquered were not civilised up to the level of modern Hindoos or Chinamen, and had not the physical stamina of the negro race. All the more remarkable is it that they have survived and multiply.

How far climate has co-operated in circumscribing the spread of the European race in America seems difficult to determine. We can hardly suppose it is accidental that the proportion of pure whites should be smallest in the tropical parts of America, Guatemala and Nicaragua, and largest in temperate latitudes. At the same time, considering the great flexibility of the human constitution, and the fact that whites can and do labour in Texas, in Mexico, and in the districts of the Lower Plate, we may probably say, that the character of the population of America has been determined more by the varying adaptability of its primitive races for civilisation than by climatic conditions. Had the native Indians of Mexico and Peru been as untameable as the Araucanians were or the Apaches are, the white man could not have existed side by side with them. He must either have exterminated them or have been driven out. In fact, however, if the Indians whom Cortez or Pizarro found had been essentially warlike, they would not have been as numerous as they were, and the work of destroying them, tribe after tribe, would have been comparatively easy, as it has been easy for the people of the United States to make a clearance of Narraganset, Mohegan, Seneca, and Seminole Indians.

It is probably safe to say, that the Chinaman, the Hindoo, and the negro are in no danger of anything like the fate that overtook the aborigines of the New World at the hands of a foreign conqueror. A compact nation of 400,000,000 may be endangered by revolts like that of the Tae-Pings or that of the Mahommedans of Yunnan — for in both those cases the war waged was one of extermination—but has little to dread from a civilised power, except temporary humiliation or tribute. Now that massacres on a large scale are not sanctified by religion, there exists no reason why a conqueror—if we can suppose a foreign conqueror of China—should do more than levy taxes, or exact a levy of conscripts or of forced labourers. India left to itself might be rent for a time by the war of Mussulman and Hindoo, but India is too populous for any large part of its people to be exterminated; unless indeed wars were waged in the Chinese fashion. That either Russians or Frenchmen, or indeed any European race, could colonise any province accidentally left desolate seems on the face of it impossible.

The climate would be fatal in a generation, except in the hills; and that a remote province like Cashmere could be cleared of its present people, settled by Europeans, and kept free from the intrusion of native labour, seems the most fanciful of speculations. There remain therefore only Central Asia, Malaysia, and Africa as possible outlets not yet used for the surplus population of Europe, and of these Africa is naturally that which is especially attracting the attention of Englishmen at the present moment. It has been opened up very much by English enterprise; its resources prove to be vaster than was at one time supposed; and the climate of large tracts appears to be tolerable. We have arranged its partition with the most important of our neighbours; and the posts we hold along the Western Coast, in the Cape and Natal, and in Egypt, are so many points of vantage for our empire. It seems as if England for the moment was a little weary of India, and disposed to regard the Colonies as rather troublesome allies than dependencies, but was actively sanguine of possibilities in the Dark Continent.

We may put aside the Portuguese and French settlements of Mozambique, Angola, and Senegambia. No one of these has succeeded in attracting colonists; but the failure may be explained by climate or by an administration that aimed rather at commerce than at settlement. The case of the Cape and the sister colonies seems to be more in point. The Dutch occupation of the Cape dates from 1652, and the early colonists were to a great extent picked men; many of them French Huguenots. The natives with whom the settlers came in contact were Hottentots and Bushmen, weak races, of whom the Bushmen were not fitted to be slaves, while the Hottentots were not very valuable.

Practically the Bushmen were exterminated; and when the English conquered the colony in 1795 the Hottentots were only as 14,500 to 21,000 whites.[1] Nevertheless, the convenience of slave labour had been found to be so great that the coloured population of the colony altogether was roughly as two in three, and that proportion has been maintained ever since or increased, though slavery has been abolished, though thousands of British settlers have been poured into the country, and though the diamond-fields have attracted thousands of immigrants. As many as 30,000 Kaffirs are said to have taken refuge under British rule during the governorship of Sir George Grey alone.[2] Meanwhile it must be borne in mind, that the outlying parts of the Cape colony have always been very largely peopled by Dutch Boers, who have to some extent stemmed the influx of free coloured settlers by their constant wars with the natives, and by their disinclination to admit them except as slaves. The Cape therefore shows us European influences at their strongest in Africa; and their strongest is for the most masterful of European races to be a decided, though at present a governing minority. Still the influx of blacks at the Cape is not yet so great as to have made manual and unskilled labour discreditable to white men.

The case of Natal is more instructive for what may be expected in Africa generally. Natal was seized by the British in 1842, the Boers who had occupied it, and to whom it was valuable for its sea-board, being a mere handful of men among natives who accepted them for the moment as deliverers from the Zulus. Nevertheless, the number of black inhabitants at that

---

[1] Theale's *Compendium of South African History*, chap. xiv.
[2] Wilmot's *History of the Cape Colony*, p. 83.

time, though great in comparison with the Dutch, was so inconsiderable as to be only five to the square mile.[1] The new possession offered great advantages of soil and climate. A great deal of it is rich land, and it rises in plateaus from the coast, so that several varieties of temperature may be enjoyed. During the first years of settlement there was no danger from the Zulus, whose warriors had almost been exterminated in Dingan's wars. From time to time assisted immigrants were poured literally in thousands into the country. In 1878-79 the presence of a large British army made the fortunes of contractors and farmers. For years the diamond-fields and gold-diggings of the Orange Free State have reflected prosperity over Natal. Nevertheless, in 1891, nearly fifty years after its first settlement, Natal has only 36,000 Europeans out of 481,000 settlers, the remainder being chiefly Zulus, though partly Hindoos and Chinamen. The lower races have nearly doubled in proportion since 1863, when one-seventh of the population was European. The reasons of this are not far to seek. British rule means order and peace, industry and trade, and the enjoyment of property under fairly equal laws. To the African native the establishment of a colony like Natal is like throwing open the gates of paradise.[2] He streams in, offering his cheap though not very regular labour, and supplying all his own wants at the very smallest expenditure of toil. Where he multiplies, however, the British race begins to consider labour of all but the highest kinds

[1] "Before the Dutch occupied it, the blacks were only as one to six square miles."—Aylward's *Transvaal*, p. 5.
[2] Although the Dutch rule is far less tender to the natives than the British, the immigration of natives began from the establishment of government by the Dutch in 1839. "In their own expressive way of speaking, they could sleep without fear under the shield of the white man."—Theale's *South African History*, chap. xxxi.

dishonourable; and from the moment that a white population will not work in the fields, on the roads, in the mines, or in factories, its doom is practically sealed. It is limited to supplying employees, merchants, contractors, shopmen, and foremen to the community. Sooner or later the black race will be educated to a point at which it will demand and receive a share in these employments and in the government.[1] Whenever that happens, the white race will be either absorbed or disappear. The mass will gradually depart, but a few, who have lost the sense of superiority, will remain, intermarry, and be perpetuated in the persons of a few hundred, or it may be a few thousand, mulattoes and quadroons.

Now the fate of Natal is bound to be the fate of those parts of the African Continent which lie north of Natal and south of the desert of Sahara. It is quite conceivable that tracts will be discovered with rich gold-fields, like those of California and Australia, and with a climate allowing white men to labour. Tens of thousands of diggers may be attracted there, and may determine to keep the gold deposits to themselves, and to debar blacks or Chinamen from working them. Even in this case the blacks will still press into the country that they may enjoy the security of English rule, and will be field-hands, domestic servants, and generally drudges of every kind, reinforcing the original negro population, so as to keep it always superior in numbers to the whites. Before long the surface and easily worked deposits will have been exhausted. Independent miners will be replaced by companies, and

[1] This is already the case, to some extent, at the Cape. Mr. Theale remarks, that as landholders the Fingoes "are entitled to vote for members of Parliament, and large numbers avail themselves of this privilege."—*South African History*, chap. xxvii.

companies will employ the cheapest labour they can secure, which will always be that of the native and inferior race.[1] Let it be remembered that a country as big as Great Britain, which would be a mere patch on the Continent of Africa, would have a native population of half a million if it were peopled as Natal was when the British Government took it over. Can it be conceived that England could send out half a million settlers to balance these, unless the attraction were as great as that of Australian gold was for a time? And even assuming the half-million to come, where would they be at the end of a century with the black race increasing faster by births, and recruited by constant accessions from the populous interior of the continent? Can it be supposed that such a state would fare better than Georgia or South Carolina has fared? The best chance for a community so constituted would be to declare itself independent, as the Boers of the Transvaal have done, and so maintain the supremacy of the white race. Such a country, however, would not escape the fate of all countries into which an inferior people is admitted in large numbers. Its colonists would soon be divided into a wealthy ruling caste, planters or miners, and mean whites; while the blacks, servile or semi-servile, would increase year by year, because their labour was necessary to maintain and extend the fortunes of the governing caste. Such a community might last for generations, but its chance of perpetuity would be far smaller in Africa, where it was surrounded by dense masses of an unfriendly population, than it was in Louisiana, where slavery might

---

[1] "In capacity the African is fit to work; in inclination he is willing to work; and in actual experiment he has done it."—Drummond's *Tropical Africa*, p. 65.

have lasted to this day if slave-owners had been content to obey the law, and had not been infatuated with the arrogance which is the curse that avenges unrighteous domination.

So far the argument has only sought to establish that no emigration of the English people, or of these reinforced by other races, can make any such impression on any part of the African Continent as to transform regions that are now peopled however sparsely by blacks into regions peopled by whites. To take an extreme assumption, however, we may suppose the whole emigration that now leaves Europe for America and Australia diverted suddenly to Africa, either because prospects in Africa became suddenly so attractive as to kindle the popular imagination, or because the people of America and Australia had restricted the influx of settlers by legislation. The whole excess of emigrants over immigrants from Great Britain may be put roughly at a quarter of a million; and the settlers carried from French, German, and Italian ports can hardly exceed 200,000 more. In the course of twenty years this would mean that a population of 9,000,000 had been transported to a new home, and the most favourable estimate of the natural increase of these settlers will not raise their number above 12,000,000. It must be admitted that a great settlement of this kind would involve organisation and administrative capacity of a very rare order. The colonists will not bear to be discharged by steamers at the rate of nearly 1200 a day at a single port, and left to find work and sustenance as they can. They will have to be distributed by railways over different parts of the continent; and the work of clearing the jungle, building roads, draining swamps, and developing mines may of course find employment for any number. Meanwhile, wherever they penetrate they will bring security and employment to the black races of the interior. These are now roughly estimated for Central Africa alone at 100,000,000. If they increase only at the rate of one per cent a year during the twenty years that have been assumed, the increase will be more than double the influx of whites. If they multiply as the blacks in the United States were once multiplying, they will have grown at the rate of 50,000,000, while the whites by an impossible rate of progression will only number 12,000,000. Under these circumstances, can we conceive any large part of the continent where the whites will be able to settle down, and develop an industrial civilisation, such as is found in any part of America and in Australia?

In all this discussion it has been assumed, for purposes of argument, that our imaginary European immigrants will be able to spread and establish themselves everywhere. No one can seriously expect this. There must be large tracts more or less like Senegambia and the parts about Sierra Leone, where only white men of exceptional constitutions, and submitting to a very strict regime, can live and do work. In the struggle for existence the African race, which can flourish everywhere in its native habitat, is bound to have an advantage over the race that can only thrive in the best parts of the continent.[1]

It has seemed important to argue out the case of Central Africa at some length, because no other part of the world is supposed to furnish so magnificent an

[1] "The really appalling mortality of Europeans is a fact with which all who have any idea of casting in their lot with Africa should seriously reckon. . . . The malaria spares no man . . . no prediction can be made beforehand as to which regions are haunted by it and which are safe."—Drummond's *Tropical Africa*, p. 44.

outlet to the teeming myriads of Europe. The assumption is, that it is to be another Australia, an assumption which leaves out of account the fact that the Australian aborigines have been weak and few, and that the climate of the settled parts of Australia is magnificent. Next in importance to Africa for western Europeans are the islands of the Malay Archipelago, which cover an extent of land equal to half Europe, and which are at present most imperfectly peopled by a population which may be roughly put at between 30,000,000 and 40,000,000. It cannot be extreme to say, that an additional 200,000,000 might easily settle in those of the islands which, like Celebes, Sumatra, New Guinea, and Borneo, are not peopled up to one tithe of what they could support.[1] It is almost equally certain that these colonists cannot be white men. After holding Java for centuries, the Dutch are still nothing more than a garrison, a civil service, and a collection of foreign traders. They number about 30,000, while the native population has more than quadrupled during the century, and is now nearly 20,000,000. Settlement by Dutchmen in Java is not prohibited, and a good many old employees live in the hills; but the climate is better suited for natives, and this is even truer of Borneo and New Guinea, the countries which offer most attraction to immigrants. These, except in favoured parts, have

[1] The four islands specified have alone an area of 837,000 square miles, and a population roughly estimated at about 8,000,000. Java and Madura with less than a sixteenth of this area have a population of 20,000,000. But besides these islands, there is Luzon as big as Ireland; "eighteen more islands are on the average as large as Jamaica" (4193 square miles); "more than a hundred are as large as the Isle of Wight" (135 square miles).—Wallace's *Malay Archipelago*, p. 3. Five years ago, Obi Major, with an area of 600,000 acres, and "apparently both fertile and healthy," was still uninhabited.—Guillemard's *Cruise of the Marchesa*, vol. ii. p. 235.

the hot damp climate which is deadly to the native of the Temperate Zone. That any great number of European immigrants could be acclimatised in them seems more than doubtful; that even if they came they could compete with the Chinese labour, which follows the English rule everywhere in Malaysia, is not to be believed. The work of the European in this archipelago is to organise government, maintain peace, make roads, and form plantations.

There is a vast tract of country in Central Asia that offers great possibilities for settlement. Eastern Afghan, and Western Turkestan, with an area of 1,500,000 square miles, have a population which certainly does not exceed 15,000,000, or ten to the square mile. Were they peopled as the Baltic provinces of Russia are—no very extreme supposition—they would support 90,000,000.[1] It is conceivable that something like this may be realised at no very distant date, when railroads are carried across China, and when water—the great want of Turkestan—is provided for it by a system of canalisation and artesian wells. Meanwhile, it is important to observe that whatever benefit is derived

[1] Marvin in the second chapter of his book on Merv brings evidence to show that the districts between the Atrek and Goorgan, and the Atrek and Sunbar rivers, the country between Astrabad and Meshed, and between Meshed and Herat, are for the most part eminently fertile. He adds on good Russian authority that great parts of the steppes that are called desert could be transformed into excellent pasture by irrigation. Schuyler says of the valley of Shahrisubs: "Kitab, Shaar, and even Yakrbak and Tchirakahi with their surrounding villages looked like forests rather than cities from the number of gardens and orchards" (*Turkistan*, ii. p. 62). Of the district between Bukhara and Varganzi, a distance of thirty miles, he says: "The whole road led through well-cultivated gardens and fields" (*Turkistan*, ii. p. 114). Bukhara, however, is one of the least promising parts of Turkestan; and Schuyler notes elsewhere, that the desert is gaining upon the cultivable land (*Turkistan*, ii. p. 312). Of Eastern Turkestan, a region containing at least 250,000 square miles, and only 1,000,000 inhabitants, Boulger says, that it has been called "the garden of Asia" (*Life of Yakoob Bey*, p. 2).

from an increase of population in these regions will mostly fall to China. That empire possesses the better two-thirds of Turkestan, and can pour in the surplus of a population of 400,000,000. Russia can only contribute the surplus of a population of about 100,000,000; and though the Russian is a fearless and good colonist, there are so many spaces in Russia in Europe to be filled up, so many growing towns that need workmen, so many counter-attractions in the gold-bearing districts of Siberia, that the work of peopling the outlying dependencies of the empire is likely to be very gradual. Indeed it is reported that Russia is encouraging Chinese colonists to settle in the parts about Merv.

Thus far the argument has aimed at showing that the most highly civilised races of the world, being those at present which are more or less purely Aryan, are not likely to wrest any large tracts of territory from half-civilised or savage peoples. That the races which now occupy the United States and Canada will people the countries they are in, with some possible exceptions to be noted hereafter, seems scarcely to be doubted. It may be hoped that this population will be numbered by hundreds of millions. That France and Italy will gradually Europeanise Algeria, Tunis, and Tripoli, seems very possible. It may even be that Morocco will be absorbed. These countries are rich and sparsely in-inhabited, and their native populations of Arabs and Kabyles may easily be assimilated to their European conquerors. In the south-east of Europe it seems certain that the Turk will sooner or later die out or cross back into Asia. His failure to establish himself permanently is incidental evidence how hard it is to change the population of a country. The Osmanli made life almost unendurable to the subject people for centuries, but though he depopulated the country, and paralysed its progress, he stopped short of extermination. The inevitable result has been that the industrial races have increased, while the military race has declined; so that the Turks proper in Europe, who were numbered at from 2,000,000 to 3,000,000 in the reign of Solyman I. (1520-1566)[1] can only now be estimated at a little more than a million and a half. The succession of the Turk at Constantinople is certain to devolve upon a civilised people, and whether it fall to Russia, Austria, or one of the emancipated states, will mean that the higher race has entered again upon part of its natural habitat, from which it had been irregularly expelled. Beyond this it is possible that Russia may contribute a large immigration to Western Turkestan; that English settlers may reinforce the white population of the Cape, so as to keep it dominant; and that the Australian feeling against Asiatic immigrants may keep Northern Australia free from any overwhelming influx of Chinamen or Hindoo coolies.

Meanwhile, the small triumphs which the Aryan race may achieve in these directions are likely to be more than balanced by the disproportionate growth of what we consider the inferior races. China is generally regarded as a stationary power which can fairly hold its own, though it has lost Annam to France, and the suzerainty of Upper Burmah to England, and the Amoor Valley to Russia, but which is not a serious competitor in the race for empire. There is a certain plausibility in this view. On the other hand, China has recovered Eastern Turkestan from Mahommedan rule and from a Russian protectorate, is dominating the Corea, and has

[1] Creasy's *History of the Ottoman Turks*, p. 199.

stamped out a dangerous rebellion in Yunnan. No one can doubt that if China were to get for sovereign a man with the organising and aggressive genius of Peter the Great or Frederick the Second, it would be a very formidable neighbour to either British India or Russia. Neither is it easy to suppose that the improvements, now tentatively introduced into China, will not soon be taken up and pushed on a large scale, so that railways will be carried into the heart of Asia, and large armies drilled and furnished with arms of precision on the European model. In any such case the rights which China has reluctantly conceded or still claims over Annam and Tonquin, over Siam, over Upper Burmah, and over Nepaul, may become matters of very serious discussion. At present the French settlements arrest the expansion of China in the direction most dangerous to the world. Unfortunately, the climate of Saigon is such as no European cares to settle in, and the war to secure Tonquin was so unpopular that it cost a French premier his tenure of office. It is difficult to suppose that France would make great sacrifices for such a possession. It seems not unlikely that she might consent to sell her rights, or to exchange them for some commercial advantage, or for some territorial equivalent, such as China might have to offer in the future. Should some arrangement of this kind ever be made, China will incontinently resume the old protectorate over Siam, and will become very much more formidable than she is even at present from her inherent strength.

Whatever, however, be the fortune of China in this direction, it is scarcely doubtful that she will not only people up to the furthest boundary of her recognised territory, but gradually acquire new dominions. The history of our Straits Settlements will afford a familiar instance how the Chinese are spreading. They already form half the population predominating in Singapore and Perak, and the best observers are agreed that the Malay cannot hold his own against them.[1] They are beginning to settle in Borneo and Sumatra, and they are supplanting the natives in some of the small islands of the Pacific, such as Hawaii. The climate of all these countries suits them, and they commend themselves to governments and employers by their power of steady industry ; and they intermarry freely up to a safe point with the women of the country,[2] getting all the advan-

[1] Baron von Hübner says: "On my first visit to Singapore in 1871, the population consisted of 100 white families, of 20,000 Malays, and of a few thousand Chinese. On my return there, in the beginning of 1884, the population was divided, according to the official census, into 100 whites, 20,000 Malays, and 86,000 Chinese."—Von Hübner's *Through the British Empire*, vol. i. pp. 387, 388. Previous attempts by the Chinese to settle had failed from time to time, in consequence of the hostility they invariably provoked. Thus Miss Bird says of Sungei Ujong : "In 1828 the number of Chinese working the mines here was 1000, and in the same year they were massacred by the Malays. They now number 10,000, and under British protection have nothing to fear."— *Golden Chersonese*, p. 188. "Throughout the length and breadth of Malaysia," says Dr. Guillemard, "the Chinaman has made his way. How he swarms in Singapore we are all aware; but that he is equally at home in the Aru Islands, and bids fair to monopolise the trade of the Philippines, is perhaps not so generally known. At Macassar he shares the mercantile plum with the German. In the Moluccas the vast amount of graves around Ternate testify to the number of his race who have lived and died there. In New Guinea alone he is not to be found ; for neither white man nor Malay has as yet fairly established himself there, and the Celestial is rarely or never a pioneer."—*Cruise of the Marchesa*, ii. p. 126. "Every town from Northern Burmah south, and throughout the vast Indian Archipelago," says Mr. Harrison, "has already fallen into his (the Chinaman's) hands. Even the farms and gardens about the towns are becoming his."—*Race with the Sun*. Of Bangkok Mr. Harrison says (p. 134): "The wily Chinese monopolise the gambling-houses, as indeed they do nearly all the avenues of wealth, and nearly all kinds of business which require industry and skill." "A considerable portion of the population" (of Palembang, in Sumatra) "are Chinese and Arabs."— Wallace's *Malay Archipelago*, p. 122.

[2] "Les premiers Chinois, qui se sont établis à Malacca, ont épousé des Malaises. Aujourd'hui ces familles ne s'allient plus qu'entr'elles. En observant rigoureusement cette coutume, ces hommes singuliers sont

tages of alliance, yet not sacrificing their nationality. Several causes have retarded their spread hitherto: the regions enumerated have mostly been too insecure for an industrial people to flourish in, until the British or the Dutch established order; the government of China has hitherto discouraged emigration; English administrations have been obliged to be rather wary in their dealings with a people who showed at Sarawak and Penang that they were capable of combining for purposes of massacre;[1] and the Chinese superstition about burial in the sacred soil of the Celestial Empire made the great majority of the emigrants birds of passage. All these causes are disappearing. Malay piracy is becoming a thing of the past; the policy of China is being modified; and it can hardly be supposed that the regard for a family burial-place will long continue to keep millions of not very imaginative men from making their homes in the countries in which their labour will be most valuable. Lastly, it is more than conceivable that some of these countries will pass under Chinese rule. The alternatives are that they should be left under foreign protectorates, as at present, till Malays and Dyaks have increased in the same proportion as the Javanese, or that they should be peopled by emigrants from Europe.

Now, the former of these is the only imaginable alternative to Chinese settlement. Europeans cannot flourish under the Tropics, and will not work with the hand where an inferior race works. What we have to consider, therefore, is the probability that the natives

parvenus à confectionner des femmes parfaitement semblables à celles de Fokien, et de Kuan Tong."—Yvan: *De France en Chine*, p. 237.

[1] Mr. Thompson points out that the Chinese guilds are not only a menace to political administration, but are apt to make war with one another.—*Malacca, Indo-China, and China*, p. 15.

who are giving way to the Chinese in the Malay Peninsula will be able to make head against them in Borneo or Sumatra. Borneo is nearly six times as big as Java, and if it were peopled like Java would support a population of nearly 100,000,000. It has actually, by recent estimates, less than 2,000,000 upon it, and these are distributed among several different races. Of these, the tribes in the interior are more likely to be exterminated than reclaimed; and the Dyaks and Malays, numbering between them about 1,500,000, are the only races strong enough to compete in industry with Chinamen. Obviously there is at present room for both in the island, and the British North Borneo Company is stimulating the immigration of coolies, both from China and from the Malay Peninsula. In the long run the Chinese, who outnumber the Malays as sixteen to one, who are more decidedly industrial, and who organise where they can in a way that precludes competition, are tolerably certain to gain the upper hand. They may not destroy the early settlers, but they will reduce them to the position of the Hill tribes in India, or of the Ainos in Japan. Assume fifty years hence that China has taken its inevitable position as one of the great powers of the world, and that Borneo has a population of 10,000,000, predominantly Chinese, is it easy to suppose in such a case that the larger part of Borneo would still be a dependency of the Netherlands? or that the whole island would not have passed, by arms or diplomacy, into the possession of China? Assume England—or it might be Germany, as administering the inheritance of Holland—to possess a nominal suzerainty, would Borneo any the less be Chinese, to all practical purposes, in its commerce, in its political sympathies, in its civilisation, and in its influence upon its neighbours?

The expansion of China towards the south and south-west seems most probable, because there is here most natural wealth to develop, and because the circumstances are specially favourable: administrations guided by commercial principles, and populations too weak to resist immigration.[1] Nothing but the vigilant opposition of the Australian democracies has kept the Chinese from becoming a power on that more remote continent; and at one time within the last forty years the Chinamen actually in Victoria numbered something like 13 per cent of the adult male population.[2] It cannot be held, however, that the Chinese are debarred from gaining territory to the north or west. Even if we choose to regard the Corea and Thibet as already Chinese, there is Nepaul, which might easily be annexed on the Indian frontier if England were crippled or occupied; and there are parts of Turkestan which might be wrested under some similar conjuncture from Russia; or, more naturally still, China might first people and then occupy the provinces along the lower course of the Amoor, which she ceded very reluctantly under pressure, at a time when she was in dire need. There are those who believe that the Chinaman is likely to supersede Spaniard and Indian alike in parts of South America.[3] Without assuming that all of these possibilities are likely to be realised, there is surely a strong presumption that so great a people as the Chinese, and possessed of such enormous natural resources, will sooner or later

---

[1] "Necessity has made the law" (against emigration) "a dead letter."—Williams, *Middle Kingdom*, vol. i. p. 278 (c. 1883).

[2] In 1857 Victoria had a total male population of 297,547. Of these the Chinese numbered 34,874.—Hayter's *Statistical Summary of Victoria from 1835-81 inclusive*; Fairfax's *Handbook to Australasia for 1859*.

[3] Or, le Chinois, ce me semble, dominera un jour ce monde, qui dès maintenant dépend de lui.—Wiener, *Pérou et Bolivie*, p. 36.

overflow their borders, and spread over new territory, and submerge weaker races.

It is difficult to suppose that the motley populations which occupy India and British Burmah can ever be welded into anything as homogeneous as the Chinese Empire. Meanwhile, it is important to observe that British rule, so far as it has any effect, is tending to obliterate the religious differences between Mahommedan and Hindoo, and the racial differences between the Bengalee and the Ghoorka, the Sikh and the Madrassee. Whether England retain her rule or be superseded by some other power, or give place to an independent state or states, it is permissible to hope that the old days of sanguinary misrule, when whole tracts were desolated by Pindarees, are never likely to recur. Even if we assume a state of things such as has been witnessed in South America, a cleavage into a number of small states, incessant revolutions and wars, there seems no reason why the Peninsula should not recover itself, as South America has to some extent done, so that population and wealth might increase in it. It can maintain a much greater population than it has within its own borders—50 per cent more if it be peopled as China is; and it is barred from any great increase to the east by the fact that its people could hardly hope to contend against the Chinese. To the west, however, there is a possibility of expansion over Beluchistan, which is not all desert,[1] and over Afghanistan, which is not all moun-

[1] Of the five provinces forming Beluchistan, Makran, the ancient Gedrosia, seems to be the worst, but the others have large patches of good land, the area of which might be increased by irrigation. Brahmi Khan (1755-95) introduced gardens with considerable success (Oliver's *Across the Border*, chap. ii.) Captain Christie says of the little district of Seistan : " The country, although now inhabited by Afghans and Beloochees in felt tents, still bears the marks of former civilisation and opulence, and there are ruins of villages, forts, and windmills along the

tain. An industrial race coming in gradually under the protection of British arms may easily reclaim large portions of these districts, and swamp the military tribes now settled in them. Those who bear in mind that Persia, with a territory three times as large as that of France, has a population not half as large again as that of Belgium,[1] will perhaps incline to believe that here also in the southern and eastern provinces are regions which may ultimately come to have their fields tilled by coolies, and their commerce carried on by Banyahs.

Some who admit the possibility that the Chinese and Hindoo races may spread over new territory and absorb other populations in Asia may doubt the future of the American Indians, and hold that Southern and Central America are as much the destined inheritance of the white man as the greater part of Northern America seems already to be his estate. Wiener, who travelled among the Indians of Peru and Bolivia, declares that the fine qualities of the aboriginal race have been destroyed beyond the power of recovery by the degradation of centuries of misrule, that the half-caste Indian is fit for nothing but servitude, and that the free Indian has reverted to savagery.[2] Professor Orton, who saw the Indian in Ecuador and along the Amazon districts, where he is perhaps at his lowest, declares that "yet a

whole route from Podbar to Dushak, the capital."—*Travels in Beloochistan*, Appendix, p. 407. Seistan is no doubt more Afghan than Beluch. However, even of Makran, Marco Polo speaks as a country where the people had abundance of food, and to which many merchants resorted by sea and land.—Book iii. chap. xxxiv.

[1] This is taking the largest estimate—that adopted by the *Almanach de Gotha*—of nearly 8,000,000 souls. It is characteristic of the uncertainty attaching to estimates of population in countries like Persia that the *Statesman's Year-Book* puts the population at only 4,400,000, or 20 per cent less than that of Belgium.

[2] Wiener's *Pérou et Bolivie*, pp. 731-738.

little while and the race will be extinct as the dodo."[1] Meanwhile Wiener goes so far as to say that the acclimatisation of the white man has only given good results where there is a cross with native blood. "Families of pure white race generally begin to die out in the third generation, and become the hopeless victims of scrofula."[2] Orton makes the admission, that few of the whites in the Amazon valley "are of pure Caucasian descent." A later American traveller, Mr. Curtis, declares that the interior of Brazil is unsuited to Europeans. "The climate is so enervating that, after an experience of two years, the German colonist will be found by his Portuguese predecessor sitting in the shade of the fig-tree, and hiring a negro to do his work." Mr. Curtis adds, that even in the southern provinces the success of colonists has been very small. "Most of the colonies have broken up," and many of the members "have succumbed to the influences of the climate and died of fever."[3] If these statements are true, and there is a good deal to support them, it would seem as if Southern and Central America, north of Uruguay, are never likely to be the home of the white man in dense masses. If the Indians are dying out, like the pure-blooded Spaniards, the country will be peopled by half-castes or by negroes, or it may be by Chinamen, who have got a footing in Peru, or by coolies, such as are working profitably in British Guiana.

Meanwhile, it must be borne in mind that some observers take a much more promising view of the prospects of the Indian than M. Wiener and Mr. Orton. Mr. Curtis distinguishes the races in Ecuador as divided

---

[1] Orton's *Andes and Amazon*, p. 316.
[2] Wiener's *Pérou et Bolivie*, p. 30.
[3] Curtis's *Capitals of Southern America*, p. 706.

into a Spanish aristocracy, half-caste artisans and mechanics, and Indian cultivators and servants.[1] Something like this seems to be the general division, and if it embraced all the inhabitants of the country, it would mean that the families of Spanish descent were an insignificant minority who must sooner or later be absorbed into the inferior population. Statistics, in fact, show that the whites so-called are only as one in eight of the whole nation of Ecuador. Now Ecuador is a good specimen of a country in which the white race holds its own. When we go farther north, we find Mr. Boyle, a very acute observer, and who spent some time in Central America, declaring his conviction, "that the descendants of the Spaniards, after the lapse of three centuries, are still but squatters in the land; round them on every side are the sons of the old races."[2] Mr. Boyle estimates the free Indians of Guatemala at 1,000,000 at least; and official statistics declare that in the capital itself only one-tenth are pure-blooded whites. That anything like an accurate census has been taken, or is possible in these countries, may be doubted. Wild Indians will not give in returns; and among the free the tendency till lately must always have been to claim affinity with the dominant caste. Meanwhile, it may be noticed of the capital of Guatemala, that Whetham declares few of the inhabitants to have Spanish blood,[3] and of Mexico, that the Europeans, who in 1810 were classed as one in six of the population,

---

[1] Curtis's *Capitals of Southern America*, p. 329.
[2] Boyle's *Ride Across a Continent*, vol. i. p. 157.
[3] *Across Central America*, p. 22. Mr. Boyle says that in Masaya, 4 miles distant from Granada, out of 18,000 inhabitants nine-tenths are pure-blooded Indians. He adds a striking testimony to the thickness of the old Indian population: "In no part of the country, savannah, shore, or forest, can you dig without encountering pottery."—*Ride Across a Continent*, p. 7.

are now set down as little more than a twentieth. If we take the popular estimates, we find Humboldt in 1790 putting the pure Indians in Mexico at two-fifths of the population;[1] while Alison, taking the date 1810, calculates the Spaniards in Mexico, Guatemala, and Caracas at about 1,600,000 in a total population of 8,500,000, or rather less than 20 per cent.[2] The numbers given for this year in the *Statesman's Year-Book* make the descendants of the Spaniard at most 1,200,000 out of a population of more than 12,000,000 in those countries. On the whole, I believe, that in Spanish America, excluding Chili[3] and the Argentine Confederation, the pure or nearly pure descendants of the conquerors are not as one in four to half-castes and Indians, and that these latter amount to about 25,000,000, pretty evenly divided.[4]

It may be admitted at once that the position of those of Indian blood is still very secondary. Still, the evidence is, that they are conquering a place for themselves in other ways than by increasing and multiplying. "General Porfirio Diaz," says Mr. Curtis, "the foremost man in Mexico to-day, and one whose public career will fill pages in the history of that republic, is the representative of mixed Spanish and Aztec ancestry, like all of the famous native leaders of the last half-century."[5] In fact, however, the most distinguished of all, Juarez, was a pure-blooded Indian, as were also Mejia and

---

[1] Humboldt, *La Nouvelle Espagne*, livre ii. chap. vi. Stephens says that the Indians constituted (c. 1842) "three-fourths of the inhabitants of Guatemala."—*Central America*, vol. i. p. 305.

[2] Alison's *History of Europe*, vol. ix. p. 185.

[3] Even in Chili the population is far from being of pure European descent. "The Chilian soldier is by race more than three parts Araucanian," says Mr. Morris (*Dark Days in Chili*, p. 283).

[4] See Appendix A.

[5] Curtis's *Capitals of Southern America*, p. 30.

Mendez, two of Maximilian's best generals. In Guatemala the pure-blooded Indian, Carera, defeated the ablest revolutionary leader, the Spaniard—with a dash of Corsican blood—Morazan; and having been raised to power by the Church, had the sagacity to discard it, and establish a secular polity. The most distinguished of his successors, Barrios, was a half-caste. Guardia, one of the best presidents of Costa Rica, was a half-caste; and even in Peru, where the tradition of Pizarro's brutality was long maintained, and assisted to depress the natives, there has been a half-caste president, Castilla. There, too, the old rule that reserved office and the priesthood for the descendants of the conquerors has fallen into disuse.[1] Wiener stayed with a half-caste priest, and Orton carried a letter to an Indian governor. Even in Mexico the ruling class is still essentially white; and everywhere the whites are fighting and intriguing for the spoils of office, while the native people remains passive and seemingly unobservant, and barely contributes here and there a successful leader to a popular movement. Meanwhile, the general level of the autochthonous race is being raised; it is acquiring riches and self-respect, and must sooner or later get the country back into its hands. The Guaranis of Paraguay, whose race is widely diffused over the south, cannot be very inferior to the Aztecs. Literature is the last growth of a new country, but more than two centuries ago a descendant of the Incas, Garcilasso de la Vega, conquered an honourable name for himself in Spanish literature.[2]

---

[1] L'Église est devenue, en effet, à Pérou depuis peu de temps seulement endurante à l'égard des métis, qui veulent embrasser la carrière ecclésiastique. Jadis tout homme de couleur en était effectivement exclus.—Wiener, *Pérou et Bolivie*, p. 299.

[2] "His commentaries are a striking and interesting book," says Ticknor (*History of Spanish Literature*, vol. iii. p. 190).

However, the question whether the Indians will people part of South America, and the whole of Central America again, is comparatively an unimportant issue. What seems certain is that no European race will take their place. The weakest of the American states, be it Honduras or Nicaragua, is protected by climate from the Anglo-Saxon or German immigrant. M. de Lesseps in 1880 defended the climate of the district through which his canal was to pass by the statement, that out of 2000 Chinamen engaged on the construction of the Panama Railway only 500 had died during the work; and that of these half had committed suicide; but even this mortality of adult males will appear considerable to most men; and M. de Lesseps was compelled to admit that the mortality among the Irish had been much greater. He explained this away as the effect of drunken habits.[1] It seems proved that Europeans who are naturally strong, and who commit no excess, have a fair chance of life in the higher parts and in the reclaimed parts of Central America. This, however, is as much as can be maintained. M. de Verbrugghe, who has vindicated the reputation of the district marked out for the Panama Canal, admits that many parts on the Nicaragua route, such as Grey Town, the mouths of the Atrato, and the marshes of the Trinidad are absolutely pestilential.[2] Generally it may be said that immigrants from the Temperate Zone are likely to repeat the experience of Paterson's party, until the jungle and the swamp have been brought back into cultivation. The work of reclaiming them, however, can only be done by races tolerant of heat, and more or less insensible to

[1] Lanier's *L'Amérique*, p. 348.
[2] Verbrugghe's *Le Canal Inter-Océanique de Panama*, cited in Lanier's *L'Amérique*, pp. 347-350.

fever, and when these have established themselves in large numbers, there will be no place left for the white man. The southern planters who subsidised Walker, intended to turn Nicaragua into another Louisiana. Now that slavery is abolished, the country can only be developed by free Indians or by free negroes coming in from the states. These are the two natural sources of the coloured labour that is indispensable.

Of the other countries—one and all—that have been classed as predominantly Indian, it may be said that they are not likely to encourage European immigration on a very extended scale, or, if they did encourage it, to attract it. The circumstances of the Argentine Republic are exceptional. "It is estimated," says Mr. Curtis, "that the extent of agricultural land in the Argentine Republic equals 600,000 square miles; an area equal to Louisiana, Mississippi, Alabama, Georgia, Tennessee, Arkansas, Kentucky, Illinois, Indiana, Ohio, Missouri, Iowa, and Wisconsin, and capable of producing every crop in these states."[1] Let it be added that these enormous tracts lie fairly near together, that they are traversed in great part by railways, that the climate is that of Southern France, and that Indians are hardly a more real danger than in the United States. It is easy to understand 600,000 immigrants pouring into such a paradise in the space of ten years. Contrast Ecuador, Peru, and Bolivia, which are in a great measure tropical Switzerlands; Quito, for instance, being 2000 feet higher than the Hospice of the Great St. Bernard in Europe, and Cuzco and Potosi and the capital of Bolivia higher still. The fertile niches of these countries are already occupied by Indians. The reclaimable parts can only

[1] Curtis's *Capitals of Southern America*, p. 584.

be developed by irrigation, and lie at a distance from one another, so that foreign immigrants could not enjoy congenial neighbourhood. There remain, of course, the states of Colombia, Venezuela, and the three Guianas. The richest parts of these, the valleys of the Orinoco, the Magdalena, and smaller rivers, are all either swamps or liable to inundation: districts that may, at some future day, maintain a population of many millions, but in which small bodies of foreign immigrants would find, under worse climatic conditions, what Dickens painted in his sketch of Eden. Venezuela is graphically described by Eastwick as "a forest larger than France, steppes like those of Gobi, and mountain tracts which it would take many Switzerlands to match."[1] Last of all, it must be remembered that it is more than doubtful if native governments or populations would encourage or tolerate immigration on a large scale. The Church would oppose an influx of heretics, and the Spanish governing caste would hesitate lest they should see the precedent of Texas repeated.

Brazil stands by itself among South American states in one important particular. Its indigenous Indians were to a great extent less docile and reclaimable than the Aztecs, the Quichuas, and the Guaranis of Paraguay have proved themselves. Brazil accordingly has a large element of negro population; how large may be estimated from the fact that, in 1850, the slaves were set down at 2,500,000. It seems probable that negroes and negro half-castes compose the better half of the 12,000,000 who are calculated to people Brazil; the pure Indians are estimated by a liberal calculation at 1,000,000; while the Portuguese, Germans, and half-caste or civilised Indians make up the

[1] Eastwick's *Venezuela*, p. 25.

remainder.[1] What all observers are agreed upon is that there are very few families of pure Portuguese blood, and the climate of Brazil, except in the Highlands, is opposed, as has been noticed, to the perpetuation of any European people in its full vigour. It seems difficult to doubt that Brazil will pass more and more into the hands of the negroes; the Indians, perhaps, maintaining themselves, and spreading in the northern and more inaccessible central parts; while the white may continue for a long time to be numerous in the cities, and in parts of exceptional healthiness.

The possibilities for Brazil may be illustrated by what is taking place before our eyes in the southern states of the Union. In 1790 the coloured population of the Union was about three-quarters of a million in an estimated population of less than 4,000,000— that is, it numbered nearly 20 per cent of the whole nation. Fortunately for the world, the American Government adopted the policy, first, of prohibiting the importation of slaves, and then of encouraging white immigration with a result which can hardly be estimated at less than an influx of 16,000,000 whites in the century. Accordingly, the proportion of the coloured population to the American people has decreased decade by decade, till it is now only about 13 per cent of the whole. Meanwhile, it is important to observe that, till lately, the negroes have increased, after a fitful and uncertain fashion, not only absolutely, but relatively in the seven states that are sometimes known as the Black Belt, that stretch from North Carolina to Louisiana inclusive, that were the seats of the old slave planta-

---

[1] The Census of 1872 gave an estimate of less than 4,000,000 of European descent; less than 500,000 Indians; and about 6,000,000 negroes and half-castes of all kinds.—*Almanach de Gotha.*

tions, and that are eminently favourable to the black race by climate or the opportunities of congenial toil, while they are at least a little dangerous or debilitating to the white man. Briefly, it may be stated that the whites were as 7 to 6·25 in those states in 1860; that they were as 19 to 18·5 in 1880; and that they are as 23 to 21·4 in 1890. The forecast of the Statistical Bureau in 1860 estimated that, in 1880, the blacks would be 6,618,350 in a total population of 56,450,241.[1] As a fact, when that year came, the blacks were as 6,577,151 in a population of 50,152,166. They had multiplied in spite of the Civil War almost up to a sanguine estimate; the whites had fallen short of expectation by 13 per cent. It was believed, for a time, that the "extinction of slavery in widening the field for white labour and enterprise will tend to reduce the rate of increase of the coloured race;" and that "the coloured population in America is doomed to comparatively rapid absorption or extinction." No such anticipations are entertained now. Professor Gilman believes that, in 1920, the blacks in the eight old slave states will be at 17,400,000 to 9,390,000 whites—that is, within measurable distance of being two to one. It is, of course, possible that the causes which were expected to operate twenty years ago in reducing negro increase will be more effectual when education is diffused, and that the black will multiply more slowly as he acquires a higher standard of comfort. On the other hand, there is also a possibility that whites will find it more and more uncongenial to live in negro states, controlled by negro legislatures, subjected to the competition of negro labour, and sometimes, it may be, overshadowed socially by

[1] See note on the Tenth Census of the United States, by F. J. Mouat (*Journal of the Statistical Society*, 1880, p. 579).

negroes. In that case, the Black Belt will deserve its name year by year more distinctively.[1] Its people of course are bound to remain a part of the Union, so that, in this case, a black commonwealth will not be constituted politically. What is remarkable is, that the blacks should be increasing so rapidly in a country where they are outnumbered vastly by the whites altogether; where the conditions are incomparably more favourable to white enterprise than in Brazil or Africa; and where the negroes possess no other advantage than immunity from fever up to a certain point, and a readiness to live cheaply. The first of these advantages must not be exaggerated. Mr. Olmsted, in 1862, brought a great deal of evidence to show that whites were really healthier than negroes in every part of the southern states, except perhaps the Rice Coast.[2] What made the negroes dense in early days was that, while they were slaves, field labour was considered dishonourable, except on a man's own land, and the whites accordingly congregated in the towns. What keeps the blacks numerous is that, in many kinds of labour, they can undersell the whites, because their standard of requirements is not high, and again, because neither race can endure to live with the other on equal terms. The blacks find the north uncongenial; the white immigrant goes to the west, or to Manitoba, rather than to the

---

[1] For fuller statistical details on this subject see Appendix B.

[2] "There are grounds for doubting the common opinion that the negroes at the south suffer less from local causes of disease than whites." Mr. Olmsted goes on to show that, by the vital statistics of Charleston, the average mortality during six years has been of blacks alone, 1 in 54; of whites alone, 1 in 58.—*Journeys and Explorations in the Cotton Kingdom*, vol. ii. pp. 258, 259. The United States Census for 1880 says, p. 1706, "In a population of 43,402,970 whites there are recorded 640,191 deaths, giving a death-rate of 14·74 per 1000. In a population of 6,752,813 coloured there are recorded 116,702 deaths, giving a death-rate of 17·28 per 1000."

more fertile south, where he has to measure himself against the negro. If the negro increases to an extent that makes the southern states of the Union too small for him, the chances perhaps are that he will overflow in the direction of Central America rather than add a new unit of population to the north and Canada.

The result of all these considerations seems to be that by far the most fertile parts of the earth, and which either are or are bound to be the most populous, cannot possibly be the homes of what it is convenient to call the Aryan race, or indeed of any higher race whatsoever. In Asia the population of India and China, with the countries inextricably bound to them, is already incomparably greater than the collective sum of Russians, Persians, Turks, Arabs, and Syrians, and the disproportion is likely to increase. A conquest by Russia of Turkey in Asia would hardly affect the populations of Syria and Karamania, except by giving Syrians and Armenians the opportunity of increasing under orderly rule. In Africa the vast regions between the Tropics, abandoned to barbarism and anarchy, as with trifling exceptions they have been, have none the less five times the population of the north and south, parts of which have enjoyed English and French administration.[1] In

---

[1] I have adopted the calculations supplied by Mr. Ravenstein to Mr. Silva White for his *Development of Africa*, and have deducted

Algeria and Tunis	5,370,000
Egypt and Tripoli	7,980,000
Cape and Natal	1,730,000
Dutch Free States	513,000
Morocco	6,076,000
Total	21,669,000

From Mr. Ravenstein's total estimate of 127,038,370 for Africa, this leaves 105,369,370 for Tropical Africa. About a tenth of this, under

America, taken as a whole, the white population is at present larger than the coloured, almost as two to one, and this proportion seems likely to be maintained for a time, till the western parts of the Union and Canada, and the undeveloped tracts of the Argentine Confederation, are settled in after a fashion. Meanwhile, the mere fact that the white race naturally prefers these parts is giving the Indians and the negroes time to increase in the tropical and semi-tropical parts of America, so that nothing short of extermination on too great a scale to be even dreamed of will be able to dispossess them. Neither must it be forgotten that the lower races of men increase faster than the higher; so that fifty years of absolute peace might mean as much for Honduras or Benguela as a hundred years for England or Italy. On the whole, it seems difficult to doubt that the black and yellow belt, which always encircles the globe between the Tropics, will extend its area, and deepen its colour with time. The work of the white man in these latitudes is only to introduce order and an acquaintance with the best industrial methods of the west. The countries belong to their autochthonous races; and these, though they may in parts accept the white man as a conqueror and organiser, will gradually become too strong and unwieldy for him to control, or if they retain him, will do it only with the condition that he assimilates himself to the inferior race.

There is perhaps one consideration which may be regarded as an offset to the enormous probabilities of Chinese and Hindoo expansion. Both China and Hindostan afford ample space for growth within their

---

French and English rule, like Senegal and Sierra Leone, or under a moderately good native government, like the Azores and Madeira, is not abandoned to barbarism and anarchy.

own limits. China proper, for instance, is as large as twenty-two Englands, or by some estimates as twenty-six, and, on the same basis of population, might maintain at least 650,000,000 or even 750,000,000, or, in other words, might increase for fifty years before it required to relieve itself by an exodus. In fact, it is supposed that from its superior fertility, China could carry more than England to the square mile, and might double its numbers before it needed to trouble its neighbours. Putting, on the one hand, the sufficiency of land at home, and, on the other hand, the conservative genius of the administration, which discourages emigration, and of the people who do not readily accept it, it may be argued that half a century, or a century hence, we shall find China no further advanced than she now is, while the English, French, and Dutch settlements in the Indian Ocean will have consolidated themselves. Those who argue in this way may be reminded that a Tae-Ping rebellion, which lasted fourteen years, is estimated to have cost China from 20,000,000 to 50,000,000 of population; and that, while the inhabitants of a single province, Szechuen, increased by 45,000,000 between 1842 and 1882, there was a loss by official estimates of 100,000,000 in the other provinces. The nation altogether is calculated to have decreased by at least 30,000,000 in this period.[1] Yet China was

---

[1] The population of China is said by official records to have been:—

> 201,013,344 in 1760.
> 414,686,994 in 1842.
> 382,078,860 in 1879.

Dr. Williams treats as specially authentic the censuses of 1762 and 1812:—

> 1762 . . . . 198,214,553.
> 1812 . . . . 362,467,183.

These seems to show that the population under favourable conditions

able during the whole time to spare colonists to Siam, to the Straits Settlements and Malaysia, to the United States and Peru, and to Australia, besides those whom the Government poured into Ili. The settlement in Siam took place under the disadvantage that Chinamen forfeited the rights of citizenship in their own country, and were not protected in case of injury; nevertheless, the Chinese element of the population is now 3,000,000, or about one-fourth. If this has taken place during a period of conservatism and decadence, what are we to expect as year by year the population of the Celestial Empire increases, and its rulers adopt the aggressive policy of the West?

It must be borne in mind, too, that a country may often find its numbers too large for it when it is very far from having reached the limits of its productivity. England in 1840 had a population of 16,000,000, and was over-peopled, so that except for America and Australia it is difficult to see how a great part of her people could have supported life. England in 1890 has a population of 29,000,000, and maintains them, if anything, more easily than she did the smaller number. No one supposes that the extreme limits of her possible increase have been reached. There can be little doubt that a large emigration from China would remove the congestion of some of its districts, and powerfully stimulate Chinese trade, as colonies needing Chinese products were formed. There seems no reason why

doubles in less than sixty years. Dr. Williams regards the census of 1879 as too high by 25,000,000.—*The Middle Kingdom*, vol. i. pp. 263-270. Mr. Smith treats every Chinese census as fanciful.—*Chinese Characteristics*, pp. 235, 236.

The population of Szechuen was 22,256,964 in 1842, and 67,712,897 in 1882.—*Arbeiten der Kaiserlichen Russischen Gesandschaft*, 1852-1857, übersetzt von Abel, Band ii. S. 193; *Journal of the Royal Statistical Society*, 1887, pp. 688-694.

millions of Chinamen should not pass over into Borneo, as freely as they transferred themselves to Siam or to Szechuen, and make themselves new homes a little outside of the empire as well as within it. Englishmen never dream of settling in Ireland, though Ireland has sometimes offered very good openings. They will have a warmer welcome and more chance of bettering themselves in America or Australia. As the provinces of China fill up gradually, that great displacement of the population which has been going on within the empire is bound to die out, and men who have to carve out new homes will naturally seek the countries where there is waste land.[1]

It is, no doubt, matter of extreme difficulty to predict what the rate of increase in any particular country, or at any given time, will be. Gibbon has estimated the number of Roman subjects under Claudius at 120,000,000.[2] If this population had doubled once in every 150 years, it would long ago have reached a total which no one supposes the world capable of maintaining. As a fact, the population of the countries that constituted the empire is not more than about 200,000,000.[3] Misgovernment, war, and pestilence

[1] It may be noticed that there is one strong reason in the genius of the Chinese people to limit fresh settlement within the empire, at least in districts that have already been settled. "Immense tracts in the north and west of the province (Yunnan) have lain waste since the Mahommedan rebellion, and owing to the antipathy of the Chinese to settle on lands which they look upon as the property of people who may still be living, or whose descendants may still be living, it must be many years before the agriculture of the province is properly developed."
—Hosie's *Three Years in Western China*, pp. 205, 206.

[2] *Decline and Fall of the Roman Empire*, chap. ii.

[3] The countries reckoned in are: Italy, 29,000,000; France, 37,000,000; Belgium and Holland, 10,000,000; Great Britain, 33,000,000; Spain and Portugal, 21,000,000; Turkey in Europe, 15,500,000; Hungary, Dalmatia, and Bosnia, 17,250,000; Turkey in Asia, 16,000,000; and North Africa, 14,000,000; altogether about 202,000,000.

have perpetually foiled nature, and it is only within the last century that anything like the annual increase, upon which we are now apt to count, has been attained. In Gibbon's time these same countries could not have mustered much more than half the population of the old empire.[1] Even now there is a great difference perceptible between them. The increase of France is very slow, and the Turkish provinces are almost stationary. England has added largely to her population in the last fifty years, and Ireland in the same period has lost one-fourth of her numbers. Neither are these changes always coincident with national advance or decline. France, for instance, though nearly stationary, is still one of the richest countries in Europe, and England has not been impoverished by her increase. The wealth of France appears to attract immigrants from other countries; but not— just now, at least—to stimulate the growth of the native French population.

What, however, we seem able to say is, that in the long run the lower civilisation has a more vigorous life than the higher, the unprivileged gains upon the privileged caste, and the conquered people absorbs the conqueror. There is no perceptible trace of ancient Greek or Roman blood in Asia Minor or in Turkey in Europe. The Turk—himself a barbarian—has destroyed or driven out or depressed all the higher races he came across, and the population under him is now Syrian or Armenian, Albanian or Bulgarian. The

---

[1] Gibbon compares them with the population of all Europe, and puts it at 105,000,000 or 107,000,000. Excluding Germany, Russia, and Poland, Scandinavia, and Ireland, this would be reduced to about 60,000,000. The African provinces would hardly exceed 5,000,000 at that time. Napoleon says that Egypt, when he knew it, had only from 2,500,000 to 2,800,000 souls.—*Mémoires de Napoléon*, ed. 1823, tome ii. p. 206.

Greece that has been restored represents a very small portion of the country in which Greeks were superior by numbers, or by social influence and commercial activity, under Alexander, or even under Claudius. In Transylvania the Saxons are being crowded out by Roumanians, and in Hungary the Magyars[1] and Germans can barely stem the uprising nationalities of Slavs and Roumanians. In Northern Africa the Carthaginian, the Greek, the Roman, and the Vandal were successively effaced, and until the French conquest of Algiers the country was given up to Arabs of a not very pure breed, to Berbers, and to blacks. The Irish were reckoned by Petty in 1672 at 1,100,000 in their own country,[2] and there cannot then have been many outside Ireland. They are now probably from 16,000,000 to 20,000,000, counting only those who can be distinctly recognised as of Irish descent. Before the time of their great dispersion to America and Australia, they had increased within the British Isles from being about a sixth to being nearly a third of

---

[1] As the Magyars are of the same race as the Turks, though with a larger admixture of Aryan blood, it seems desirable I should point out that from first to last I use the words "higher" and "lower" with no reference to the essential value of a race, which it would be hard to determine, but with regard to its actual position in the world. The Slowack may have finer natural capabilities than the Magyar. At present, I believe, it is correct to say that the Magyar population has a larger proportion of educated men, and of men owning property, and is more capable of self-government.

[2] Mr. Hallam calls Petty's conjectures "prodigiously vague" (*Const. Hist.* vol. iii. p. 392, note *y*); but Swift in 1729 says, that the popular estimate then was 1,500,000 ("Letter on Mr. M'Culla's project about halfpence"). Macaulay seems to follow Petty, and estimates the Catholics at 1,000,000 in 1686, whom Petty had put at 800,000 in 1672 (*History*, chap. vi.) I have estimated their present numbers at 5,250,000 for Ireland, 1,000,000 for England and Scotland, 800,000 for Australasia, 1,000,000 for the Dominion of Canada, and from 8,000,000 to 10,000,000 for the United States. They are also well represented at the Cape and in South America.

the population.[1] Compare the increase of Sweden, with a population of the highest type, at once warlike and industrial, during a rather longer period, and it will seem very small indeed. Sweden with its old province Finland has increased at most fourfold; the Irish people at least fifteenfold.[2]

Lest it should be supposed that these are speculative calculations, or based upon casual instances, it may be pointed out that under present conditions of society, a class or a people which values comfort and position highly cannot possibly increase as rapidly as the class that contents itself with bare existence. The English aristocracy is a typical example of the way in which a close corporation dies out. Its members are almost always wealthy in the first instance, and their estates have been constantly added to by favour from the Crown,[3] by something like the monopoly of the

---

[1] By the highest estimate, Mulhall's, they were as 13·2 to 64 in 1672. In 1849 they were as 8·19 to 18·65.

[2] "It has been calculated," says Fryxell, "that at the beginning of Charles XI.'s reign the population of Sweden and Finland of those times consisted of 1,775,000 persons."—*Svea Rikes Historie*, xviii. s. 155. Sweden and Finland—the latter enormously benefited by the neighbourhood of St. Petersburg—contained in 1880 a population of about 6,500,000. The emigration from these countries will not add more than half a million to this estimate.

[3] It is generally supposed that William III.'s grants to Bentinck, Keppel, and the husband of Lady Elizabeth Villiers, are the last instances of royal gifts on a large scale to favourites. This, however, is not quite the case. Mme. de Walmoden had a peerage and money from George II. Lord Bute is supposed to have received at least £300,000, which the Princess of Wales had saved out of her large revenue (Walpole's *Last Journals*, i. p. 19), and Greville says of Lady Conyngham, whom George IV. admired: "The wealth she has accumulated by savings and presents must be enormous" (*Memoirs*, vol. i. p. 212). George III. wrote to Lord North in 1777: "I must insist you will now state to me whether £12,000 or £15,000 will not set your affairs in order; if it will, nay, if £20,000 is necessary, I am resolved you shall have no other person concerned in freeing them but myself."—*Letter* 410, ed. Donne. But this is a very small part of what the North family got from royal favour. Compare George III.'s letter of December 12, 1778:

best Government appointments, and by marriages with wealthy heiresses. They are able to command the field sports and open-air life that conduce to health, and the medical advice that combats disease. Nevertheless, they die out so rapidly that only five families out of nearly six hundred go back without a break, and in the male line, to the fifteenth century.[1] It is sometimes thought that the untitled landed gentry represent a more permanent aristocracy, better blood, and longer connection with land than the peers. This is only the conceit of county notabilities. The late Mr. Evelyn Shirley made a list of all the families in England who could show unbroken connection with the squirearchy since the Wars of the Roses terminated, and though he was most liberal in his inclusions his list went easily into a single thin volume. It is perfectly true that a certain number of Englishmen with large landed estates descend from ancestors who held land anciently somewhere; but it will generally be found in such cases that the ancestors were yeomen, or at most squireens. An analysis of modern landowners in a county will habitually prove that not more than six or eight, owning 3000 acres,[2] descend from ancestors who owned as much in the time of Elizabeth. The peers, modern as they are, represent a larger average of old families than the country squires. The great device for perpetuating untitled families has been the law of entail, which has really been a most potent

"Lord Barrington is to wait on Lord North to know what can be done for him. I therefore authorise you to make such a provision as you may think fit."

[1] Stanley (of Derby), Neville (of Abergavenny), Courtenay (of Devon), Lumley (of Scarborough), Stourton (of Stourton).

[2] 3000 acres is the amount taken by Mr. Bateman in his *Great Landowners of Great Britain and Ireland* to be the qualification of a great landowner.

engine for destroying them, by forcing successive generations to saddle the land with encumbrances. On the other hand, the fascination of a title for Englishwomen is so great that peers, beggared by the prodigality of their ancestors, are constantly able to retrieve their fortunes by marriage with heiresses.

Now, if we inquire why it is that noble families die out, we shall find that the reason lies in the desire of all their members to maintain themselves in the class they are born into. It is an unwritten law that they must marry money, or not marry at all; and the result is, that when the heir to the title, marrying perhaps late in life, finds his wife sterile—and heiresses are the outcome of families that tend to be sterile—it may easily happen that his younger brothers have not married at all. Often, of course, it is not too late for them to take wives; but if the peer in possession has daughters on whom the unentailed property will be settled, a man confirmed in bachelor habits will often hesitate before he marries only to continue the title. Now it is the boast of Englishmen that our aristocracy is a supremely reasonable one, that there is no nobility clinging to the children of cadets, and that the highest peer marries freely into the commercial classes, and has done so for centuries past without requiring sixteen quarters in a wife, or even two generations of gentility. All the more noteworthy is it that family after family passes away as if it were laden with a mysterious curse. The instance cited above, which shows how few of our nobles are as old as the first Tudor, may seem an unfair one, as the sixteenth and seventeenth centuries were times of unsettlement, when many families were deprived of the peerage by attainder, or ruined by confiscations. An example from comparatively modern times will therefore be more instructive. 155 peers were summoned to the first Parliament of James II. In 1825, only 140 years later, only forty-eight of these nobles were represented by lineal descendants in the male line. The family has in several instances been continued by collaterals begging the peerage, which they could not have claimed at law, and in this way the change may seem less than it has really been; but the broad result appears to be that left to itself from 1688, with new creations absolutely forbidden, the House of Lords would by this time have been practically extinguished. Of Charles II.'s six bastards, who were made dukes, only three have perpetuated the race. Three peerages have been lost to the Howard family, three to the Greys, two to the Mordaunts, two to the Hydes, two to the Gerards, and two to the Lucases. A religiously-minded antiquary of Queen Elizabeth's time attempted to show that a curse attached to all the families which had been enriched by sharing the spoils of ecclesiastical property. At the present day, we know that a normal percentage of those families is still enjoying the fruits of the Parliamentary settlement, which it has pleased divines to call sacrilege. What was really valuable in Sir Henry Spelman's researches was the proof they afforded, that men high placed enough to enjoy court favour are rarely the founders of long-lived families. It is in the lower strata of society that we have to seek for the springs of national life.

It is a very small matter to the world at large whether titled and landed aristocracies show a tendency to gradual extinction, but it cannot be accounted matter of indifference if the higher races increase very much more slowly than the lower. Even if we assume higher and lower to be merely relative terms, and that the negro is capable of becoming as fine a specimen of humanity as the Englishman or the Frenchman, it has to be recognised that very favourable conditions and a long period of time are required for the transmutation, which, after all, is more than a little doubtful. Now to take two extreme instances, the French, who are a very important factor in civilisation, will only double themselves in two centuries if they retain the rate of progression of the last seventy years; while the negroes of the Southern States are doubling themselves once in forty years. Wealth is supposed to have increased more than fivefold in France since the peace of 1815.[1] This wealth is to a great extent distributed by the stringent law of succession; and the position of the small landowner, and of the artisan, is incomparably better than it has been at any previous time. The population does not emigrate to avoid the conscription, or because the pressure of the taxes is intolerable. It shows its sense of enhanced national burdens, if indeed it shows it at all, by increasing from decade to decade more slowly. Perhaps, what really retards the growth of families is the tacit but universal resolve on no account to submit to a lower standard of food or clothing, or of whatever conduces to comfort and self-respect.[2] At any rate, for one reason or the other, either because the State, or because the family and the individual make greater claims on economy now than they made in past times, France is receding, year by year, from her old high place among populous states.

---

[1] From £1,800,000,000 in 1815 to £9,070,000,000 in 1882. Fournier de Flaix on the national wealth of France.—*Statistical Journal*, March 1886, p. 197.

[2] Mr. Hamerton mentions thrift and luxury as two causes that retard the growth of population in France.—*French and English*, pp. 252, 253.

In a more or less small degree, what is true of France is true of Continental Europe, taken as a whole, exclusive of Prussia; and, if we allow for immigrants of the white population, in America. At the end of a long term of prosperous years, none of the great nations have increased in numbers, as negroes and Hindoos have increased, or, as there is reason to think, Chinamen would have multiplied under similar circumstances.

England has been a singular instance of an old country that has increased its numbers at something like the Oriental rate of progression, while it has carried on exhausting wars, and sent out millions of emigrants. It may be contended, therefore, that an equally wise administration, promoting manufactures and colonies and adopting free trade, may do for Europe in general what England has achieved. On examination, it will be found, however, that precisely the poorest and most backward part of the British Isles, Ireland, is the part that increased most rapidly, till its progress was arrested by famine and wholesale emigration. The population of Ireland is given by Mulhall as 2,373,000 in 1752. In 1841 it was 8,195,000, that is, it had increased between three and fourfold. During the same period, England had increased from 7,000,000 to 16,000,000, or from two to threefold, and Scotland from 1,265,000 to 2,620,000, that is, had just about doubled itself. The most thrifty and progressive of the three countries showed the smallest increase. Such as this increase was, however, it was undoubtedly due in part to an immigration from Ireland. Since the peasantry of Ireland have earned higher wages, and acquired a larger proprietorship in their native land, they have ceased to increase at any rapid rate. England, therefore, is now the capital example of a highly civilised country that doubles in sixty years; for even Germany cannot exhibit anything like the same rate of progression. The average for all Europe is to double in about a century.[1] Against this, we have the negro doubling in forty years, and the Hindoo in about eighty,[2] under circumstances which have no doubt been highly favourable, but which are not unlikely to last. China, down to 1842, doubled at the rate of once in eighty years. Her progress was then suspended by a gigantic calamity. If she can preserve peace and benefit by the outlets which England offers her in the Indian seas, is there any reason why she should not increase even more rapidly than in the best period of the past?

It has been no part of this argument to consider whether an inferior race may not to some extent displace a superior in a country where the superior race has been supreme in power, and unapproached in numbers for centuries. Such a case as that of the Mauritius, where the French colonists are dwindling away, and where such civilisation as they had established is giving place to the inroads of Chinamen and Hindoos, who are gradually acquiring land and trade, may be regarded as on too small a scale to be conclusive.[3] Russia shows

[1] In 1849 Alison wrote that the population of the Russian Empire was about 64,000,000, and was likely to be 130,000,000 by natural increase before 1900. In 1887 it was returned as 107,000,000, but of these 5,000,000 are accounted for by acquisitions in Central Asia. Russia, however, confirms the general rule that nations with a low standard of comfort increase faster than nations with a high standard under fairly similar conditions of peace and order.

[2] In 1881 the population of British India amounted to 198,790,853 persons. In 1891 it was estimated at 220,500,000. The acquisition of Upper Burmah accounts only for 3,000,000.

[3] In 1832 the population of the Mauritius was 89,610, of whom 63,500 were slaves, Africans by race, the rest being mostly of European descent, pure or mixed. In 1888 the population consisted of 260,000 Hindoos and 117,000 of all other nationalities, including Chinamen, who are a new and noticeable element. It is evident, that in fifty-six

us the curious spectacle of a race that is credited with the possession of high qualities, that has not been outrageously ill-treated in the immediate past, and that is only slightly inferior in concrete civilisation to its rulers, increasing so rapidly as to be thought a danger to the Empire. The Jews have spread into Russia from Poland, where they enjoyed exceptional privileges, and though they suffered in 1832 for their supposed complicity in the Polish War of Independence, they have generally been protected by the law, and only restricted from settlement in certain parts of the Empire. They were for a time encouraged to colonise parts of the Ukraine, and though it may seem futile, and even tyrannical to settle Jews on the land as agriculturists, it must be remembered that instances were on record in which Jews had taken to a country life of themselves, or had been induced to adopt it. Clarke, who travelled through Poland in 1778, tells us that there "Jews cultivate the ground, and we frequently saw them engaged in sowing, reaping, mowing, and other works of husbandry."[1] Maria Theresa actually established Jewish agricultural colonies with partial and temporary success in Bohemia. Therefore, we need not assume that the race is incapable of husbandry; and that the Jews in Russia have generally abandoned or sub-let their land in the Ukraine[2] is probably due to the fact that they have seen more profitable and congenial employment open to them in the cities. Their position, though not a dignified or pleasant one, has been, till

years there has been no increase of the original population; and all who know the island are aware that a great deal of the land has passed from its old French proprietors to companies, and is passing from companies to the Hindoos.—Lanier's *L'Afrique*, p. 862; *Colonial Year Book*, 1890, p. 354.

[1] Clarke's *Travels in Poland*, book ii. chap. vii. p. 237.
[2] Wallace's *Russia*, pp. 374, 375.

lately, tolerably endurable to a people that has no recent memories of independence. As long as they retained their faith they were shut out from the court, from office, and from society; but as contractors, merchants, tradesmen, money-lenders, middlemen, and smugglers, they have been able to do a great deal of profitable business. They were trusted and employed by the police during the unsuccessful Polish rising of 1864-65; and now and again some of the brighter of them, such as Jessy Helfman and Aaron Zundelevitch have sympathised with the plans of the Nihilists, and have worked with Russians for reforms, as the more ardent Russians conceive them. It is almost needless to add, that in a country like Russia it has always been possible to evade the laws restraining Jewish industry or settlement by bribing officials.

Now the conditions just described are precisely those which are most favourable to an increase of population. Given security to life, limb, and property, which there has been till very lately, the power to enjoy wealth being limited, while its value as a safeguard is enhanced, and all the checks of self-restraint being removed, the Jewish population has had no motive to limit its reproductive powers. There is reason to think that the Jewish people is exceptionally healthy and fertile; but any race would increase which had the wit to make money—a strong stimulus for making it in the need to purchase protection—and no private use to spend it on, except food, and the rearing of a family. The Jew has no reason for living in a palace, for keeping up unnecessary servants, or for spending extravagantly on social pleasures; and is, indeed, wise if he avoids all ostentation. His risk of attack from the populace, and the percentage he pays to officials, will be less in proportion as he is shabbily dressed and poorly housed. Naturally he accumulates money, and naturally, also, he marries young and does not dream of limiting his family. Is it wonderful if the rapid increase of the race has begun to provoke alarm? In 1778 the Jews of Poland and Lithuania cannot have much exceeded from 300,000 to 400,000.[1] Those in the other parts of Russia were at that time an inappreciable quantity. The smallest estimate now puts the Jews of Russia at more than 3,000,000, and the highest makes them amount to 6,000,000.[2] Rejecting as extravagant the calculation which makes them double every fourteen years,[3] we may surely admit that the ruling powers have some cause to be alarmed if a race that dislikes agriculture, mechanical industry, the life of a sailor, and the profession of arms, that does not intermarry with its neighbours, that does not share their traditions, or aspirations, or faith, increases, let us say, twice as rapidly. Eighty years ago it might have been sufficient to deal with the Jews of Russia, as the wise policy

[1] According to the last capitation there were 166,871 Jews in Poland, exclusive of Lithuania (c. 1778) Clarke, *Travels in Poland*, book i. chap. vii. p. 119. The population of Lithuania was probably about half that of Poland at this time. This would make the number of Jews about 250,000; but it is safer to put it higher, as they were reputed to be skilful in evading the capitation tax.

[2] The *Statesman's Year-Book* for 1891 gives the number of Jews in Russia as 3,000,000, but the calculation is manifestly inadequate, as only 80 per cent of the population of the Empire is accounted for in the table of faiths. Lanier puts the Jews at 3,100,000, but his calculation is defective in the same way. M. Metchersky, as quoted in the *Contemporary Review* (March 1891, p. 320) declares that there are 6,000,000 Jews in Russia. It seems as if 4,000,000 would not be an excessive estimate. In that case they have increased tenfold, while the rest of the population has increased rather less than threefold. If this rate of relative progression is continued, they will be one-ninth of the population, instead of as now one-twenty-sixth, in 110 years.

[3] Prince Metchersky, indeed, goes further, and says: "There are already in Russia 6,000,000 Jews; in twenty years time there will be 20,000,000 Jews."—*Contemp. Review*, March 1891, p. 320.

of Napoleon dealt with those of France, and to give them absolute social and civil equality. The Jews of France are Frenchmen of another faith, and show no tendency to disproportionate increase, being, in fact, as nearly stationary as the rest of the population. The remedy is not as simple in Russia, because the Jews are now a nation in themselves — herding together, too numerous, and, it may be feared, too detested to be absorbed into the general population. However, it is not an object in this place to discuss how the Jews in Russia ought to be treated. What is desired is to show that since it has become impossible to deny inferior races the protection of the law in civilised communities, they are bound to increase faster than the privileged part of the nation. The case of the Jews in Russia is peculiarly instructive, because they were a mere fraction of the population when Lithuania and Poland were first incorporated, and are now numerous enough to appear a danger to the Empire. Nevertheless, even now they would hardly provoke any general hostility if they were not swamping the middle-class in cities. Were they content, like the Roumanians in Hungary, to do field drudgery, their increase would hardly have been noticed till it had become irresistible.

It may be said that the arguments of this chapter assume the progress of the world to be henceforth in an opposite direction to that which has been pursued in the past. Taking Europe, for instance, we find here and there the remnants of inferior peoples, whose ancestors were once widely spread, and whom invaders of a higher type have exterminated or supplanted. The Basques, the Lapps, the Letts are familiar instances; and a very superior race, the Kelts, though they continue to exist, and have always been an appreciable element in Europe, have been Romanised and Teutonised into partial conformity with more vigorous conquerors. It may seem to some as if we might expect the same process to be repeated in Asia and Africa; even if we concede what has been contended for above, that under the conditions which exist in a British or Dutch colony in tropical zones, the native is bound to increase faster than the European. Those who argue in this way must bear in mind that the modern world differs so entirely from the ancient in certain conditions of primary importance, that we are bound to expect a different evolution. For instance, Cæsar is said to have killed a million Gauls, and made slaves of another million.[1] Even if we reduce these estimates by half and allow for Gaul having been a fourth larger than France, it will yet seem probable that a fourth of the male population was either killed or sold out of the country. The last war of modern times, conducted as pitilessly as war was by a Greek or Roman general, was the Thirty Years' War in Germany; and it cost that country four-fifths of its population. "Wurtemberg, which before had a population of half a million, was reduced after the

---

[1] The estimates given are Appian's, but according to Pliny (lib. vii. cap. 20) Cæsar used to boast that 1,192,000 had fallen in battle against him, besides those who perished in the civil wars.—Hume's *Essay on Population*. Cæsar tells us that 368,000 Helvetii entered Gaul; and that the survivors allowed to return home were 110,000. In the case of the Nervii their senators were reduced from 600 to 3, and their fighting men from 60,000 to 500.—*De Bello Gallico*, i. 29; ii. 28. Procopius declares that the wars of Justinian destroyed 1,500,000 persons in Italy alone. "Μυριάδας πεντακοσίας ἐν Λιβύῃ . . . Ἰταλία δὲ οὐχ ἧσσον ἢ τριπλασία Λιβύης οὖσα ἐρῆμος ἀνθρώπων πολλῷ μᾶλλον," etc.—*Anecdota*, c. 18. Even if we admit the compiler of the *Anecdota* to be not Procopius, as seems probable, it is noticeable that he writes of Africa, where he estimates the losses at 5,000,000, from personal observation, and in language that might almost have suggested Burke's description of the Carnatic.

battle of Nordlingen to 46,000."[1] Now it may be rash to say that the world is really better than it was; but it is undoubted, that for more than two centuries—and even in countries where regulars were fighting against partisans—nothing has occurred to parallel or recall these horrors of old time. Neither is this mitigation of war confined to Europe. Burke tells us that when Hyder Ali ravaged the Carnatic, "a storm of universal fire blasted every field, consumed every house, destroyed every temple." When the British armies traversed this district eighteen months later, "through the whole line of their march they did not see one man, not one woman, not one child, not one four-footed beast of any description whatever."[2] Less than a century later, when there was a mutiny in India, which roused the worst passions of religious fanatics and the ferocity of insurgent soldiers, fighting with the halter round their necks, neither the Sepoy outrages nor the terrible reprisals of English soldiers were even comparable to Hyder Ali's style of warfare. The last specimen of the old style of war was seen when the Chinese troops stamped out rebellion in Yunnan and in Ili. Now, although it would not be wise to calculate that there will be no revival of the old savagery, it is reasonable to expect that the accepted practice of civilised nations will on the whole maintain itself, and will influence the procedure of conquerors in Southern Asia, in Africa, and in South America. Meanwhile the effect already produced has told visibly in favour of the growth of population; and its chief effects have naturally been seen in the increase of those who suffered most from war formerly.

---

[1] Niebuhr's *Lectures on Ancient History*, vol. ii. p. 234.
[2] Burke's *Speech on the Nabob of Arcot's Debts*, vol. iii. pp. 160, 161, Bohn's ed.

China and India are the two most striking instances. The Tae-Ping war, which cost China many millions of people, was put down practically by British aid. Our policy could not allow the Chinese trade to be paralysed, and our humanity was horrified by the news of massacres which Gustavus Adolphus, Cromwell, or Turenne would have looked upon as the regrettable but necessary consequences of war. Then, again, in India, for one war that we have waged, we have prevented twenty by the mere establishment of a strong central authority. Accordingly the population of India has increased at least fourfold, probably fivefold, within a century.

There is another way in which we are the blind instruments of fate for multiplying the races that are now our subjects, and will one day be our rivals. We carry the sanitary science and the engineering skill of Europe into the East. The Indian official who wishes to obtain favourable notice at headquarters is very apt to promulgate a new plan of some crowded native town, by which broad streets are to replace the sinuous alleys, and before which the worst quarter will disappear. No native can be compelled to build in conformity with the new regulations, but every native who refuses to do it knows or thinks that he will be a marked man with the police, and compliance is very general. The system does not make our "Raj" popular, but it compasses great good for the people at a comparatively small cost, and familiarises the masses with elementary notions of decency. Five years ago a Governor of the so-called "benighted Presidency," Madras, Sir M. E. Grant Duff, put it on record, that "nearly all municipalities are now willing to undertake the" (sanitary) "conservancy of private dwellings for a small fee."[1] Accordingly, though

[1] Review Minute of 20th September 1886, by H.E. the Governor.

India is still the breeding-place of cholera, its epidemics are much more manageable than they were; and this though the conditions of health in an increased population are more difficult to compass. Anciently, there were periodical famines, sweeping away, it might be, millions at a time. At present, what with irrigation works and enhanced security, the produce of the country is far greater than it used to be, and railways enable it to be more rapidly distributed. A famine, like that which destroyed three-quarters of a million and one-fourth of the population in Orissa as lately as 1866,[1] is becoming every year more and more improbable. Meanwhile, the people, as is only natural, are taking advantage of the prosperity by multiplying rather than by raising their standard of comfort. The education, the contact with other people, that could make the present form of existence appear deficient, are wanting. The ryot asks for little more than to be freed from the worst exactions of the money-lender, to be secured a continuance of peace and reasonable prices, and to be let alone by the English official.

The day will come, and perhaps is not far distant, when the European observer will look round to see the globe girdled with a continuous zone of the black and yellow races, no longer too weak for aggression or under tutelage, but independent, or practically so, in government, monopolising the trade of their own regions, and circumscribing the industry of the European; when Chinamen and the nations of Hindostan, the States of Central and South America, by that time predominantly Indian, and it may be African nations of the Congo and the Zambesi, under a dominant caste of foreign rulers, are represented by fleets in the European seas,

---

[1] Hunter's *Orissa*, vol. ii. p. 185.

invited to international conferences, and welcomed as allies in the quarrels of the civilised world. The citizens of these countries will then be taken up into the social relations of the white races, will throng the English turf, or the salons of Paris, and will be admitted to intermarriage. It is idle to say, that if all this should come to pass our pride of place will not be humiliated. We were struggling among ourselves for supremacy in a world which we thought of as destined to belong to the Aryan races and to the Christian faith; to the letters and arts and charm of social manners which we have inherited from the best times of the past. We shall wake to find ourselves elbowed and hustled, and perhaps even thrust aside by peoples whom we looked down upon as servile, and thought of as bound always to minister to our needs. The solitary consolation will be, that the changes have been inevitable. It has been our work to organise and create, to carry peace and law and order over the world, that others may enter in and enjoy. Yet in some of us the feeling of caste is so strong that we are not sorry to think we shall have passed away before that day arrives.

CHAPTER II

THE STATIONARY ORDER IN SOCIETY

The break-up of the Roman Empire has shown that a splendid political organisation may be destroyed by the concert of inferior or less highly developed races.—Although this was the birth of a new world, it involved the extinction of thought, art, and style for centuries.—Parallels may be found in the histories of Greece, of Peru, and of Cambodia.—The fortunes of Spain and Turkey are striking illustrations of the same law from modern times.—The supremacy of the inferior races in the future is likely to be achieved by industrial progress rather than by military conquest.—The Englishman is changing from faith in private enterprise to faith in State organisation.—The change is likely to affect the character of the race for vigorous originality.—We see the beginning of decadence in the decline of speculative thought.—We find a decay of mechanical invention, and even more, that a less hearty welcome is given to it.—With impaired faith in himself, the Englishman will trust more and more to the State, and to State Socialism, which is likely to be accompanied with a change to the stationary order, population and wealth ceasing to increase.—This change may not necessarily be bad, but it will be great.—Yet, in fact, great parts of State Socialism have already been adopted, and the arguments against the remainder, even if valid, are not demonstrably irrefutable.—What democracies really aim at, that Governments shall give immediate effect to the popular will, need not be a source of unrest and instability if some satisfactory order can be achieved, and if there are the conditions for maintaining it.—The military spirit will not die out, because the instinct of existence is driving every State to aggrandise itself, that it may not be absorbed.—It seems certain, too, that sooner or later China must become a formidable military power.—For all nations, except perhaps the United States and England, military strength means a strong executive organisation, large forces, and the power to mobilise them rapidly.—The belief of some Liberals, that a strong militia may supersede the necessity for a highly trained army, is refuted by the precedents of

American history.—In revolutionary France the Republic was not saved by raw levies, but by militia and regulars, commanded by trained generals, and operating in superior numbers.—Napoleon disapproved of short-service men, and lost battles from the time he began to employ them.—The Spanish volunteers were of no use, except behind walls.—The partial successes of the Boers against England admit of easy explanation.—Therefore military absolutism will be combined with industrial Socialism in the communities of the future. When they are not State soldiers, citizens will very commonly be State servants.—This form of polity is congenial to Eastern nations; and these, as they become powerful, will begin to influence European habits and thought.—As, however, the Englishman has a higher standard of comfort than the Chinaman, he cannot hold his own, other things being equal, against the Chinaman.—The ideal of the European Socialist is, however, not to intensify toil, but to diminish it, and to increase the material and moral well-being of the man.—Throughout Europe this may be done by industrial combination; but Chinese competition will force the European either to protect himself by hostile tariffs or to limit the increase of population.—The belief that the stationary state has been reached will produce general discouragement, and will probably affect the intellectual energy of the people concerned.—If the Mahommedans succeed in becoming dominant in China, China will be an aggressive military power; but this is perhaps less to be dreaded than its industrial development.

THE preceding pages have aimed at showing that certain races which we regard as inferior, and the highest of which is certainly our inferior in military and political organisation, are likely to increase very largely in comparison with the races which at present constitute what claims to be the civilised world. Such an event has happened once before under such circumstances, that its character and results are tolerably well known. An old order, which we call in the first period of its existence the Roman Empire, broke up as invaders poured down upon it from Germany and Russia, from Central Asia, and from Persia. It seems at first incredible that so magnificent a polity as Trajan succeeded to should not have been able to maintain itself. Lying centrally round the sea which was then the great highway and artery of commerce, the Roman dominion was traversed by roads, which gave its armies the great advantage of concentrating rapidly on any point that was menaced. Its population was incomparably greater than that of any neighbour; its generals and engineers and the equipment of its troops were unsurpassed in the world; and the emperors of capacity were sufficiently numerous to have atoned for the incompetence of a few. An observer speculating upon manifest destiny, and knowing nothing more of the earth than was known a little earlier to the elder Pliny, might surely have said with reason in Trajan's time, that sooner or later the eagles would certainly fly in triumph over the whole habitable world. Even now, though we can trace the stages of decadence, it is difficult not to be astonished at the completeness of the ruin. Summing up the most obvious causes, we seem to see that the institution of slavery deprived Italy of a large part of her natural and best defenders; that the burden of taxes produced a depopulation in the provinces, as men ceased to marry, or escaped across the border and joined the barbarians; and that while Rome was thus losing her life-blood, Germans and Parthians were acquiring the arts of war, and becoming conscious of their strength. Even so, we have to fall back upon other explanations—upon famines and pestilences that desolated provinces, and upon an upheaval of peoples in the far East, resulting in an exodus of Tartars across Europe—fully to understand why the attack on the Roman Empire became so strong, and was at last so weakly combated.

Optimists are fond of showing that, after all, all happened for the best in the best of all possible worlds.[1] A larger polity, making country life and local institutions possible, supplanted the rule by municipal garri-

---

[1] Guizot, *La Civilisation en Europe*, Leçons 2 and 4.

sons, the centralisation under prefects and emperor, which Rome had imposed upon her provinces. The German, whom Tacitus had admired, superseded the polished, servile, and profoundly immoral society which Tacitus and Juvenal had denounced. The cross surmounting the Capitol; Telemachus sealing with his blood the decisive protest against the atrocities of the Coliseum; the guild-hall taking the place of the basilica; charitable institutions sown broadcast over the earth; freedom for national life everywhere, and, after a time, freedom for industry, are the obvious contrasts between the old order and the new.[1] There is an element of truth in all this, but it is not a complete statement of the case. We are apt to forget that the process of transformation lasted over centuries. One of the first results of the conquest of the Roman world was that all the highest science and thought, the tradition of the public opinion of the best men, died out with the upper classes, who were its depositories. In Roman law the world lost the jurisconsult while it retained the notary; in the arts of construction, it kept the mason and lost the architect; while in art, in poetry, in philosophy, and in history, it unhappily lost everything. Whether the Germans of a generation later than Arminius were quite as virtuous as Tacitus thought them may reasonably be doubted. What admits of no doubt is, that the Germanic conquerors of France were as vicious and sensual as Tiberius or Vitellius, without being educated up to the level which made a Roman patrician capable of carrying on the government of a civilised country. Even the times of Roman decadence give us Marcus Aurelius,

[1] The late Professor Maurice put these ideas very happily when he said that the title of Gibbon's great work had expressed its limitations; that Gibbon had understood the decline and fall of the old order, but had not appreciated the birth of a new society.

Lucian, and a succession of great fathers, with Appian, Arrian, and Dio Cassius among historians; and Roman poetry may be said to have died out worthily in Claudian. The six centuries that succeeded the invasion of Attila are almost absolutely barren of thought and style. The races that produced Charlemagne and Alfred, Eginhardt and Bede, and to which we owe the Nibelungen Lied, and a host of minor poems, were certainly not wanting in original power, or even in literary capacity. Only criticism, and the appreciation of the best models, and the instinctive apprehension of perfect form had died out; and though the fraternity of great thinkers began again with Anselm, it was not till the thirteenth and fourteenth centuries that the new world seemed able to create poets of the first order, or historians like Joinville and Froissart, whom the charm of expression has endeared to all time.

Now the disastrous gap made in civilisation by the destruction of the Roman Empire has many parallels in history on a smaller scale. There can be little doubt that the wars of Alexander's successors, and the Roman conquests in Greece and Asia, destroyed a very high form of Greek literature,[1] and that Roman supremacy arrested the spread of Greek influence in the East. In Germany, the terrible Thirty Years' War threw back the country in the estimation of good judges for two centuries at least,[2] though in this case the eclipse of

---

[1] "Professor Thiersch, with whom I once discussed this period, said that in his opinion there never existed a period more charming, in an intellectual point of view, than the age of Menander at Athens."—Niebuhr, *Lectures on Ancient History*, vol. iii. p. 49.

[2] "When Germans tell us, as they often do, that their country is only just recovering the ravages of the Thirty Years' War, we are, at first, tempted to smile; but if we examine into the matter closely, we shall find that the statement is literally and perfectly correct."—Grant Duff, *Studies in European Politics*, p. 249, published in 1866.

literature was less noticeable than the injury inflicted on population and industrial progress. A striking example of the way in which a people civilised up to a certain point may be plunged again into barbarism, is exhibited by the fate of the native Peruvians. This people could build roads and aqueducts, such as the Spaniards only knew of by inheriting them from Rome; and the Temple of the Sun at Cuzco was admitted by the Spanish historian, Sarmiento, to be surpassed only by two buildings in Spain, which at that time possessed all really good that it has now.[1] A Spanish conqueror has left it on record, that the Government was so admirable that there was perfect administration, absolute security of property, and a morality far higher than that of the Christian conquerors.[2] It was all swept away within a generation, and we only know of it by the labours of antiquaries. Cambodia and Cochin China are covered with magnificent ruins, which the present occupants of the country cannot account for, and do not claim for their ancestors.[3] No one knows

---

[1] "The road from Quito to Peru is variously estimated at from 1500 to 2000 miles long, built of heavy flags of freestone."—Prescott, *Conquest of Peru*, p. 27. "The aqueduct that traversed the district of Condesugu measured between 400 and 500 miles."—Prescott, *Conquest of Peru*, p. 57. The aqueduct of Chimu is still more than 60 feet in height.—Squier's *Peru*, p. 118. Mr. Squier says that the fortress of the Sacrahuaman can only properly be compared with the Pyramids, or Stonehenge, or the Coliseum. He also calls it "the most massive among monuments of similar character, either in the old or the new world." Of Chimu Mr. Squier says, that a plain from 12 to 15 miles long, by 5 to 6 broad, is thickly studded over with the ruins of the ancient city.—Squier, *Peru*, pp. 468, 469, 118; Prescott, *Conquest of Peru*, p. 41.

[2] Will of Manco Sierra Lejesama.—Prescott, *Conquest of Peru*, Appendix iv.

[3] For good popular descriptions of these ruins, discovered in 1861 by M. Henri Mouhot, see Thomson's *Malacca, Indo-China, and China*, pp. 135-152; Cotteau's *Un Touriste dans l'Extrême Orient*, pp. 409-414; and Vincent's "Rival to Solomon's Temple," printed in his *In and Out of Central America*, pp. 146-181. The date is conjecturally assigned to

whether the race which constructed them was exterminated, or has emigrated, or has relapsed into barbarism. We can only say that a people of eminent architectural genius, and wielding great resources, and probably Buddhist in faith, once occupied these regions, and that its place is now taken by a mongrel population of the Chinese type, and which has contributed nothing to the world's history.

The illustrations of complete ruin in the cases of Rome, Peru, and Cambodia, may seem to belong to times when the forces of the world were not properly equipoised, and when it was impossible to predict how the balance of strength would ultimately incline. At present, large states are very much contained within natural boundaries, and there is a general consent that none shall be aggrandised by inordinate extensions of territory. Napoleon himself, though he was ruined by aiming at too much, did not propose to keep Spain, or any large part of Germany in his own hands; and the annexation of Alsace-Lorraine by conquest may still be regarded as a hazardous experiment. Those who think in this way, may turn profitably to two instances of comparatively modern history.

The Spain of Queen Elizabeth's time possessed Portugal, Naples, Milan, Franche-Comte, and Flanders in Europe; the greater part of what is now called Spanish America, and a line of important settlements in Africa, India, and Malaysia.[1] Its European dominions included

between 1295 and 1373. Mr. Wallace notices similar ruins in Java, and states that they far surpass those of Central America, perhaps even those of India. He also notices that the present inhabitants "look upon these relics of their forefathers with ignorant amazement, as the undoubted productions of giants or of demons."—Wallace's *Malay Archipelago*, pp. 104-106.

[1] "From Borneo to California the great ocean was but a Spanish lake."—Motley's *United Netherlands*, iii. p. 485.

most of the highly civilised and wealthy parts of Europe; the tribute of gold and exotic products that it received from its colonies appeared fabulous to its contemporaries.[1] Spanish state-craft was more highly esteemed in courts than even Italian subtlety; Spanish armies were the best in the world; and Bacon, who held that "no nation which doth not directly profess arms, may look to have greatness fall into their laps," declared that of Christian Europe, only the Spaniards had an effective military organisation.[2] Neither was the greatness of Spain only material. It was the Spaniard Ignatius Loyola who restored the old faith, making it again a militant power, even among thoughtful men; and no country of that day, except England, can show such names in literature as Cervantes, Lope de Vega, and Mendoza.

What Spain was for the western world, Turkey with even greater pageantry of power was for the eastern. "While its Sultan reigned in the palace of the Cæsars by the shores of the Bosphorus, his viceroys gave law in the halls of the Caliphs at Bagdad in the east, or collected tribute beneath the shadow of Atlas in the west. From Aden in the south, his banners emblazoned with the cross scimitars were unfurled to the Indian sea; and at Buda in the north his pashas quaffed their sherbet in the libraries and the galleries of the poet-king, Matthias. The Shah of Persia, the chief of the Holy Roman Empire, and the proud republics of Genoa and Venice were reckoned among the vassals whose tribute swelled his

---

[1] "Contarini estimates Philip II.'s American revenues for the year 1593 at 2,000,000 of scudi, which is certainly not too high."—Ranke's *Spanish Empire*, p. 96. Motley estimates the revenue from Mexico at from 2,500,000 to 3,000,000 of dollars.—*United Netherlands*, vol. iii. p. 487. The English public expenditure in years of peace averaged about £400,000 in the first part of the reign of James I.—Gardiner's *History of England*, vol. ii. Appendix viii.

[2] Bacon's *Essays*, No. xxix.

annual revenue."[1] The observer, who looks to moral conduct as one of the forces of empire, must have admitted that Turk and Spaniard were distinguished in private life by intense religious conviction, by loyalty to the chief of the State, by a temperate habit of life, such as monasteries profess and the service of arms exacts, and by scrupulous fidelity to their word once given. Their vices were those of soldiers in every age, lawlessness to all but their own chiefs, a cynical licentiousness and ferocity; drawbacks no doubt to a perfect character, but not very much in excess of what was held to be permissible at the time. With all these elements of strength, the Spaniard and Turk were justly regarded as a menace to the existence of other nations. Luther spoke of the Turk as the personified wrath of God,[2] and modern criticism declares that the Turk saved Europe by curbing the power of Spain.[3] No one doubted the strength of the two great Empires. Yet within a century from the death of Philip II. the cabinets of Europe were discussing in what way Spain should be dismembered, as they have been discussing for two generations past on whom the inheritance of the Turk in Europe shall devolve. It can hardly have been religious bigotry that destroyed Spain, for its place in Europe was taken by France, which, under Louis XIV., was almost as intolerant of heresy as Spain had ever been. It can hardly have been the drain of colonies, for those colonies were fostering Spanish trade and contributing revenue to the exchequer; and colonies, poorer and not much more wisely administered, made England a great power. It can scarcely have been

---

[1] Stirling-Maxwell's *Don John of Austria*, vol. i. pp. 289, 290.
[2] Luther's *Tisch-Reden*, Band iv. S. 656.
[3] Michelet's *Histoire de France*, Réforme, chap. xv.

comparative barbarism that ruined the Turk, for the conquerors of Constantinople compared as well for civilisation with the degenerate race they overthrew as the Poles and Russians, who have inflicted the severest losses upon them, compare with the Turks. The truth surely is, that we may extend Bacon's axiom, by saying, that if the nation which cultivates war absorbingly is bound to achieve great success, it is bound also to do it at the cost, within measurable time, of its place among the nations of the world.

It may be argued that all the instances quoted are those in which the immediate agent of dissolution has been defeat in war. It is easy to imagine the inferior races increasing more rapidly than they do upon the higher, but difficult to suppose that they will ever be in such numbers as to crush superior skill and energy by brute weight. It is not, however, the purpose of this argument to assume that Europe is ever likely to be overrun by the Chinese, or North America subject to insurgent negroes. Each century has its own way of doing its appropriate work, and though in the face of Europe under arms it may seem perilous to count upon any dying out of the military spirit, every year seems to increase the pre-eminence of industrial over essentially martial nations.[1] The Chinese would be

[1] Even as regards the size of armies, it would be a mistake to suppose that the armies now maintained in time of peace are much larger than was the case anciently. Prussia, in 1740, had an army of 83,468 men to a population of 2,240,000. This is larger in proportion than the Prussian army on the war footing now is. Russia, with a population estimated at 12,000,000, had a peace establishment of 92,000 regulars and about 80,000 irregulars. It has now a population of 107,000,000, and a peace establishment of 841,000. France, in consequence of Fleury's pacific policy, had the smallest army proportionally of any great power at that time—only 130,000 regulars and 36,000 militia, to a population a little under 20,000,000. But the peace establishment in the last years of Louis XIV. had been 360,000 men to a smaller popula-

less dangerous than they are if they were as warlike as the Turks in the sixteenth and seventeenth centuries, because, in that case, they would waste their reproductive forces in arms. The danger for Europe, and for the higher races everywhere, if the black and yellow belt encroaches upon the earth, will not be the risk that St. Petersburg or London may be made tributary to Pekin, but that the expansion of Englishmen and Russians and other like nations will be arrested, and the character of the peoples profoundly modified, as they have to adapt themselves to a stationary condition of society. Beyond this there is the more subtle danger that, while the lower races are raising themselves to the material level of the higher, the higher may be assimilating to the moral and mental depression of the lower.

It is fashionable to talk regretfully of the unrest of modern civilisation. We have become conscious of the cravings for something better than they have which animate almost all classes of society, but especially those who toil with the hand. Emigration to America or Australia is the great outlet for the most energetic in Western Europe; the less imaginative merely go from the country into the large towns, and many of these latter, as they find their hopes disappointed, are seized with the desire to reconstruct society. "If the Englishman," said Fortescue, four hundred years ago, "be poor, and see another man having riches, which may be taken from him by might, he will not spare to do so."[1] The Englishman is a little less disposed now to right himself by violence, but he has a power of righting himself by law which he did not possess in

tion.—*Histoire de mon Temps, Œuvres de Frédéric II.* chap. i. The numbers given by Frederic for Prussia have been altered in accordance with the corrections of the editor, Herr Preuss.

[1] Fortescue on *Monarchy*, chap. xiii.

Fortescue's days, and which may be used with very notable consequences. His tendency in Australia, where he is carrying out modern ideas with great freedom, is to adopt a very extensive system of State Socialism. He goes to the State for railways and irrigation works; the State in Victoria provides him with costless schooling for his children; the State in New Zealand insures him; the State everywhere provides work for him if times are bad; and it is more than probable that the State will soon be called upon to run steamers, to work coal-mines, and at least to explore for the miner in any kind of ore. In Victoria, and more or less in all the colonies, though least of all at present in New South Wales, the State tries to protect its citizens from foreign competition. These changes from English policy have been adopted gradually, and are partially explained by the peculiar circumstances of a young country. What is noteworthy is that they entirely recommend themselves to public sentiment. It is difficult to suppose, that if emigration from England suddenly received a great check, the mother country, confronted with the task of providing for its yearly surplus of population within its own boundaries, would not gradually and cautiously resort to a Socialism like that of Australia. Even as it is, English statesmen have had to make remarkable concessions. The very existence of a Poor Law is the affirmation of the right of every man to have State support in the last extremity. The rights of property and the right of free contract have alike been disregarded in Ireland, when it became a question of the many against the few. The landlord has been assisted to drain with cheap money out of the public exchequer; English diplomacy and arms have been freely employed to open up new markets for

H

British manufactures. The corn of India has been transported at unremunerative rates upon Government lines, in order that the food of the people might be cheapened.[1] There is now a cry for giving free primary education to every one. All these are absolute departures from the time-honoured English principle of leaving every man to do the best for himself, and fare as he may. Some of them are unconscious concessions, and others are conscious approaches to State Socialism. It is scarcely conceivable that we have seen the end yet. There seems nothing overstrained in supposing that the State in England, as elsewhere, may undertake the construction of railways, or the reclaiming of land from the sea; and may, in fact, engage largely in industrial enterprises, so as to ensure work and support for a large part of the population. Again, it may buy up existing railways, as it has bought up telegraphs; and in this case a great body of workmen possessing votes will look to the State as paymaster, and will have a voice in determining what they are to get. Lastly, it is more than conceivable that education of every kind will be made free. The expediency of giving intellect, in every condition of life, its chance to assert itself will recommend this change, and the upper classes are certain to contend that if the State relieves parents in one class of life from the charge of their children's schooling, it is bound to relieve all.

Now, it is impossible to say beforehand whether these changes will be for good or ill. What seems

[1] "The railways, so far from being a commercial success, have entailed the very heavy burden of over £47,000,000 on the Indian taxpayer. . . . The Indus Valley and Sind-Punjab and Delhi Railways are the most signal instance of bounty-supported lines, but to a less extent; all the wheat-carrying lines are only worked by the help of the State."—Connell on "Indian Railways and Indian Wheat," *Statistical Journal*, 1885, pp. 244-253.

evident is that they are bound to affect the character of the whole people. Nowhere in the world has the struggle for existence been so fierce as in Great Britain; and it has been the mainspring of English energy. In the sixteenth century Meteren declared that Englishmen were as lazy as Spaniards.[1] They were, in fact, like the Spaniards of that time, ready for adventure, able to endure great hardships, unsurpassable explorers and privateers, but indisposed to the plodding industry for which Germans and Flemings were conspicuous. Two centuries later Holberg declared that the greatest examples of human indolence were to be found among the pauper class in England, and the best examples of well-applied toil among the English adventurers and merchants.[2] The praise, though Holberg uses the word "industry," is evidently directed to English enterprise. A greater thinker than Holberg, Kant, was peculiarly impressed by the factitious self-reliance and capricious originality of the English character;[3] and taking the general estimate of our nation in that century, we may say that it was a popular reflection of Kant's judgment, though commonly more favourable. The Englishman of old French novels is habitually an original, disregardful of the opinion of the world, ready to measure

[1] Quoted in Motley's *United Netherlands*, vol. i. p. 291. This is the criticism of a foreigner, but it is incidentally confirmed by the negative testimony of the Venetian Ambassador, Andrea Trevisano, of Nicander Nucius, of Borde, and of Lely, who agree in omitting all mention of industry as a feature in English character. It must be borne in mind that the ploughman was scarce in times like the sixteenth century, when most of the land was in pasture, and that we owe our manufactures to Flemish settlers. The two classes most distinguished for steady toil were, therefore, scantily represented.

[2] Holberg's *Betänkning over nogle Europäiske Nationer*, S. 232.

[3] Kant's *Anthropologie*. Kant's estimate is distinctly an unfriendly one. He calls the English "a people of whim:" glances at their "brutal pride:" (*stolze Grobheit*) and suggests that English self-assertiveness is not natural, but the result of circumstances.

himself against any odds, and taking nothing upon trust. Peterborough and Clive, the knights-errant at the head of armies and councils, were in fact glorified instances of the Englishman, as his contemporaries appraised him. The reputation which the Englishman of Great Britain enjoyed has now been in great measure transferred to the Anglo-American. The original race has grown "bulbous, heavy-witted, material,"[1] as Hawthorne cynically puts it; is careful of its bank-balance and of the proprieties; is weighted with an ever-present sense of responsibilities. No Peterborough or Clive would now be allowed a free hand by his Government. The first impetuous act would provoke a recall by telegram. The conquest of an Empire would only terrify the British Cabinet with an apprehension of Parliamentary criticism.

Now, this change, which we see most conspicuously in matters of foreign policy, is one that may be traced in every direction. "The English," says Holberg, "as soon as they hear of anything they are not familiar with, take hold of it at once, examine it, accept it, and teach it publicly." Holberg referred to new opinions; and the contrast between the English school of free thought, which moulded religious enlightenment in the eighteenth century, and the utter sterility of our literature in the nineteenth, except for a single name, is sufficiently remarkable. Heine has said, that the most stupid Englishman can talk sensibly about politics, and that it is impossible to extract anything but nonsense from the best educated Englishman when religion is discussed.[2] The reason is not that educated Englishmen are unconscious of the movement of speculative thought all the

---

[1] Hawthorne's *Our Old Home*, vol. i. p. 99.
[2] Heine, England : *Die Emancipation der Katholiken*, Band xi. S. 115.

world over, but that they deliberately shrink from the impulse to explore new regions, at the cost of surrendering certain accepted and acceptable conclusions. Certainly no one can now say, as Holberg did, that there is a ready taking in and promulgation of new thought. The results of Biblical criticism in Germany have never been tolerated in England, till they were so nearly superseded in their native country as to appear comparatively Conservative; and even the scientific conclusions of the Englishman Darwin were being disseminated in text-books on the Continent while English society was reading refutations of them, or at best taking refuge in half-hearted attempts to reconcile the doctrine of evolution with the teaching of Genesis. Still, it is probably true to say that English speculation is more fearless in physical science than in metaphysics or Biblical exegesis, or the critical reconstruction of history. A great many persons are glad to acquiesce in the view that the conclusions of science may be allowed to stand by themselves, and that when they are absolutely opposed to those of faith, it is not necessary to disbelieve either.

Perhaps one of the best instances of the decadence of English energy is in the imperfect welcome accorded to mechanical invention. The end of the eighteenth century and the beginning of the nineteenth were conspicuous in England by the number of new inventions given to the world. The industrial supremacy of the globe was achieved almost at a bound by the men whose catalogue of names includes Arkwright and Hargreaves, Watt and Bramah, Brinsley and Stephenson, Wedgwood, Maudsley, and Davy. There is no reason why this inventive faculty should not have continued in the country. Nasmyth, Bessemer, Whitworth, and

Armstrong are conspicuous instances that the race retains the power of magnificent conceptions, and the great multiplication of factories and workshops in Great Britain ought to have stimulated the thought, as it has trained the eyes and hands of a large industrial population. Indeed, it may be said that England still contributes the larger half of the world's inventive fertility; but England no longer gets or deserves the credit for it. If we look back to actual history, we shall find that many of the best patents, such as the steam-plough, the sewing-machine, and the electric telegraph had to cross back to England from America before they could obtain recognition.[1] Even Nasmyth's steam-hammer was employed in Creuzot before the foundries of his own country adopted it.[2] The English inventor is still more than the equal of his rivals; more fertile in expedients than the German, and more patient than the American. Where he fails is when he carries his work to market. The instinctive feeling in England is, that if an invention were really valuable it would have been hit upon before; the feeling in America, that

[1] It may be added that the electric telephone was first invented by Mr. Graham Bell of Edinburgh, who had studied the subject under his father in Scotland, though he took out the first patent in America.—Moncel's *Le Téléphone*, pp. 6, 33. A reaping-machine, resembling the Australian stripper, has been traced back to the Belgae as known by Pliny; and Mr. Smiles shows that one was in use in France in the sixteenth century (*Industrial Biography*, p. 173); while the present form was invented by Commin of Denwick (1812), and Patrick Bell of Dumfries (1827), before M'Cormick patented it in America. The sewing-machine was first invented by Saint in England, c. 1790. Howe in America improved it, and sold the patent for a trifle (£250) to Thomas in England. Thomas neglected to bring it out, and Howe bought it again and made it a success in America.

[2] Smiles's *Industrial Biography*, p. 287. Compare Goethe's remark: "Der Engländer ist Meister das Entdeckte gleich zu nützen, bis es wieder zur neuen Entdeckung, und frischer That führt. Man frage nur, warum sie uns überall voraus sind."—*Ueber Naturwissenschaft*, Band iii. S. 268.

whatever is new ought simply because it is new to have a trial. Naturally, perhaps, the Conservative impulse is strongest in our military administration. In 1848 the Prussian needle-gun attracted so much attention in the campaign against Denmark, that a committee of officers was appointed to report upon it. They agreed that it was quite unnecessary to give up Brown Bess, and the change to a long-range rifle had accordingly to be made during the Crimean War.[1] We hold our empire and preserve national existence on the condition of being stronger at sea than any other power, and yet France—a formidable rival and possible enemy—was allowed to outstrip us for a time in the construction of ironclads.[2]

Now, the Conservatism of an ancient society, which shrinks instinctively from change, because any change may lead to dangerous combinations, is most remarkable in England, because England has in many matters been the principle of ferment in the modern world. It has changed Catholicism for Protestantism, and tempered Protestantism with free thought; it has limited monarchy; it has given a peculiar meaning to aristocracy, making that elastic and flexible which is rigid everywhere else; it has associated the working classes with government; it has experimented in making labour free, and in freeing the exchange of labour from fetters ; and it has popularised the feeling,

[1] My authority for this is an officer who was on the committee.

[2] In the summer of 1866 the English ironclad fleet consisted of 36 vessels, carrying 637 guns; the French ironclad fleet of 33 vessels, carrying 777 guns. Even if ships chiefly valuable for coast defence were deducted from these lists, the French still remained superior in guns by 613 to 526, though inferior in the number of sea-going ships by 17 to 27.—*Statesman's Year-Book*, 1886-87. " France undoubtedly was the first to construct sea-going ironclads, a policy we at first thought folly, and then were constrained to follow."—Eardley Wilmot: *The Development of Navies*, p. 249.

that men may make themselves a country anywhere under the sun. It has boasted that it makes the functions of the State small in order to leave the widest possible sphere to energy and enterprise. Therefore, if England becomes temporising in her policy, if her best literary work is circumscribed to the criticism of style, and the construction of literary mosaics; if her wealth is more and more withdrawn from speculative adventures; if her industry is less and less originative; if her people appear to be losing the impulse to better themselves outside of England, or are denied the opportunity, we may surely assume that these changes will be accompanied with a transformation of character. Crushed or cowed by the forces that surround him, the Englishman will invoke the aid of the State. Universal suffrage, which was inevitable, has given him the machinery for moulding all the forces of Government to his purpose, and he will in all likelihood employ them to introduce an extended socialism of the Australian type. It is quite possible that these changes will be worked out slowly, temperately, and wisely. There is no reason why they should be attended with any forcible confiscations of property or cancelling of national obligations. It is conceivable that the soil of England and Scotland might be bought back from its present proprietors, as different statesmen have proposed the soil of Ireland should be, by the creation of a large three per cent stock, the interest on which should be paid by a peasant proprietary. The coal-mines of England might be resumed in the same way, and worked for the State. The question is not whether these changes are desirable and would answer the ends expected, but whether they are not possible and even likely. The case assumed is, that the races of Europe have very nearly reached the extreme limit of expansion, that they will wrest nothing from the inhabitants of tropical countries, and are even likely to lose a little to them, and that when the Temperate Zone is fairly peopled, so that immigration on a large scale will be discouraged by every country, England, which unites a small territory to a dense population, will find itself face to face with the problem how to feed and clothe its people. If we assume a nation, so circumstanced, to become stationary, as France is tending to do, that in itself involves a very great change in character and habits of life—a change, perhaps, quite as great as the adoption of State Socialism. If, on the other hand, we suppose, as perhaps is more probable, that the passage to a stationary condition has to be spread over several generations, in that case there must be some means of supporting the ever-pressing burden of fresh lives.

The case of England has been taken because England is of all countries that which has benefited most by emigration, that which will suffer most when emigration is checked, and that in which socialistic theories have so far found least favour. There are some European countries, like Spain and Russia, which will admit of a very large increase within their own boundaries, and which accordingly need not feel the pressure of population till long after it has become a factor in British politics. There are others again, like France and Italy, which will perhaps readily adapt themselves to the stationary state. Meanwhile we may surely say of all, that it means a great deal for them if dispersion over the earth is checked, and a great deal also if liberty and enterprise come to be powerfully trammelled in the country which hitherto has furnished the greatest argument for their utility. It is possible, of course, that the new order, in which the individual withers and the man is less and less, may have compensating advantages of its own. To some it has seemed that the struggle for existence, which the English theory of unlimited competition involves, is unutterably brutal, and that the survival of the fittest in industrial war means the extinction of all who are weak, of all who have other interests than gain, of all who are scrupulous. It is not the purpose of this argument to consider whether there is any truth in this point of view. All that is contended is, that if anything like the democratic programme of the day comes to be realised; if every man, weak or strong, skilled or unskilled, is assured work on fairly equal terms; if the hours of labour are limited; if the State takes the employment of labour more and more into its own hands, buying up lands and factories and mines, the change will practically be as great as that which has transformed serfs or slaves all over the world into free labourers.

It will also be a change that will reproduce many conditions of primitive society and conditions that we associate with inferior races. The proprietorship of land by communities, as distinct from private property, has existed, to quote M. de Laveleye, "in Germany and ancient Italy, in Peru and China, in Mexico and India, among the Scandinavians and the Arabs, with precisely similar characteristics."[1] A change in the practice of the Western nations has accustomed us to regard this stage in a nation's life as a rude and ephemeral one. It is difficult even to assume a modern State deriving rent from all the land in the country, and running all

[1] Laveleye on *Primitive Property*, p. 2.

the factories. Yet, as a matter of fact, we administer India in conformity with the primitive rule;[1] and every State has been compelled to organise great establishments for the construction of ships, or for providing warlike stores. In addition to this, there are numerous instances of mines belonging to the State, like the saltmine of Wieliczka, and the quicksilver mines of Almaden. The railways are owned by the State half the world over, and there are cases where the State runs commercial steamers,[2] though the more usual practice is for the State to subsidise them. Habitually, the European Governments have only instituted manufactures when the article to be produced was one of limited demand, like the porcelain of Sèvres and Meissen, or the tapestry of the Gobelins, or when it was important to naturalise a new industry, as was the case for some time in Russia. Frederick the Great's practice, approved by Mirabeau and by Mr. Carlyle,[3] of forcing the rich abbeys to establish manufactures, was the action of an exceptional man, more vigorous than economically intelligent, in an exceptional time. If, however, we ask why the best economists, especially in England, have always disapproved of the State mixing itself up in industrial undertakings, we shall find the reasons to be such as would not weigh much, if at all, with Trades-Unionists. Mr. Mill, for instance, argues, that a people whose work is found for them become deficient in initiative; that as a general rule the business of life is better performed when those who

[1] The State in India derives more than £23,000,000 from the rent of land.
[2] The Russian Volunteer fleet—seven ships, bought by subscription, and presented to the Crown—is used for commercial purposes in time of peace.
[3] " Friedrich was not the least of a free-trader," etc.—Carlyle's *History of Frederick the Great*, vol. vi. p. 365.

have an immediate interest in it are left to take their own course, uncontrolled either by the mandate of the law, or of any public functionary; above all, that it is exceedingly dangerous to multiply State functionaries, and concentrate all the power of organised action in a dominant bureaucracy.[1] It is a corollary from these principles that Government work cannot be as cheaply done as the work in private establishments. A Socialist, however, will only regard the first of these arguments as important, and will probably demur to its validity. He will argue, that in private establishments the workman's improvements are habitually confiscated for the use of the master; and that if men continue to invent, where they reap only trifling advantages, they will probably have their wits sharpened when their work is secure of recognition, because the Government has no interest in defrauding them. He will maintain that the logical tendency of unlimited competition is to make profits by sweating the operative, and that the State, which can command its own market, is not liable to this temptation. A Socialist is not afraid of increasing the power of the State, or of multiplying State functionaries. He wishes the interest of the community to be paramount, and that all should be in the State's service. Neither does he think cheap production the main object to be aimed at. It is important, because it economises the wage-fund of the administration; but the real essentials are that the work done should be good, and the workman adequately requited.

This argument has assumed throughout that the progress of the world is not, as is commonly taken for granted, to democracy, but to some form of State

---

[1] Mill's *Political Economy*, Book iii. chap. xi. s. 26; Hearne's *Plutology*, chap. xxiii.

Socialism. It is not contended for a moment that democracy may not be, or indeed is not likely to be, a temporary form of political growth. What, however, does democracy mean? Not necessarily the extinction of hereditary kingship, for a sovereign, and even a line of sovereigns, may be approved the best possible exponents of the popular will. Not necessarily, or perhaps conceivably, the destruction of social inequality, for even if a House of Lords be swept away, men who are pre-eminent by practical ability or by wealth will always make their superiority felt, and if they use their power wisely may count upon a generous recognition. What democracy seems really to mean is the vesting of power in the people in such way that their changes of purpose may have instantaneous effect given to them. It is this approval of mutability which statesmen dread. It may mean that a war will be declared wantonly, and given up disgracefully; that an alliance of long standing will suddenly be discarded; that ruinous expenditure will be incurred; that a national debt will be repudiated, or property confiscated to relieve temporary pressure; that inexperienced men will be put at the public helm in virtue of a certain talent of voluble speech, and a fertility in plausible expedients. Perhaps all these dangers have been exaggerated. The most real of all seems to be the risk of profuse expenditure; and even in this respect it would be difficult for a democracy to transcend the extravagance of the old military monarchies. At any rate, it seems likely that two great causes will so far modify the democratic unrest as to make political society in the rather distant future more stable, more wary, and more compactly cemented than it is now. In the first place, the growth of new military powers, such as China, or the augmentation of old empires, if we assume Hindoos and negroes to be subject to European States, will make it more and more necessary for every country to keep its armies and fleets in a high state of efficiency. In the next place, Socialism, which gives an industrial programme, is almost certain to be the complement of democracy, which only gives the power of adopting a programme. Socialism, however, which strives to annihilate the struggle for existence, competition, and the collision of capital with labour, aims at a millennium of orderly progress from which the pressure of want and the stimulus of ambition shall be excluded.

It may be argued, that as the nations of the world become more and more enlightened, the barbarism of war will tend more and more to be discarded; and the fact noted above, that purely warlike nations cannot hold their own against the industrial races, seems to indicate that the earth may some day be covered with States, all of which desire peace. Unhappily, the dream of peace, which was very prevalent fifty years ago, has been succeeded by a period of wars causing more eventful changes than have been known for many centuries; and Europe is now little better than a camp of instruction. The great cause that has determined this activity seems to be the conviction that only powerful empires can maintain themselves in the immediate future; and that for purposes of self-preservation the weak must unite, and the strong secure themselves by anticipating their neighbours. The gross results are, that Prussia, which could be disregarded thirty years ago, is now a first-rate Power; that Italy has become important as an ally, and that Russia is as strong as ever in Eastern Europe, and incomparably stronger in Central Asia. Meanwhile,

France, Austria, and Turkey are all weaker than they were. Unless we assume the Powers that have gained strength to be satisfied with what they have got, and the nations that have lost to be convinced they cannot retrieve their losses, the war which is always being anticipated is certain some day to break out. The accident of a military sovereign, or an ambitious minister, of troubles at home or possibilities abroad, will be sufficient to determine it. More than this, the great Powers see what they may gain by annexing dominions which will give them soldiers or revenue, or outlets for their commerce. Russia is as certainly working for a harbour in the Persian Gulf as for one in the Dardanelles. Even if we assume that the next fifty years will bring a settlement of all these questions, can any one believe that finality will have been reached? The larger any empire becomes, the more numerous will be the points of contact with its neighbours and possible enemies. There will always be the little adjoining province that is desirable to round off the Imperial territory.

Neither does it seem possible to imagine that the great inert force of China will not some day be organised, and rendered mobile and capable of military aggression. Almost the most secluded of the nations in early times, China was barred from a career of conquest by the mountains of Thibet, the desert of Gobi, and the snows of Siberia. She was swept over by Tartar conquerors, and the repeated attempts of her people to trade or colonise in the Malay Archipelago were met with restrictive measures,[1] or foiled by massacres. Gradually, her policy became one of deified

---

[1] Thus at Bantam, in the 16th century, the Chinese used to be confined to a quarter of their own outside the town.—*Voyages des Hollandais*, tome ii. p. 41. Kerr's *Travels*, vol. viii. p. 143.

inactivity. She tried to concentrate all the energy of her people upon her own soil, and was as unwilling to let the labourer depart as to welcome the merchant. Her great resources went to feed the luxury of a court and the greed of officials. We have compelled her to come into the fellowship of nations. She has adopted steamers, and European artillery and army organisation; she has accepted the telegraph; she is about to introduce railways; and she has credit enough to carry out the changes she needs with foreign capital. On three sides of her lie countries that she may easily seize, over which very often she has some old claim, and in the climate of which her people can live. Flexible as Jews, they can thrive on the mountain plateaux of Thibet, and under the sun of Singapore; more versatile even than Jews, they are excellent labourers, and not without merit as soldiers and sailors; while they have a capacity for trade which no other nation of the East possesses. They do not need even the accident of a man of genius to develop their magnificent future. Ordinary statesmanship, adopting the improvements of Europe without offending the customs and prejudices of the people, may make them a State which no Power in Europe will dare to disregard; with an army which could march by fixed stages across Asia; and a fleet which could hold its own against any the strongest of the European Powers could afford to keep permanently in Chinese waters.

It is not the purpose of this argument to anticipate what the career of military conquest may be in Europe or Asia. All that is aimed at is to show that, though the world may become more and more industrial in its tendencies, the most powerful States will still continue, and indeed must continue, to keep up large armaments, and to be prepared at a moment's notice for defence or aggression. This, however, implies a strong and tolerably permanent Executive. The cases of the United States of America and of England offer no parallel to the condition of the continent of Europe, of Asia, and of part at least of Africa. The United States have no neighbour who can threaten them, and can afford to run the risk of being over-mastered at sea for a few weeks. The Power that ventured on such an experiment would be apt to expiate its short-lived triumph severely. England has a first line of defence for her own shores in her navy. But England is compelled, even now, to keep her Indian army more efficient and more easily mobilised than her forces at home; and this obligation will grow upon her with every decade. For the rest of the world outside the American continent, something like the state of preparation in which France, Germany, Austria, Russia, and Italy keep themselves at present, seems to be inevitable to all time. Even if a general reduction of armaments were agreed to, it is doubtful if it would much alter the equilibrium. One administration would always be in advance of another, by giving more instruction during the same term of service in the militia; so that, when war was declared, it would have an advantage of six weeks over an opponent. But, beyond this, it is difficult to conceive how a great reduction of armaments could ever be effected. Russia, for instance, may need less defence than was once the case on the side of Turkey and Sweden; but she has to guard an infinitely larger frontier against Germany and Austria, against England and China, and against the allies which any one of these powers might succeed in influencing. From the moment China becomes as strong as Roumania is now—that is, can dispose of a corps of 100,000 trained men, or their equivalent, she becomes a power that must enter into the combinations of England, Russia, and France. It seems, therefore, as if the utility of armies was likely to endure; and, if so, it can hardly be doubted that, under present conditions, the ability to handle them promptly and vigorously will also be indispensable. In other words, every State must have a strong military executive more or less independent of party combinations, and more or less autocratic. The alternative is that it ceases to exist, and in this case it will be organised by its conqueror.

It may be argued, on the other hand, by a few Liberals who love peace, that, under free institutions which endear the existing order to every man, it will be easy to enforce an universal conscription of volunteers, militia, or landwehr, on such a scale as to make invasion a danger only to the invader. Unfortunately, the conclusive evidence of history shows that half-trained troops are perfectly valueless in the open field against trained; that even where the troops are fairly matched enthusiasm is a very imperfect substitute for generalship; and that, other things being equal, those who wage a purely defensive war are at a disadvantage. If we take the most thoroughly accepted of the views referred to, the belief in volunteer soldiers, we shall find it to rest very much on the success of the Americans in the War of Independence against England; on the victories of the French Republican armies in 1793-94; on the tenacious resistance of the Spanish guerillas to the French armies; and on the defeat of a body of English soldiers by the Boers at Majuba Hill. Now every one of these supposed instances can be shown to tell the other way. Whether the Americans, many of whom had seen active service against the French, were not more than an ordinary militia may be fairly questioned. It may be conceded that they were less than regulars, and they were accordingly beaten, not dishonourably, but decisively, at Bunker's Hill, at Brooklyn, at Chatterton's Hill, at Germantown, at Brandywine, at Camden, and at Guildford, though the English generals were never more than second-rate, though half the English troops were German mercenaries, and though the Americans latterly were, of course, trained soldiers. The one great success that the militia really achieved was in the third year of the war, when, with an army of 13,216 effectives, it obliged a British force of 3500 to capitulate at Saratoga. Except for the support of the French army under Rochambeau, it is more than doubtful if the Americans could have maintained the struggle in the last year of the war against an English army which never mustered more than 8000 in the field. In this instance, we must bear in mind that the Americans, from their great poverty, were unable to keep their forces together the whole year round, so as to give them the habit of concerted action which distinguishes regular from irregular troops. In 1812 their militia did incomparably worse against the veterans sent out under Ross of Bladensburg, and a little body of 4500 men marched where it liked, defeated armies of 7400 and 6400 successively, burnt Washington, and would probably have taken Baltimore in the teeth of 15,000 militia, if the enemy had not sunk ships to make the co-operation of the British fleet impossible. It may be said that the same year witnessed the defeat of a highly-trained British force under Pakenham before New Orleans. In that case 6000 men, without artillery, and without fascines or scaling ladders, were hurled against strong works defended by twice the number, and were shot down.[1] It is no discredit to the Americans to say that, with equally good strategy, and an equally strong position, almost any troops in the world could have repelled the attack which Pakenham ought never to have made.

The second supposed instance of a defeat of regular soldiers by insurrectionary levies is when France was invaded by the Duke of Brunswick in 1793, and by the Prussians, Austrians, and British in 1794. The popular assumption is that the old French army had been disbanded or allowed to disappear, and that under the influence of revolutionary excitement hundreds of thousands of citizen soldiers sprung to arms under the command of citizen officers, drove the invaders back, and overflowed Italy, Spain, and the Low Countries. "O youth, O hope, O infinite strength of the consciousness and the feeling of right—who could resist them?" says M. Michelet poetically, while he develops this view;[2] and General Foy, a much higher authority on military matters, says that from "the year 1794 inclusive, our young army, commanded by new men who had escaped from studies and counting-houses, was seen to demolish the reputation of old armies and old generals."[3] General Foy probably refers to Moreau, who had been a lawyer, and to Jourdan, who, after serving as a private in the American War, had settled down as a draper. Taking now the facts of history, we shall find that the poetical view requires to be largely discounted. The army of the monarchy was never disbanded, though it lost a great many of its officers and men by emigration, or otherwise, and was more or

---

[1] Gleig's *Washington and New Orleans*, chaps. vii.-xiv. and xxi.-xxiii.
[2] Michelet, *Hist. de la Révolution*, tome iv. p. 68.
[3] Foy, *Guerre de la Péninsule*, tome i. p. 100.

less demoralised. The work of reorganising it was constantly going on. "The regulation of the infantry manœuvres of 1791," says Foy, "is a model of concision and clearness," and he explains that in that year a change, bringing privates into closer contact with their officers, was introduced.[1] "If in 1792," says Napoleon, "France repelled the aggression of the first coalition, it is because she had had three years to prepare in, and in which to levy 200 battalions of the National Guard; it is because she was only attacked by armies of at most 100,000 men. If 800,000 men had marched under the orders of the Duke of Brunswick, Paris would have been taken, in spite of the energy and the onward rush of the nation."[2] What really happened then in 1792 is that a very inadequate though efficient army, under the Duke of Brunswick, prepared to march upon Paris, capturing fortresses and defeating armies on its way. The French troops, though not good enough to be called soldiers, were a great deal better than volunteers. They consisted partly of regiments out of the old army, and partly of the National Guard, under experienced officers. Dumouriez, Kellerman, Rochambeau, Lafayette, Luckner, Montesquieu, Dillon, Beurnonville, Custine, Biron, and Beaurepaire—the men who are responsible for the failures and successes of 1792—were all old officers of the aristocratic *régime*. They could not at first give cohesion or self-confidence to the troops under them. Brunswick's army advanced, taking Longwy and Verdun, and winning two victories at Grand-Pré and Vaux,—in the latter of which 1500 Prussian hussars scattered a whole corps of 10,000 men in a disorderly flight which carried

---

[1] Foy, *Guerre de la Péninsule*, tome i. p. 109. Compare Stephen's *French Revolution*, vol. ii. pp. 197-200, and 451.
[2] Napoleon, *Notes et Mélanges*, tome ii. p. 294, edition of 1823.

some of the fugitives to Paris.[1] Gradually, however, Dumouriez received reinforcements, and was able to keep his men together in the entrenched camp of Valmy under a cannonade which only cost each side 800 men out of 70,000 or 80,000 brought into the field. The mere fact that the French forces were able to hold their position was equivalent to a victory under the circumstances. From that time forward the French were on the aggressive, and before the end of the year the victory of Jemappes, in which, however, they were two to one against the Austrians, gave them possession of Austrian Flanders.[2] Valmy and Jemappes, such as they are, are the only victories that can be claimed for the French insurrectionary levies. They were won by soldiers and militia troops under veteran officers; and if their leaders had had a little more time in which to weld together their excellent but discordant materials, the army would have been a more than average specimen of a well-trained French force of those days. During the years next succeeding its composition steadily grew better. Carnot, a man of genius, organised it; and the opportunities given to privates and young men of rising to important command were taken advantage of by a number of able officers. Still, Moreau is perhaps the one instance of a civilian who rose rapidly to distinction in the army. Hoche, Ney, Jourdan, Junot, Massena, Bernadotte, and Berthier, had all been privates or non-commissioned officers in the Royalist army before they rose to command under the Republic.

---

[1] "At the very outset the French encountered the most ludicrous reverses. The French troops had proved as worthless as their leaders were incapable. Whole brigades turned tail, crying that they were betrayed, casting away their weapons as they ran, and betraying the most abject cowardice and terror."—Griffith, *French Revolutionary Generals*, p. 4.

[2] Alison says 40,000 to 19,000.—*Hist. of Europe*, vol. ii. p 188.

We know what Napoleon's opinion of short-service men was. Decrès once said to him in council, "I cannot extemporise a sailor as you do a soldier. It takes seven years to make a sailor. You turn out a soldier in six months." "Taisez-vous," said Napoleon. "Such ideas are enough to destroy an empire. It takes six years to make a soldier."[1] On another occasion he wrote of himself: "The First Consul did very good things, he put everything in the right way, but he did not work miracles; the heroes of Hohen-Linden and Marengo were not recruits, but good and old soldiers."[2] Evidently Napoleon's knowledge of the levies of 1792 and 1793 had not inclined him to suppose that enthusiasm can be a substitute for drill. His own experience was, in fact, very significant. The French navy, deprived of its best officers and gunners, who were largely Royalist, had to trust to reconstruction under such administrators as the man who wound up his official report with the words, "Legislators, these are the impulses of an ingenuous patriot, who has no guiding principle but nature, and a truly French heart"; or the other, who appended a marginal note to his acceptance of resignations from the old staff: "there are plenty more to be got."[3] The result was seen in those engagements when ships, officered and manned by men who for courage were worthy foes of Nelson and Collingwood's heroes, were constantly out-manœuvred and destroyed in the first engagement.[4] Napoleon's fall is

---

[1] Thiers quoted by Senior, *Conversations*, vol. i. p. 291.
[2] Napoleon, *Notes et Mélanges*, tome ii. p. 218.
[3] Jurien de la Gravière, *Guerres Maritimes*, tome i. pp. 138, 139.
[4] "In 1810 or 1811," said Admiral Mathieu, "I was on board a French corvette, which fought an action with an English vessel, the *Lively*. We passed three times under her stern, and raked her each time. We ought to have cleared her decks. Not a shot touched her."—Senior's *Correspondence of A. de Tocqueville*, tome ii. p. 202.

the record of a struggle by volunteers handled by some of the best leaders in the world against men only a little better drilled, and who scarcely dared face them. If half the conscripts who fought at Leipzig could have been exchanged for an equal number of the veterans sacrificed in Russia, the map of Europe would be very different now from what it is. Raw levies did not save the Republic in 1792, but they ruined the Empire in 1814.

As little can it be said that irregular levies or guerillas saved Spain during the war with the French that began in 1808, and only ended when Wellington crossed the Pyrenees in 1813. The capitulation of Baylen and the defence of Saragossa are the only important instances during the whole of that period when raw Spanish levies did good service against a regular force. At Baylen, where the French general was incapable, perhaps half-hearted, where his forces were divided, and where two Swiss regiments turned against him in the battle, the Spanish regulars were twice as numerous as the French actually engaged, and the presence of a few thousand armed peasants only gave solidity and confidence to the regular force.[1] At the first siege of Saragossa the defenders were as two to one compared with the investing army, and, in spite of a heroic defence, must have capitulated if the news of Baylen had not forced the French to retire. At the second siege, where the besieged were as many in number as the besiegers, they were forced to surrender

[1] Foy reckons the French force actually engaged under Dupont at 12,000 against 40,000 Spaniards. After Dupont's surrender, Vedel's division came up, and was forced to capitulate.—*Guerre de la Péninsule*, tome iv. p. 68. Alison puts the army of Castanos at 28,000 foot and 2000 horse, who appear, however, to have received reinforcements. Alison ascribes the victory to the Swiss and Walloon guards, and to the Spanish artillery, all regulars.—*Hist. of Europe*, vol. vii. pp. 359-362.

after a defence in which three-fourths of their number had perished.[1] In short, even behind walls, and when they were largely mixed with regular troops, volunteers could not hold their own against military experience and discipline. Of the guerillas, Napier tells us that they could do nothing against even a house or church, of which the French had barricaded the entrance.[2] They were excellent for cutting off stragglers, intercepting communications, and generally giving annoyance, especially when they were backed by a regular army; but as a rule they were more formidable to their friends than to the enemy. The attempt to employ them has never again been made, except during the French occupation of Mexico, and then also it was a complete failure. Under generals of very ordinary talent, a small body of French troops kept the country down, as long as they were allowed to remain there.

The successes of the Boers in the Transvaal against British troops have revived in some quarters the belief that men who are good shots, and know the country, may be employed against well-disciplined troops, even in the open field. It must be borne in mind that one of the great sources of weakness in irregulars—their liability to get in one another's way—scarcely occurs when only handfuls of men are brought into action. The Boers had also seen service enough in Kaffir wars to be free from the liability to sudden panics. The force which Sir George Colley led to three separate defeats consisted altogether of less than 1100 men. They were

---

[1] Thiers estimates the troops actually before the walls at 18,000 (*Consulat et Empire*, livre 33); Alison at 16,500 (vol. vii. p. 243); while the troops inside Saragossa are put by Thiers at 40,000 to 45,000, and by Alison at 40,000. French troops, variously estimated at 17,000 to 26,000, were, however, employed in keeping open communications.

[2] Napier's *Peninsular War*, book xv. chap. i.

wasted in attacks on strong positions in the hills, and at Majuba Hill a portion of them were sent to occupy ground of which they knew nothing, surrounded by an enemy in superior force, whom they had neither cannon, Gatlings, nor rockets to dislodge.[1] Such defeats, however creditable to the Boers who inflicted them, could not have affected the issue of the campaign. The English forces within striking distance of the enemy were overwhelming, and must have dispersed the insurgents, if a peace, politically defensible, but more remarkable in its surrender of military honour than the capitulations of Kloster-Zeven or Baylen, had not been hastily rushed through by the British Government.

It has seemed important to discuss this question of defence without defiance at length, because if there be any organisation by which a great State can secure itself from attack, without spending large sums on its army and navy, and using up many years of its subjects' lives in forced service, there can be no doubt but that the wisest statesmanship will adopt it; and in that case the military influence, which is essentially absolutist, would be withdrawn from politics. What, however, we have to anticipate is, that every State will have to be constantly on its guard against dismemberment or subjugation; and this not only as now, but more than now, because some new States will have been formed, or even more, because some old ones will have become very formidable. If, however, the industrial requirements of old States have led to something like State Socialism, we may expect this to take an all-pervading form. The child will be taught at State schools, and, perhaps, taught the elements of a craft, and drilled there. The youth will be compelled to take service

[1] Bellair's *Transvaal War*, chap. x.

in the State forces; when he is discharged from service will have employment found for him by the State; and will be supported in sickness or old age from a State Insurance Fund. He will find it increasingly difficult to emigrate; and as the principal forms of labour will have been monopolised by the State, he will find it difficult to invest his savings in anything but the purchase of State funds. It is conceivable that loafers and vagrants will be hunted down and punished under this *régime*, with incomparably more severity than any modern State attempts. Even the institution of an idle Monday may be put down, when labour is regarded as a due to the country, and not as the private property of the individual, which he may sell or withhold at pleasure. States organised on the democratic basis for giving labour its greatest possible return, and citizens compelled to submit impartially to military discipline, are likely to approach the problems of life with great seriousness, and to be very intolerant of the Bohemian element in rich and poor. Besides, if private speculation has been to a great extent extinguished by the State monopoly of some form of enterprise, large fortunes will gradually be subdivided, and the privileged class, that spends lavishly and claims to exempt itself from the ordinary burdens, from the conscription or the obligation to work, will become very unimportant.

Now it is noticeable that this form of society will be an approximation to old forms, which are eminently consonant to the genius of those races—the Chinese, the Hindoo, and the American Indian—which it has been shown are likely to increase in numbers and become strong. If we can assume a really powerful China, and an united India, independent, or practically so, and a strong Central African State, or federation of

States—suppositions which are at least possible—we can hardly suppose that they will be without influence upon the States of European growth. The conquest of India not only introduced the Nabob into English society, but naturalised the vulgar profusion to which adventurers in the East had become accustomed. Algeria was a very small province to have any effect on French society, but many Frenchmen declare that it infected their soldiers with what is known in France as "the vice of Algeria." To take the strongest instance of all, no one can doubt that the planters and mean whites of the Southern States were powerfully modified by their contact with the black race, becoming imperious, licentious, and disdainful of patient toil. It is the habit in England to assume that the reprobation of Chinese vice—from opium-eating and gambling to nameless immorality—which Australians and Californians feel is mere political affectation, because there is a vicious white class in every great city. The fact, however, is, that a community is distinctly injured by the introduction of new forms of immorality, which attract some for whom the old would have no fascinations. In all the instances cited, the foreign element and influence have been comparatively weak. If, however, China were organised, as she is likely to be; if her flag floated on every sea, and her naval officers visited every great port as honoured guests; if her army was an important factor in the peace of the world, and her diplomatists respected in consequence; if her commerce was world-wide; if her literature was achieving a success of esteem for style and thought, it is inconceivable that these influences would not tell upon the character and conduct of mankind. It is not assumed that this effect would necessarily be all evil. The Chinaman might, for instance, be an example of patient toil; and this, with certain reasonable limitations, is to be admired. What, however, seems probable is, that as the Chinese race forced itself into a position of equality with its neighbours, the spectacle of lives consumed in labour, lives rewarded by nothing but the supply of animal wants, would cease to be considered repulsive and humiliating. European Socialism aims at distributing labour and wealth, so that every man may have leisure and the opportunity of becoming better than he is. The practical Socialism of the East has never aimed at more than the satisfaction of material needs. The question is, whether, when the two forces are measured one against the other, that which has the lowest aims is not bound to starve the other out of the field.

No one in California or Australia, where the effects of Chinese competition have been studied, has, I believe, the smallest doubt that Chinese labourers, if allowed to come in freely, could starve all the white men in either country out of it, or force them to submit to harder work and a much lower standard of wages. In Victoria, a single trade, that of furniture-making, was taken possession of, and ruined for white men within the space of something like five years. Only two large employers excluded Chinamen altogether; and white men, where they were retained, were kept on only to supply a limited demand for the best kind of work.[1] Now, what Chinamen can do in Melbourne, where only

[1] See the evidence upon Technical Education in Victoria taken before a Commission in 1888. Mr. Svenson, a cabinetmaker, was asked, "You think that the Chinese competition has interfered with you." "Yes; very much. I hardly know one of what I may call my mates in the cabinet-making line. They have all gone to other occupations." Mr. Harwood, a cabinetmaker, said, "The lower branches of the trade are monopolised by the Chinese."—*Blue Book*, pp. 37 and 46, published 1889.

the worst workmen go, and where these receive wages which would be thought high in China, Chinamen at home could do incomparably better, if they worked in establishments fitted up with the best machinery, and were directed by foremen knowing the European taste. Does any one doubt that the day is at hand when China will have cheap fuel from her coal-mines, cheap transport by railways and steamers, and will have founded technical schools to develop her industries? Whenever that day comes, she may wrest the control of the world's markets, especially throughout Asia, from England and Germany. The alternative will be that England—having adopted and developed the principles of State Socialism—will enforce a rigidly protective tariff against the cheap industry of her rival. How far this can be practicable with the races subject to England may be a question. The Hindoo may strongly resent having to purchase English muslins, if he can get a better article at half the price from Canton. What, however, it is really important to notice is, that a reversion by England to a protective tariff would be a very powerful modification of English thought and policy; and, if there be any truth in Free Trade, would be financially disastrous to England herself in the long run. Probably, however, it would be evaded, as regarded the East, by the establishment of Chinese factories upon English soil in some part of the Straits Settlements.

It will be observed that both the changes at work within English society and the change resulting from the organisation of labour in the Black and Yellow Belt will tend to intensify toil, and to diffuse it more uniformly throughout the strata of society. Socialism, however, is aiming at something very different. Its desire is to abolish competition, to secure a fair day's work at a fair day's wage to every man, and to arrange for intervals of toil,—a day and a half or two days in every week,—when the body may recruit strength, and the attention be relaxed. It is certain that neither the days of slavery, nor those of serfdom, nor the palmy times when capital and labour were left to make their own terms, have ever given the workers an even tolerable existence, except it may be now and again for brief intervals. The best Professor Rogers is able to say for the thirteenth and fourteenth centuries is, that it was tolerably easy to support life, and that "the poorest and meanest man had no insurmountable and absolute impediment put in his career, if he would seize his opportunity, and make use of it."[1] The most grudging requirements of modern legislation demand that a family shall live in wholesome tenements, that children shall be educated up to a certain low level, that children shall not be stunted by overwork, and that women shall not be allowed to unsex themselves by certain kinds of rough labour. Practically, however, only a part of all this is enforced. Is it too much to say that, in the general interest, separation of the sexes in homes might be insisted on, with the result that, instead of families living in a single room, there should be three bedrooms at least to every married man's domicile? Ought not the average of wages to be such, that every able-bodied man could bring up his family in a house good enough for self-respect, on food good enough to maintain the body at its highest efficiency, and at the same time to make a provision against sickness and old age? Is it not for the interest of the State that every child should be well taught, that the most capable should be able to rise out of the ranks,

[1] Rogers, *Six Centuries of Work and Wages*, pp. 183, 184.

and that all should have a little sunshine, some respite from toil during their early years? There is so little in all this that is extravagant, that in fact everything suggested is being cared for in one country or another by philanthropists or the law. It would, no doubt, be a great step to see all carried out together in the same society, but it would not be as great a change as the transition from slavery to free labour has been.

For Europe and North America to be brought up to this state of development—other things being as they are—would imply a levelling-up of wages that is not at first sight impossible. Practically, the highest-paid artisans hold their own in the race for supremacy, so that England and the United States have nothing to fear from the competition of Russia and Austria. Indeed, in America the opportunities of money-making afforded by a young country are so great, that private enterprise is not as yet seriously threatened by Socialism, except in the bastard form of Protection. In England the principle that men who will work must not starve has always been admitted, though in a somewhat grudging fashion: law and the unions are limiting the hours of labour and fixing the wage-rate; and little remains to be done beyond providing State employment on a large scale. Probably the Continental workman would require to be content with a little less than his rival in Birmingham or Manchester, because his employer would have to get similar results to the English on a larger expenditure upon coal; but it cannot be impossible to adjust differences of this kind. In that case, we may assume that all the races possessed of the same, or nearly the same civilisation, will belong, so to speak, to the same trades-union, so far as production is concerned, but will more or less rigidly exclude one another's manufactures by protective tariffs. England, of course, might not conform to this policy; but if England stood alone in her Free Trade, the exception would be unimportant. She would not be able to force her products upon her neighbours; she might lose to some of them, and find her industries dying out one by one. It is quite conceivable, for instance, that she might lose the carrying trade in the eastern seas to China, as her steamers there are already very largely manned by Lascars and Chinamen.

Now, it is surely probable that the European nations, with their production limited, and its price enhanced by Socialism, and with exchange among themselves fettered by protection, would find themselves at a great disadvantage in competing with a really industrial China. The resources of China are immense, the capacity of its people for toil is almost unlimited, and their wants are of the slenderest. The great mass of the people lives ascetically, and retains its habits, even when it is thrown among wasteful races like the English of America and Australia, who despise and distrust asceticism. The organisation of labour appears to be largely in the hands of employers, who maintain their ascendency by murder. We may assume all this to be modified, but we cannot assume the change to be so sudden and complete that Chinese industry will conform to the standards of the western world. What is true of the Chinese is true more or less of Hindoos and negroes. A hundred years hence when these races, which are now as two to one to the higher, shall be as three to one; when they have borrowed the science of Europe, and developed their still virgin worlds, the pressure of their competition upon the white man will be irresistible. He will be driven from every neutral market and forced to confine himself within his own. Ultimately he will have to conform to the Oriental standard of existence, or, and this is the probable solution, to stint the increase of population. If he does this by methods that are inconsistent with morality, the very life-springs of the race will be tainted. If he does it by a patient self-restraint that shows itself in a limitation to late marriages, national character will be unimpaired, but material decline will have commenced. With civilisation equally diffused, the most populous country must ultimately be the most powerful; and the preponderance of China over any rival—even over the United States of America—is likely to be overwhelming.

Let us conceive the leading European nations to be stationary, while the Black and Yellow Belt, including China, Malaysia, India, Central Africa, and Tropical America is all teeming with life, developed by industrial enterprise, fairly well administered by native governments, and owning the better part of the carrying trade of the world. Can any one suppose that, in such a condition of political society, the habitual temper of mind in Europe would not be profoundly changed? Depression, hopelessness, a disregard of invention and improvement would replace the sanguine confidence of races that at present are always panting for new worlds to conquer. Here and there, it may be, the more adventurous would profit by the tradition of old supremacy to get their services accepted in the new nations, but as a rule there would be no outlet for energy, no future for statesmanship. The despondency of the English people, when their dream of conquest in France was dissipated, was attended with a complete decay of thought, with civil war, and with a standing still, or perhaps a decline of population, and to a less degree of wealth.[1] The discovery of the New World, the resurrection of old literature, the trumpet of the Reformation scarcely quickened the national pulse with real life till the reign of Elizabeth. Then, however, there was revival, because there were possibilities of golden conquest in America, speculative treasures in the reanimate learning of Greece, and a new faith that seemed to thrust aside the curtain drawn by priests, and to open heaven. It is conceivable that our later world may find itself deprived of all that it valued on earth, of the pageantry of subject provinces and the reality of commerce, while it has neither a disinterred literature to amuse it nor a vitalised religion to give it spiritual strength.

The foregoing argument has assumed that the growth of China will be gradual and peaceable, and that India, if it ever becomes independent of England, will split up into a cluster of states, federated it may be, but not capable of an aggressive foreign policy. There is one possible alternative to this future too important to be disregarded. We are not yet able to say whether Mahommedanism has ceased to be a ferment and a great organising influence. It was beaten in the Indian Mutiny; it has been stamped out in Yunnan and Ili,

---

[1] "The population of this island does not appear to me to bear any proportion to her fertility and resources."—*Italian Relation of England*, c. 1500, p. 31. "Hereof is much experience had in England, France, and other lands, and cause hereof is this that evermore the world decreaseth in people."—Pecock's *Repressor of overmuch blaming of the Clergy*, p. 306, c. 1449. When we remember that the population of England was "never in excess of 2,500,000, and was often less," down to the end of the sixteenth century, it will be evident that the Wars of the Roses, when as many as 30,000—by one estimate 38,000—perished in a single battle, that of Towton, must have reduced the population for a time nearly one-half. It is noticeable, that while 108,000 men were brought into the field at Towton, not more than about 30,000 were present at Bosworth.—Pauli's *Geschichte Englands*, Band v. SS. 359, 360, 511; Lingard's *History of England*, vol. v. pp. 173, 174, 270.

after wars in which millions of lives were destroyed; and its solitary success in the Soudan has not been followed up, and was due very much to the fact that it was combined with a national uprising against a detested foreign rule. Still it is impossible to forget that an active Mahommedan propaganda is being carried on in China, and that the province of Yunnan was, at one time, almost in the hands of the followers of the Prophet. Father Girard says that, in a single instance, when there was a famine in the province of Chan-tong, the Mahommedans bought ten thousand children, whom they educated in their own faith.[1] The whole number of Moslems in the Empire "is estimated by some officials at 20,000,000 to 25,000,000."[2] Observers agree that the Mahommedan may commonly be distinguished from his Buddhist countryman by his erect bearing and fearless tones. Islam, in this country also, transforms its votaries into military fanatics. As the popular Buddhism is nothing more than Paganism of a rather gross kind, though, with a fairly good ethical code, it may, in spite of the advantage it possesses of being the faith of the large majority, and backed by the Government, go down before a monotheism that has already been embraced by the Turkish division of the Tartars, and which is the predominant religion in Malaysia. The accident of a leader of genius arising to combine the Mahommedans in a common organisation might conceivably transfer sovereignty to a follower of Islam. In that case it is difficult to suppose that China would not become an aggressive military power, sending out her armies in millions to cross the Himalayas, and traverse the Steppes, or occupying the islands and the northern

[1] Girard, *France et Chine*, tome ii. p. 250.
[2] Balfour's *Waifs and Strays from the Far East*, pp. 31, 32.

parts of Australia, by pouring in immigrants protected by fleets. Luther's old name for the Turks, that they were "the people of the wrath of God," may receive a new and terrible application. It seems reasonable to suppose that such a visitation can only be possible in the distant future, and not unreasonable to hope that it may never occur. Should it, however, take place, the ultimate effect would probably be to drain China of population and wealth, which die out gradually wherever the Crescent floats in triumph. The military aggrandisement of the Empire, which would provoke general resistance, is, in fact, less to be dreaded than its industrial growth, which other nations will be, to some extent, interested in maintaining. Still, even a ten years' conflict against forces far greater than Tamerlane's, and inspired with as ferocious a spirit, would be something so horrible that we may well pray for it to be never anything more than an evil dream.

CHAPTER III

SOME DANGERS OF POLITICAL DEVELOPMENT

Large armies, large towns, and large national debts are said to be causes of national decline.—As nations increase, large armies will be more and more a necessity, even though statesmen may be pacific.—There are compensations to standing armies in the education given and the feelings called out by military training. Neither is war itself an unmixed evil—The tendency of populations to concentrate in towns is becoming more and more marked.—People flock to towns for work, for large profits, and because the growth of railways tends to concentrate business in a few large centres.—Beyond this, excitement, amusement, social intercourse, economy, are determining motives; and the townsman, once formed, contracts a dislike for country life.—The ancient idea was that city influences elevated and civilised men. Many remarkable men have found their only congenial sphere in a city.—Cities, however, though they attract great men, and develop the life of society, have no tendency to create genius or intellectual distinction.—One drawback to city life is that it destroys physical stamina, though science has done a great deal to eliminate disease and protract life.—And though legislation has promoted the well-being of the labourer, and though some descriptions of city labour are not unwholesome.—On the other hand, the city type is changing for the worse, though the cities are still vitalised by the best life-blood of the country districts.—As cities become of monstrous dimensions, the higher society that grows up in them is too various, and habitually too frivolous, to be of much civilising potency.—Even more does the lower class suffer by being shut out from nature and debarred the sympathy of neighbours.—The conditions of life in large cities are unfavourable to the privacy and self-respect without which family life cannot grow to any perfection.—Social reforms may counteract some of the evils arising from this tendency, but cannot be a cure for all.—Women are special gainers by the great wealth and variety of amusement in towns.—Nevertheless, amusements in towns are not more intellectual than they were, but less so. The lecture has been killed by the book or newspaper; the higher drama by the novel.—It is only an apparent exception that the drama maintains itself in Paris, and that Ibsen has had a success of esteem.—The city music-hall is not appreciably superior to the city tavern.—The sordid frugality of a country population is due to its circumstances, and the changes imminent in city life are such as will naturally engender avarice.—National debts may be incurred for justifiable and good reasons.—Countries with great natural resources appear to be warranted in mortgaging their future, in order to develop their resources.—There may, however, be periods of depression, even of decline for prosperous states.—Under the influence of theories of State Socialism, a country may engage in a vast speculation, such as buying up the land and leasing it to small cultivators; and this speculation may prove to be unremunerative.—In such a case, there might be a danger of the taxpayer repudiating his engagements to the fund-holder, and, indeed, that he could not fulfil them.—Examples of national bankruptcy are very numerous in the past.—Repudiation lowers the tone of national character; and the impoverishment of the fund-holders would extinguish a class that is very conservative of certain valuable qualities.—Whether large armies, large cities, large debts are to ruin modern society, depends upon how we use the armies, how far we can neutralise town influences, and whether we allow the indebtedness to corrode national morality.

THE late Mr. Ticknor, a learned student of history, and who was also a sagacious observer of modern society, used to express the opinion that the "ancient civilisations of the world had been undermined and destroyed by two causes—the increase of standing armies, and the growth of great cities; and that modern civilisation had now added to these sources of decay a third in the hypothecation of every nation's property to other nations."[1] It has been a part of the argument in these pages to show that the maintenance of large armies, easily mobilised, is as much a necessity now as it has been in past times. For many years to come the nations of the Temperate Zones will be trying to encroach upon one another, or on the uncivilised parts of the world, not necessarily because the spirit of an Alexander or a Napoleon animates any modern monarch, but because

[1] Ticknor's *Life*, vol. ii. p. 403.

every statesman has come to believe that national existence is only possible for great Empires. Meanwhile, the nations of the Tropics that have adopted European improvements, and it may be solidified and grown strong under European control, will inevitably adopt the policy of large armaments; all the larger because the individual Hindoo, Chinaman, or Negro is inferior to the individual European. It is quite conceivable that the soldier may be rather less of an obtrusive element in the future than he has been in the past. This, however, is not likely to be because armies will be relatively smaller, but because universal conscription will have become the rule, and military education, up to a certain point, will be part of the stock-in-trade with which every citizen is equipped when he enters life.

This conception of a world always ready for war is, of course, very different from the dreams which pacific optimists have nursed. We have been told that, as the military caste of kings and nobles is dispossessed; as society becomes more sensible and understands the waste of war; as it is informed with a higher morality and comprehends its wickedness; as the class to which war means privation and misery is able to make itself heard in the councils of the State; perhaps, too, as the risks of dismemberment to States and annihilation to combatants become more formidable, war will be replaced everywhere by international arbitration. All this may be true, but, even so, it is difficult to suppose that arbitration will not be influenced by a calculation of the forces every power interested can bring into the field; or that war will not now and again be resorted to where arbitration fails to reconcile conflicting interests, or where a decision is opposed to a high-spirited people's sense of justice. We are bound to remember that wise and good statesmen have constantly endeavoured to promote a general peace. It may be instructive to take two comparatively modern instances. In 1736 England was administered by the peace-loving Walpole, and France by the peace-loving Fleury, Austria had almost disbanded its army, Russia was only dangerous to the Turks, and the South of Europe was profoundly lethargic. Five years later the whole civilised world was in flames. A Parliamentary intrigue had embroiled England and Spain, and the ambition of a petty German sovereign had begun a war which immediately spread beyond the limits of Germany, and led to changes that remodelled the map of Europe. Cuba and Puerto Rico and Georgia, Scotland and Bohemia, were among the countries that suffered for quarrels about which the inhabitants knew and cared little. In this instance, it may be observed that the Spanish war would have been a trifle in itself. The real trouble was the ambition of Frederic II., whose army, before his accession, was scarcely regarded as a factor in European politics, and was chiefly talked of for its pedantic discipline, and its regiment of tall men. Rather more than a century later, the same experiment was renewed. The generation that remembered Napoleon's wars was passionately anxious for peace, and English statesmen, in particular, had learned by bitter experience that the glory of animating Continental alliances was dearly purchased at the price of overwhelming debt and general jealousy. In 1847 England was almost without army or navy; the King of France was as peace-loving as any English Premier; the King of Prussia was perpetually irresolute and unready; Austria desired only to avoid complications of any kind; and the King of Belgium was always ready to mediate when difficulties sprung up. It is doubtful if even the Emperor Nicholas would deliberately have risked a great European war.[1] Nevertheless, in 1848-49, there was war, or rumour of war, everywhere, and in 1853 the three greatest races of the civilised world, as it then was, were waging a very desperate struggle for supremacy. The advent to power of an adventurer, who believed that he would consolidate his position by short and brilliant campaigns, was sufficient to transform Europe into a cockpit or a camp of instruction; and at this moment the standing armies of the Continent are 50 per cent more than they were forty years ago, and the forces kept in reserve, and ready to strike, incomparably greater. The vision of inspired Manchester men, that the angel of Peace was to descend on the world in a drapery of untaxed calico, is still as far from accomplishment as the vision seen in Patmos. Trade is no freer than it was, and war is a more pervading presence.

Meanwhile, an optimist is entitled to claim that a state of military preparedness is not an unmixed evil. The Archduke Constantine, who objected to a campaign because it spoiled his troops,[2] probably meant something more than that drill was neglected and that uniforms were ruined during a campaign. He meant that the mortality of war fell upon men whom the regiments and the country could not spare. There can be little doubt that the army has been a very

---

[1] Martin, *Hist. Populaire de France*, tome v. p. 408. As late as February 12, 1854, Thiers thought the Emperor would give way.—Senior's *Conversations*, vol. i. p. 232. On his deathbed Nicholas told the Empress that it had been his wish to leave the Empire at peace.—Oustrialoff's *History of Russia*, vol. ii. p. 508.

[2] The words reported are: "I do not like war. It spoils the soldiers; dirties their uniforms, and destroys discipline."—De Cusine's *Empire of the Czar*, vol. ii. chap. xv. p. 28.

admirable school for the lower orders of European society. The recruit is forced to acquire habits of cleanliness; has his frame developed by athletic exercises; is taught some elements of knowledge in the regimental schools; learns implicit obedience, and acquires traditions of honour and loyalty to his colours and his comrades, that on critical occasions raise him above regard for this perishable life. The French cuirassiers who rode time after time to certain death at Reichshoffen and Froeschwiller;[1] the German cavalry that courted annihilation in order to win time for a movement of the infantry at Mars-la-Tour; the English infantry at Inkerman; and, even more perhaps than the heroes of any war, the men of the *Birkenhead*, are among the innumerable evidences that the service of arms can transform generous feeling and irresolute impulse into a steady and exalted heroism. Neither is war all savagery. When England first declared war against the French Republic, the feeling in France was so bitter that the Directory issued orders for no quarter to be given; orders which the French generals, to their honour, refused to obey.[2] After nearly thirty years of struggle, the feeling between Wellington's and Soult's soldiers became one of cordial respect; acts of chivalrous consideration were common on both sides, and the outposts used to mingle freely whenever there was a halt or an informal rest of any kind.[3] A civil

---

[1] Martin's *Hist. de France*, tome vii. pp. 183, 184.

[2] A single naval officer, the captain of *La Boudeuse*, carried this order into execution in the case of a prize. On his return to France he found himself universally shunned, and committed suicide.—De Vigny in Napier's *Lights and Shades of Military Life*.

[3] Thus at San Sebastian Sir T. Graham told the officer charged to arrange a capitulation: "Sir, when people defend themselves as your troops have done they are not conquered; they have a right to dictate their own terms; write what you will."—Brialmont, *Life of Napoleon*,

war is in general one of indiscriminating bitterness; but scarcely a reproach of violence to non-combatants rests upon the great armies that decided the War of Liberation in the United States. So, again, the Germans who entered France under Von Moltke were appreciably more humane and better disciplined than the soldiers whom Blücher commanded, and this to an extent that is not altogether explained by the absence of recent provocation. It seems, therefore, possible to hope that war, terrible and to some extent pitiless as it must always be, may come to be conducted without intentional injury to non-combatants, and with the smallest possible damage to private property. When horrors, like those which attended the storm of Tarragona by Suchet, and that of San Sebastian by Wellington,[1] are reprobated as atrocities by public opinion—even in military circles—and punished with unsparing severity by courts-martial, the worst influence of war will have been abolished. Lastly, when all is said, we cannot escape from a certain truth in Shakespeare's view of war, that it is "the great corrector of enormous times." Many

---

vol. ii. p. 140. During the inactive interval of a fortnight that elapsed before the battle of Salamanca, "the soldiers of both sides bathed together, and frequently swam over, and interchanged civilities with each other."—Secret Despatch quoted in Buckingham's *Memoirs of the Court of England*, vol. i. p. 385. "Towards the close of the war . . . so good an understanding prevailed between the outposts of the two armies, that Lord Wellington found it necessary to forbid all communication whatever. . . . It was a sort of custom the French and British guards visiting each other by turns."—Gleig's *Subaltern*, p. 158.

[1] Of Tarragona, Napier says: "That every barbarity commonly attendant upon the storming of towns was practised may be supposed . . . and it would be unjust to hold Suchet responsible."—*Peninsular War*, book xiii. chap. v. Of San Sebastian, where some circumstances were of unusual atrocity, Wellington writes only: "I am convinced it is impossible to prevent a town in such a situation from being plundered."—Letter to Right Hon. Sir H. Wellesley, K.B., October 9, 1813.

a nation dates its moral regeneration from a defeat that seemed to shatter it. Russia emancipated her serfs because she was beaten before Sebastopol; Austria tore up her Concordat and liberalised her government because she was vanquished at Solferino; France rid herself of the impurities of the Second Empire at the price of Sedan. There are also communities that have been the better for success. The United States became a nation with a consciousness of great destiny and of her duty towards the human race after the War of Independence. Italy conquered liberty and self-respect on the same battlefields. We may stop short of the splendid paradox of De Maistre, that war is divine in virtue of its supernatural results,[1] and content ourselves with believing that it has its place in the economy of human society, as volcanoes and earthquakes have in the physical world. It took all the courage of Voltaire, less than a century and a half ago, to explain that an earthquake was not necessarily the judgment of God upon an immoral city.[2] At present not even a theologian sees anything outrageous in Herschel's statement that "earthquakes may form part and parcel of some great scheme of Providential arrangement which is at work for good and not for ill."[3] It seems not unreasonable to suppose that a warlike spirit is as inseparable from human nature as the love of money or sexual impulse, and that like these it may have its uses, though its excess is lamentable.

[1] "La guerre est divine par ses conséquences d'un ordre surnaturel; tant générales, que particulières."—De Maistre, *Soirées de St. Pétersbourg,* Septième Entretien.

[2] "Direz-vous en voyant cet amas de victimes,
   Dieu s'est vengé; leur mort est le prix de leurs crimes?"
                    Voltaire, *Poème sur le Désastre de Lisbonne.*

[3] Herschel's *Familiar Lectures,* p. 2.

That the growth of large towns is bound to go on in a constantly increasing ratio seems more than probable. England, the greatest example, is in some respects exceptional, because the existence of large properties there has hitherto been accompanied with a system of farming which only men with some capital could attempt, and because the passion of a wealthy class for field-sports induces them to make some sacrifice of rental, and deny themselves the profits which small tenants might bring. Moreover, the old poor-law system and the doctrines of Malthus co-operated in inducing many squires to keep population down on their estates. It was a direct gain that the land should not be charged with the support of paupers, and a prospective advantage that population should not increase beyond the means of support. Then, again, the development of mines and the growth of manufactures have constantly drawn rustics from their native villages, and as the towns have been able to relieve themselves when they were over-peopled by exporting emigrants to America or Australia, there has been no reason to suspect the practice gradually established of unsoundness. The urban population of England is accordingly now nearly double the rural, and would undoubtedly be larger still if a great many miners and sailors were not included in the population of the country. No other country, except Scotland, shows anything like this ratio; but Holland, Belgium, Australia, France, and the United States are making rapid progress in the same direction, and the townsmen in these highly prosperous communities are from one in five to as many as two in five of the nation. Naturally, the towns are least prominent as a rule in the nations that have an extensive area. Altogether, however, the tendency to congregate in towns seems strongest in Anglo-Saxon countries. For instance, the proportion of townsmen in the United States (22·5 per cent in 1880)[1] and in Australia (25 per cent) is very large, though in both of these countries the area of land is considerable, and there is a great deal not taken up.

Now, if we inquire into the causes that attract population to towns, we shall find them very various, and for the most part sufficiently simple. One is, that the discoveries of science in many cases enable the farmer to substitute machinery for hand-labour. The steam-plough, or common ploughs of improved construction, reapers and binders, and threshing-machines have now come largely into use in all highly-developed countries, and the result is that a few well-trained and well-paid labourers are substituted for a great many poorly paid. Then, again, the gradual evolution of macadamised roads, canals, and railways has enormously diminished the proportion of men engaged in the transport of produce, and has also diminished the need of over-production. Formerly, there might be a famine in Gloucestershire when corn was rotting in Kent,[2] because communication between the different parts of England was so difficult and costly, and then every district had to keep corn stored, or to sow

---

[1] *United States Census for* 1880, p. 8. Mr. Bryce, excluding the small towns, makes the urban population only one-seventh; but raises it to one-fourth if towns of 8000 inhabitants are reckoned.—*American Commonwealth*, vol. iii. pp. 45, 676.

[2] Thus in 1261 the *Annals of Bermondsey* say, that the quarter of corn (*frumentum*) was sold for 24s. in London, and all over England. The average for England, however, according to Professor Rogers, was only 4s. 3d. to 9s. 9d. "The prices from Oxfordshire," says Mr. Rogers, "are exceedingly low."—*History of Prices*, vol. i. pp. 187, 226.

more than was likely to be needed; but now the best-developed countries can produce with the nicest economy. Again, science has not only cheapened production and transport, but it has increased production. An acre in England yields at least three times as much at present as it did in the fourteenth century,[1] and though deep ploughing and draining and the use of artificial manures involve rather more labour than was needed under the old system, there is still a large margin to the benefit of the modern farmer. We may add to this that railways give the shops and professional men in towns a great advantage over their rivals in the country. Every new line that is opened induces a certain number of the country people to make their purchases where the stores are largest, and where the goods can be sold cheapest; and a man troubled about his health or his property prefers to consult the ablest city practitioner of whom he has read or heard. So it happens that the small country stores are reduced in number and importance, and that the professional class gets more and more averse to a country practice. It is scarcely wonderful if for these reasons alone large towns appear to absorb all the natural growth of the community. It is rather wonderful that the remoter and less attractive parts of the country should not be generally deserted, and that the building up of towns should not go on even more rapidly than it does. We must allow, however, for the tendency of some townsmen to make their

[1] "In 1333-1336, the average produce in cheap, that is, abundant years, as all these years are, is nine bushels of wheat and fifteen of barley.—Rogers, *Economic Interpretation of History*, p. 52. "I do not believe that the average yield of England at this time" (1868) "exceeds twenty-eight bushels."—Caird in *Statistical Journal*, vol. xxxi. p. 130. The average for four recent years (1886-1889) has been 29·22 bushels.

actual homes outside city precincts, and also for the disinclination of most men to change their careers and habits suddenly. The exodus to towns takes place very much through the young, who have come to think that their best chances of employment and enjoyment are great cities, and whom their elders do not care to dissuade, and do not like to keep back from what seems certain gain.[1]

There is, however, another very potent cause that is contributing to build up towns. Every great country has established State schools, and made education of some kind compulsory. The instruction given is in no case very profound or far-reaching. It is generally more or less confined to reading, writing, and arithmetic, with so much knowledge of geography and of the national history and literature as can be given in popular text-books. Still, what difference there is between the primary education of our own days and the "sound commercial education" of a few years back is rather to the advantage of the primary State school, which professes to teach a little less, but, as a rule, teaches what it does thoroughly and expeditiously. Accordingly, the children of the poorest classes in all English-speaking countries, and in parts of the Continent, have been raised in one important respect to the level of a higher class, have acquired its tastes and ambitions, and are able to compete with it in commerce. Naturally, the cleverest boys of the village school do not care to remain plough-boys; they yearn for the speculative

---

[1] Dr. Ogle, who has made the question a study, takes this view. "The decline was brought about by the migration of young people, mainly under twenty-five years of age, from the rural to the manufacturing districts, and of young men in greater proportion than young women."—"Ogle on the alleged depopulation of the rural districts in England," *Statistical Journal*, vol. iii. p. 231.

gains of commerce, for the "large excitement" of city life, or at least for the fleshpots and the shelter from sun and rain that are incidental to existence as a town models it. To the yokel, London or New York or Melbourne is an inexhaustible romance; to the cockney of every nation, the country, except as a suburb or an ornamental farm, represents only what is repulsive in toil and uncongenial in society. Even more do the amusements of towns, the club, and the theatre, the exhibition, the race-course, and the ball, create wants that it is almost impossible to relinquish. Anciently, there were some compensations in the sweetness of village homes and the rough abundance of country life. At present, the educated person of small means, widow or school-teacher, or country surgeon's wife, who is doomed to live at a distance from a town, finds that the country is mostly tenanted by those who are too unintelligent to succeed elsewhere; and that the price of necessaries is at least as high as in the city, while the price of luxuries is greater, and many conveniences or economies, such as tram-cars and co-operative stores, and the teachers of accomplishments, are unattainable. Of course this state of things is in some respects bound to be transitory. The farmer is rapidly changing into a highly-educated man; the primary school-teacher is rising in the social grade; State inspectors and employees of the higher class are being multiplied; and railways are already carried into almost every small district in England. Still, the attractions of town-life very much overbalance those of the country even now; and the industrial reasons which urge the rising generation to throng into the metropolis, or at least into towns of some kind, are powerfully enhanced by the requirements which education and a higher refinement bring with them. It seems difficult to doubt that for many years to come towns will grow everywhere at the expense of villages. They would grow even if they were not more attractive, because rural labour does not expand as rapidly as factories and shops; but they have a fascination of their own, and they rarely relax their hold on those whom they have drawn in. A year's life amid "the crowd, the hum, the shock of men" is apt to give a distaste for that life amid green fields and pastures which poets have consented to praise; the years that make a man a confirmed townsman unfit him, morally and physically, for any other life than in populous streets. It is not often that he wishes to change, but he cannot if he would. Even the passion of the wealthy Englishman for field-sports only draws him into the country during the months sacred or possible to these. Habitually he prefers, like Dr. Johnson, to "watch the full tide of life at Charing Cross."

Now, the influence of cities on civilisation is embalmed in language itself. Almost every word that designates the higher life among men implies town-breeding; every word appropriated anciently to country use has acquired a certain savour of contempt. To the Greeks man was by nature social, or a city-dweller (πολιτικός); the polite townsman (ἀστεῖος) was contrasted with the rough dweller in fields (ἀγροικός). The Romans repeated and enforced the idea that the body politic was in the fashion of the city (*civitas*), and that the city man was naturally courteous (*urbanus*), while the dweller outside was uncouth in manners (*rusticus*), and the maintainer of an outworn creed (*paganus*). Later on, we find the legal synonyms for country labourer ("*colonus*" and "*villanus*") passing into our language as "clown" and "loon" and "villain." The French vocabulary is at least equally rich in terms of this kind. We cannot disregard the historical fact, of which these etymological trifles are confirmation, that what we call progress was in antiquity at least the outcome of city life under certain favourable conditions. Something, no doubt, has to be allowed for the perpetuity of order, which at the time was scarcely possible except within city walls or under their shadow. If Attica had been as open to an invading army as Lacedemon, we can hardly imagine that Athens would have been of much more account in the world's history than Sparta. Still, the contact of mind with mind is perhaps the main factor in intellectual development; and the incomparable benefit of Athens to its poets, its thinkers, and its orators seems to have been, that it supplied them with a society that was quick to catch at ideas, and keen to sift them. To us, who confound writers of ten centuries and fifty different places under the convenient name of "classical," it is difficult to understand why a man banished from Athens or Rome felt that the whole world was, so to speak, closed to him. The lamentations of Cicero when he was forced to leave Italy, but had nearly every great city, except Athens, open to him in Greece or Asia;[1] even the complaints of Ovid at being sent to a garrison town in what is now Bulgaria,[2] seem as unmanly and incomprehensible as the wailings of Philoctetes over his wound would appear to the maimed private of an English regiment. Yet Cicero and Ovid only expressed the feeling of every educated Roman. Later on, Juvenal winds up the panegyric of a country life by remarking that it cannot

[1] "Quod si auderem, Athenas peterem." "In hunc me casum vos vivendi auctores impulistis."—*Epist. ad Atticum*, iii. 7 and 9.

[2] "Vix ope castelli defendimur."—*Tristia*, lib. v. 10.

be endured for five days continuously.[1] The Greek and Roman had a feeling for Athens and Rome which only Paris among modern towns has inspired in a similar degree, and for something of the same reason. When Mdme. de Staël would have sacrificed everything but conviction for the right to live again in the Rue de Bac, what she regretted was the French salon, which could give her nothing superior in kind to what she found in Germany, in Russia, and in England, but which yet gave her the only intellectual atmosphere in which she could breathe freely. Half her shades of meaning, all that was best in her style, and much that was good in her thought, could only be understood by the people of whom she was one. Only they could tell her, and they only in the indirectness of social intercourse, how far she had gone home to the hearts and minds of her countrymen. It is quite conceivable that she really did better work for being thrown upon herself, just as we may assume that Dante drew concentration and energy from the "salt savour" of bread eaten in exile, and Milton from the enforced seclusion of his later years. There can be little doubt that genius is now and again apt to fritter itself away on things that are of the earth earthy; and Dante might have been squandered away in municipal intrigues, Mdme. de Staël in party-giving, if the poet had not been driven from Florence, and the publicist from Paris. All that is contended for is that minds of the highest order are very sensible to the need of human intercourse, and are apt to feel their own want of criticism and sympathy to an extent that is sometimes incompatible with self-reliance. City life has been praised, perhaps beyond its deserts, because

[1] "Facere hoc non possis quinque diebus continuis."—Juvenal, *Sat.* xi. 206, 207.

it has brought thinkers into touch one with another, and has stimulated the divine impulse to originate by sympathy or antagonism.

It must be noted, however, that the instances of societies in which men of the highest distinction have been fairly numerous are so few and far between that it seems impossible to deduce any law from them. The popular examples are Athens from Aeschylus to Demosthenes, Rome from Lucretius to Juvenal, Florence in the time of Michael Angelo, London in the period from Elizabeth to Anne, Paris in the latter half of the seventeenth century, and perhaps some circles in Germany for part of the eighteenth century. No doubt a long and brilliant list could be filled with names that do not belong to any one of these times and places. Homer, Dante, Cervantes, Voltaire, Darwin, and Victor Hugo may almost be said to make epochs in themselves; and no one dreams of disputing their ability or the influence they have exercised on style and thought. The point contended for, however, is, that individuals cannot be claimed as the direct outcome of city life in the same way that a literary set can be. Homer may have owed more than we suspect to the comments of crowds in Asia Minor, Dante may have been a representative Florentine, and Voltaire certainly seems a representative Parisian; but even Voltaire, though he founded a school of thought, had no rivals or critics or colleagues comparable with himself, except, perhaps, Rousseau, who was quite dissimilar, and who derived whatever was best in him from Geneva. The remarkable point is that even in modern society, when population is so much larger, when thought is comparatively unshackled, when burning questions are in the air, when the public is a better Maecenas than Martial prayed for, there are periods in the life of large communities which seem almost as sterile as the later centuries of the Roman Empire. Whom did England produce between Swift and Byron, outside of politics, who will be read for either power or beauty of form as an imaginative writer? What Frenchmen, except Chateaubriand and Courier, were literary in the real sense of the word in the fifty years that elapsed after Voltaire's death?[1] Is Italy adequately represented in literature by Alfieri and Leopardi for the three centuries that have passed since the death of Tasso? and is Spain represented at all for two centuries? It is easy to say that the genius of England had a worthy expression in Gibbon and Burke during a time otherwise barren; and it is perhaps true that the nation was throwing itself into politics and invention at that period. France may reasonably claim that she put her life and thought into the glory and waste of the Revolution and of the First Empire. What is difficult to explain is the complete break of intellectual continuity. No one can suppose that Brindley, Wedgwood, or Watt would have been poets if they had not been inventors; and it seems accordingly difficult to understand why one order of genius comes to the front, while another, not necessarily, but often, recedes, and is lost for a time. The natural inference would appear to be, that neither ordinary city life, nor the presence of one or two great thinkers or artists in a community is a guarantee that

[1] The possible exceptions seem to be Mdme. de Staël, Joubert, Senancourt, and Bichat; all, it may be said, more remarkable for thought than for form, and of whom only Bichat is in the first rank for thought. Yet this decadence was not from want of interest in literary matters. De Tocqueville told Senior that when he was a boy politics were never talked of, and "literature was one of the standing subjects of conversation. Every new book was read aloud."—*Correspondence of A. de Tocqueville*, vol. i. p. 137.

there will be any general activity or real elevation of thought. We have examples of countries where millions of men have succeeded one another for generations, even for centuries, and produced nothing more than a few competent administrators without statesmanship, soldiers without strategy, and literary men without the power to originate. Civilisation, such as is the outgrowth of populous communities, appears to guarantee little more at best than a wise habit of municipal administration, some energy and deftness of commerce, and certain gracious formalities in human intercourse. The official, the merchant, and the diner-out represent the outcome of city life when society is torpid.

Now the compensating drawbacks to these advantages of general acuteness and occasional distinction are sufficiently formidable. It is very doubtful whether townsmen of many generations do not lose stamina, and decline in stature, to a degree that implies perilous degeneracy.[1] The question, no doubt, is not a simple one. So far as the evidence of coats of armour goes, the ancestors of the English people must have been smaller-chested and of less stature than average men at present. On the other hand, the prowess of the English archers shows that their small stature was compatible with great muscular strength; and it is perhaps reasonable to suppose that incessant wars reduced the average height, as the tallest men were the first picked off. The wars of the first Napoleon produced an effect which is sometimes thought to be still noticeable in the conscription. Yet this argument cannot be pressed, as on the Continent, where the object is that no man should be exempted from military service, it is important to keep the standard of height as low as possible; while

[1] *Wealth of Nations*, book i. chap. viii.

in England the reductions that have been found necessary to keep the regiments filled may be due to the fact that the attractions of private employment are now greater than they were. It must be admitted also that the average of life in England is now longer than it was,—a fact which seems inconsistent with reduced vitality. Still, it may be questioned if we can infer more from this than that science, to some extent, compensates the disadvantages that result from the city life carried to excess. What science has done cannot easily be over-estimated. Leprosy, smallpox, the Black Death, the plague, and the sweating sickness, are little more than memories of the past. In 1349 the Black Death carried off at least a third of the population of all England, the deaths in London alone being reckoned at 100,000.[1] The cholera of 1831-32 only carried off 5275 in a ten times larger London, and was scarcely felt except in the slums of great cities.[2] The sufferers from plague in old times used to comfort themselves with the expectation that if they recovered they would be disease-proof for the future;[3] but the records of mortality show that these terrible visitations carried off not only two-thirds of those who were attacked, but left the remainder with debilitated constitutions. As late as Adam Smith's time the mortality among the children of the poor was enormous. "In some places," he says, "one-half the children born die before they are four years of age; in many places before they

---

[1] Pearson's *English History in the Fourteenth Century*, p. 154. Compare Hecker's *Epidemics of the Middle Ages*. "It probably killed a third of the population."—Rogers's *Economical Interpretation of History*, p. 22.

[2] Martineau's *Thirty Years' Peace*, vol. ii. p. 486.

[3] "It was the opinion of the most eminent physicians of that time that the plague was itself a sufficient purge, and that those who escaped the infection needed no physic."—Defoe's *History of the Plague*, p. 198. Compare Thucydides, ii. cap. 51 and 58.

are seven, and in almost all places before they are nine or ten."[1] The mortality of children under five is still very great, but it is not half of Adam Smith's highest estimate, and the mortality between five and ten is not so great as that of ordinary adults.

Not only have sanitary conditions been improved, but labour has been regulated with the best possible results. The horrors of the factory system have been mitigated or removed by the legislation Lord Shaftesbury initiated; and the increasing power of Trades-Unions is making the revival of overwork on a large scale impossible. Compulsory education is assisting to keep children from that toil in stifling rooms which used to be the fruitful cause of stunted frames and impaired vitality. Some occupations that were poisonous have now been made reasonably safe. A certain proportion of the workers in large towns—such as dock labourers, coalheavers, workers in foundries, and men in the building trade—work under conditions that are favourable to muscular development as well as to health, and are in a great many cases better fed than they would be in the country. Mr. Booth's very careful analysis of the population in some of the poorest parts of London has shown that only a fraction are paupers or loafers, and that not quite 20 per cent are casual or intermittent wage-earners.[2] It is probably correct to say that even in London, the typical instance of concentration, the poverty is still manageable, though now and again, in hard times, many thousands of men and women willing to

---

[1] It is already found necessary to pick the members of the London Police Force chiefly from men born in the country. The following statistics were obtained by Mr. Llewellyn Jones in 1888 :—

    London born, 2910.   Country born, 11,606.

—Hobson's *Problems of Poverty*, p. 56.

[2] *Statistical Journal*, vol. l. pp. 326-391, and vol. xli. pp. 276-331.

work are within measurable distance of starvation. Still, if we could be certain that great cities would not continue to increase even faster in the future than they have done in the past, we might fairly hope that the wisdom of statesmen would contrive a remedy for present evils.

Unhappily, there is another side to the question. We have to take into account that the great English and Scotch towns have been draining the life-blood of the country districts for more than a century. Forty years ago the population of towns and country districts in England was nearly equal. In 1881 the towns were to the country as three to two; and in 1891 they are as seven to four. We must either assume that during this period the natural increase in the country has been very small, or that it has all been carried off by emigration, or that a portion of it has been attracted to the towns. Dr. Ogle, who has made a study of the subject, gives reasons for supposing that there has been a "continuous migration of the most energetic and vigorous members of the rural communities into the manufacturing districts."[1] So long as this lasts, and is on a large scale, we are not in a condition to appreciate how far town-life tells upon the physique of the people. Not only do the vigorous countrymen replenish the towns with new life, but they have a tendency to crowd out and starve the weaker and more stunted specimens of humanity, who are the outcome of several generations that have grown up without proper access to light and air, and without muscular exercise. Before long, however, the country immigrants will be an imperceptible addition to any great English or Scotch city. What,

[1] *Statistical Journal*, vol. lii. p. 231. "An estimate, based upon returns from thirty-one of the largest cities of Europe, shows that of every 1000 increase in urban population, 215 only spring from excess of birth-rate over death-rate."—Adams's *Public Debts*, p. 349.

for instance, will 20,000 immigrants a year mean to the swarming life of a metropolis with four or five millions of inhabitants? Is it not unavoidable that the city type should become more and more pronounced? Is it not probable that the type elaborated will not be so much that of the mobile, critical, originative Athenian, who was practically an aristocrat among slaves, as of the Manchester or Bellevue operative, with an inheritance of premature decrepitude, with an horizon narrowed to parochial limits, with no interests except those of the factory or the Trades-Union; with the faith of the Salvation Army, that finds expression in antics and buffoonery, or with that even more lamentable scepticism to which the bestial element in man is the only reality?

It must be borne in mind that the city life which we associate from history with ardent public spirit and susceptibility of great ideas was never trammelled by the limitations which cramp a great capital in modern times. The Athenian could pass in a couple of hours from the Acropolis into a country solitude; he was perpetually serving as soldier or sailor, or was traversing mountain paths to consult an oracle, or to attend a festival. The free population of Rome may have amounted to nearly three-quarters of a million in part of its best literary period; but these numbers were closely packed within a circuit of thirteen miles;[1] the country with its breezy plains or umbrageous forests or little townships was close at hand; and society was so small that, for one period at least, we know all about its leaders and their family scandals, and the places of amusement, and the chief professional

---

[1] Ramsay's *Antiquities*, p. 2; Gibbon's *Decline and Fall*, vol. iv. chap. xxxi. p. 89; note by Smith.

men, as well as we know about the England of Queen Elizabeth's time. In Rome, as in Paris and London during their best days, though the city was too big for a single set, and though we can perceive that the younger Pliny and Tacitus moved in a different world from Juvenal and Martial, just as Fox and Sheridan scarcely ever met Dr. Johnson, there were still points of contact between the salons, and in this way there was, as it were, a literary commonwealth, whose members exchanged ideas and reproduced each other's thoughts with variations. Boston, not being overgrown, has been able to combine this best feature of town intercourse with a singular charm of its own during our own generation. At present London is either too vast for such a society to exist, or if it exists it is effaced by the multitudinous life of statesmen, professional men, millionaires on every side. There may be even more talent than there was in the days of Burke and Gibbon and Horace Walpole; but it is dissipated in space, or attracts no attention outside. The successful proconsul, the daring traveller, the scientific discoverer, are now passed round for a season from salon to salon, invited to air themselves in reviews, and relegated to the second place. The world at large is just as reverent of greatness, as observant of a Browning, a Newman, or a Mill, as it ever was; but the world of society prefers the small change of available and ephemeral talent to the wealth of great thoughts, which must always be kept more or less in reserve. The result seems to be that men, anxious to do great work, find city life less congenial than they did, and either live away from the metropolis, as Darwin and Newman did, or restrict their intercourse, as Carlyle and George Eliot practically did, to a circle of chosen friends. The same feature of human intercourse appears to be noticeable in France, though in France the Second Empire broke up the thinking and talking world so completely, that even the semblance of that brilliant society which existed under the last monarch has never been reconstituted. An outside observer, at least, remembers that Littré and Renan and Victor Hugo have been relics of the old world, and that Lamartine and De Musset, De Tocqueville and Michelet and Thierry, George Sand and Balzac have left no counterparts.

It is, perhaps, too early to decide whether town life is dying at the top. It may well be, that even in one of our overgrown capitals a society may spring up which shall not allow itself to be absorbed in the riot and the ennui of fashionable gatherings, which shall find better use for its thought than to tone it down into commonplace, and nobler use for its style than the affectation of epigrammatic smartness. Such a body of men might easily recover the influence and dignity which was enjoyed by the best circle of George III.'s reign during the American War; by the French Liberals under the House of Orleans; and by the Boston Transcendentalists while the struggle of slavery was undecided. All that can be said with certainty is, that as towns grow to dimensions never dreamed of as possible, it must be increasingly difficult for a few men, however brilliant, to give direction to the thought of the whole urban community. What, however, can admit of no doubt is, that if wealth and numbers and uniform habit of life and speech and opinion may tend to set aside genius or cramp originality even when they act on a small coterie, they are incomparably more calculated to exercise an influence for evil upon the masses. The dweller in a great city is tending more and more to become a very small part of a very vast machine. It is not only that his daily work is less varied, and makes less demands on resource and fertility of expedient than it did, but his whole horizon is narrowed. Put, on the one hand, the elevating influence of the State school, which has taken him through a primary reader series, and add, it may be, an occasional visit to the museum; and assume, on the other hand, what is becoming more and more a fact, that the artisan's daily walk from the house to the factory represents his knowledge of God's earth; that he has never wandered by the seaside, or in the woods; knows nothing such as village children know of life in the hedges and the farmyard; never sees the dawn whiten and flush over heather, or has looked up at the stars except through an intervening veil of smoke and fog. Does any man dream that an excursion train, with its riotous mirth and luncheon-baskets, and few hours' freedom to stand on a pier or stroll through the streets of a country town can compensate to millions of human beings for nature quite shut out? What kind of children will those be who grow up when the best sanitary laws have restricted the intercourse with animals even more than is now customary in towns; who have never picked buttercups and daisies; who read in poems of the song of birds that they cannot hear, and of a beauty in the seasons which they only know by vicissitudes of hot and cold? Will not their eyes be dimmed for all sights but those which a shop window can afford? and will not their minds be the poorer by many bright memories which their mothers had? Yet these are not even the chief losses which a city life entails. There is an inevitable companionship in country life which draws rich and poor together. At the cricket-ground and in the hunting-field, in church and in social gatherings, from harvest-home to school-feast, squire and parson, farmer and hind, meet together animated for the hour with the same kindly thoughts. In the great majority of villages, at least, the cottager looks for sympathy in his troubles to the Rectory and the Hall. Even where the clergyman has been torpid and the landowner non-resident, the village has still been a community of neighbours interested in one another. In the multitudinous desolation of a great city contact between rich and poor is scarcely possible, and as there are no abiding homes there are no real neighbours. Strangers who will help with relief, or, it may be, close the dying eyes of the destitute, are a poor exchange for families that have lived near one another, toiled together, taken holiday together for generations.

In very small communities the family life is deepened and intensified by isolation. Families intermarry, and it comes to be thought a scandal that any one should marry out of the clan. The result is seen in a certain rough loyalty of all who are so connected to one another, in a storing-up of family traditions, and in an enhanced self-respect. The obvious drawbacks to this kind of life are, that the interbreeding is sometimes carried to excess, though this is not often the case where the conditions of life are healthy, and that feeling for the parish or the district seems to supersede national sentiment. In large towns this sort of family life is impossible, and the traditions of old burgher families, tradesmen, or artisans, who lived in the same street for generations, is rapidly becoming extinct.

The apprenticeship system that gave young men a family training of a kind has to a great extent disappeared. The workman is very constantly a bird of passage; at least an immigrant from the country or abroad. He marries, or forms an irregular connection with some chance acquaintance. The lodgings are constantly changed, so that no home associations can grow up; the husband may be absent for weeks or months at a time; the children live, out of schooltime, in the court or the streets, their homes being mere feeding and sleeping places; the boys scatter as they grow up, and the girls find work in a factory, where it is impossible for the mother's eye to follow them. Of course there are thousands of cases in which the conditions are even less favourable to domesticity; where two or more families live in a room, so that not only is no separation of the sexes possible, but that an entire family cannot enjoy the privacy without which the communication of thought in counsel or sympathy is impossible. No doubt the imperishable instincts of human nature will assert themselves with perpetual miracles of gracious spontaneity in the slums as well as in Arcadia. Hermann and Dorothea will rehearse the "old, old story" in whispers or hints, and during hours when all is hushed; the mother will glow with all the hope and love of womanhood as the babe, predestined to scrofula or typhus, smiles up or crows in her face; and the father, worn out with the week's toil, will feel a Sabbath rest as he looks round upon his children, even though he cannot talk freely, or pray, or walk in green fields with them. No one can doubt that the moral sentiment is inextinguishable who reflects how the instinct of purity has maintained itself among English women, living as they have done for the last three generations in conditions of domesticity that even in the country were often only a little better than they now are in the less crowded parts of our great cities. What it seems impossible to question is, that the old family feeling, with which self-respect, loyalty to kindred, discipline and sexual purity were intimately associated, must in course of time disappear from large towns, unless some radical change should make home-life possible to the toiling and thrifty part of the population.

Now the State Socialism which is growing upon us, and the scientific teaching which we are all disposed to admit, are combining in some respects to a hopeful solution of some of these difficulties. Science, disregarding the "let-alone" theory, which declared that the State had no right to interfere with the workman's demand for lodgings, or the capitalist's supply, is instructing us that it is at our own peril if we allow the conditions of disease to exist anywhere, and that the lives and fortunes of the whole community are at stake if we overlook crowded rooms, bad drainage, foul drinking-water, or diseased food. The scientific man will probably content himself with very practicable requirements, but he will hardly be satisfied with less than a proportion of cubic feet that means separation for every family, and an abundant water-supply. The temperate State Socialism that is coming in goes naturally beyond this, and asks that the State shall make itself a large employer of labour, so far as to assure a reasonable wage to every man ready to work. We can already see tendencies of progress towards a more advanced point. Philanthropists are trying to get large spaces reserved as parks or recreation-grounds in the neighbourhood of our towns, to get gymnasiums attached to our schools, and to arrange for occasional excursions into the country. If we assume every family to be living in a five-roomed house,[1] every working-man in England to be earning his thirty shillings a week, the Saturday half-holiday to be introduced, every child to be trained in gymnastic exercises, and every young man to have the opportunity of football, cricket, or drill, we shall assume no more than would seem very moderate and perhaps inadequate in Australia; and yet changes of this kind would mean a new life for millions of human beings in such cities as London and Glasgow, Paris and Lyons, Berlin or Vienna, New York or Chicago. Nevertheless, even these reforms, which perhaps are possible and probable, would only be of partial efficacy as regards health. They would restore the sanctity of family life, but they could not bring back the old authority of family ties; and they would scarcely touch the deplorable isolation of the townsman from that world full of sweet sights and sounds, that divinity of hill and glade and running stream which were anciently the inheritance of the whole human race.

Let us now set off against these positive losses the advantage in variety of amusements which operates so largely in attracting the youth of the country districts to a town. For women, in particular, the gain seems to be incalculable. There are the theatre, the music-hall, or the opera, the picture-gallery, the comic entertainment, the lecture, the class-room, and a very considerable resource in what is known as "society" for all, except, of course, the very poor. Even if we admit that the racket and incessant change of life in very fashionable circles are carried to excess, and that

[1] I assume three sleeping-rooms, a kitchen, and a sitting-room to be the smallest amount compatible with health and decency.

the very poor are apt to be thrown upon worse associates than they would find in the country, the broad fact remains that to the great mass of women the streets within a mile of their town-house contain greater variety than they can find in a whole county. That the town acquaintanceships are as a rule perfectly superficial, that a large visiting list may not contain a single friend, or one with that sympathy of custom which neighbourhood in the country is apt to engender, may be said to be partially compensated by the comparative absence of small rivalries and petty scandals. Then, even if we assume that the old paramount influence of the best set in a metropolis has ceased to be as noticeable as it once was, there is an immense wealth of secondary, and even very high talent. The city absorbs the most practical intellects of the country, and competition keeps them from rusting. To put the case briefly, if human life in the great centres has less intensity and tenderness than in the provinces, it has also less ennui; and to the nervous, excitable, modern temperament relief from ennui is the primary condition of a healthy and desirable existence. We must probably console ourselves with this reflection, for it seems likely that the amusements of a large town rather lose than gain in character as it grows. To take the lecture-room, which is perhaps the most intellectual of all, it is noticeable that Coleridge and Carlyle had very moderate success, that Thackeray and Dickens were better received in the provinces than in London, and that Matthew Arnold was a failure in America, and had no encouragement to lecture in England. The fact probably is, that most people prefer to read a lecture in the columns of a newspaper or in a book; and if they go to a lecture at all, go only from curiosity to see or hear a distinguished man. There is nothing unreasonable in this view, but if it becomes universal, one kind of amusement that stimulated the mind in no unworthy way will be retrenched. The theatre is not likely to suffer in this manner. Hardly any one derives as much pleasure from reading a play as from seeing it well put on the stage. Even a very ordinary cast of actors, giving only the trivial stage tradition with no original renderings, will present one of Shakespeare's plays in such a way as to stimulate or instruct a critic. Unfortunately, the age is no longer tolerant of work with a high aim. It has become a proverb that Shakespeare spells ruin, and the exceptions to this are where popular actors give the stage version more or less infamously garbled, with such gorgeousness of costume and surroundings that the mind is diverted from the words to the presentation. Putting aside Shakespeare, and admitting that where Shakespeare is only tolerated his great contemporaries cannot claim to be heard, we find that the serious work of modern times is never even regarded. Shelley, Browning, and Tennyson are experimented on from time to time, and put away almost instantly; Byron's name has not recommended his dramas; Swinburne has never even been tried; and the comparative success of Bulwer Lytton and of Sheridan Knowles, if we can draw any inference from it, would seem to show that the public is really tolerant of the drama only when it is bad. It may be said that the world has become unfamiliar with strong emotions and incredulous of violent effects; that the hardness of Lear's daughters, Othello's jealousy, Iago's villainy, Macbeth's crimes, are too sensational properly to impress a society that is no longer prone to stormy impulses, and that can hardly understand impulses that outrage decorum. This, however, will not account for the fact that even the highest style of comedy has fallen into disrepute. Modern counterparts of *Much Ado about Nothing*, or *The Merchant of Venice*, of *Tartufe* or *Le Misanthrope*, seem to be as little attempted as the old form of tragedy. The popular form of amusement in England is broad farce or the extravaganza; and some of Mr. Gilbert's work in this last direction is so admirable as to show that genius may impress its own stamp upon its masterpieces, and yet be popular, if it consults the spirit of the age. Perhaps it is most reasonable to assume that the novel has killed the drama as a delineation of human energy and suffering. The novel makes less demand upon the attention, can reiterate strokes and deepen colours where the first effect has failed, and can be produced in endless variety. There is a certain class of work, the minute and progressive analysis of a character undergoing change, that the novel perhaps achieves better than the play. Meanwhile, the substitution of the book for the counterfeit presentation in the higher range of subject may surely be said to have debased one large and important class of amusement by restricting it to pageantry and sensational effects or vulgar allusion; to shifts of dresses, to the jokes of a Jack-Pudding, to pugilistic encounters, or to the bringing of a whole farmyard in feather and fleece on the stage.

It is, no doubt, to be borne in mind that although the English drama was incomparably the best in the world at one time, and though the English dramatists are the only moderns who will bear comparison with the Greeks, the French have excelled us for two centuries and a half in the average excellence of their work, and in the capacity for criticism. Now, the decadence of the drama in France is by no means so marked as it is in England. Victor Hugo's best dramas seem to many of us who are foreigners superior for dramatic situations and for the expression of fine feeling even to Corneille; and of the younger Dumas and Sardou we may at least say that they are good enough to be read and reproduced or plundered everywhere. No one supposes that a Corneille or Victor Hugo can be born in every generation; and therefore, if the best work of these men is still appreciated in their own country, if there are men, however inferior, still working upon the same lines, it would not be safe to say that the character of the drama in that country has deteriorated. Let us admit this, and allow that Paris—even though it is an overgrown city—retains one very perfect form of amusement which has seemed to decay in England as the novel superseded it for the highest work. Still, Paris is only one city, and the taste of the French people may have given them an exceptional advantage, though it has not saved even Paris from being the home of opera-bouffe. The other apparent exception to the proposition, that the taste for serious dramatic art is declining, is to be found in the vogue that Ibsen's dramas have attained to. Writing in a tongue almost unknown to the world, translated at first only into German, as careless of popular taste and as reflective as Browning, as prone to violent effects as Webster, Ibsen has nevertheless obtained a moderate recognition even in England, where his best works are comparatively unread; altogether, I believe, unacted.[1] Probably it is fair to say in this particular instance that the generous appreciation of scholars and experts has forced Ibsen's

---

[1] The reference is to *Brand* and *Peer Gynt*, though the latter is partially known as an opera.

plays upon the attention of a public that grudges the time it gives them, and would prefer *Orpheus in Hell* to *Peer Gynt*.

It is scarcely necessary to inquire if the music-hall or the comic entertainment minister to a sound or elevated taste. What may probably be urged, however, with truth is, that they are to a great extent the relaxations of a class that had no relaxations anciently, or only such as were coarse and brutal— the bear-bait, the bull-bait, or the cockpit. It may even be better that men and women should listen to a stupid and indelicate song trolled out by a professional singer than that there should be a large literature of tavern catches and obscene songs, such as have come down to us from every century, of which we have copious literary remains, and such as were freely sung at private parties. It may reasonably be contended that the popular music-hall production of to-day never sinks quite as low for grossness as songs that Shakespeare and Ben Jonson have embalmed, and that the decay of literary form in this lowest phase of brainwork is due to the enhanced self-respect which prevents any but the lowest craftsmen from pandering to the most debased taste. All that the present argument seeks to establish is, that certain forms of amusement which a city provides, and which are considered among the attractions of a city, are really not more intellectual or elevating, though they are unquestionably more garish and fascinating, than the riot and coarse jocularity of a village tap-room.

Perhaps the most genuine advantage of city life is, that though the greed for gold is naturally as fierce in towns as in the country, it has a tendency to be less sordid. The French peasant as Balzac has painted him, the Spanish villager as Galdos describes him,[1] are very intense types of what country toil tends to produce everywhere—an absolute concentration of the mind upon small economies, or, it may be, small pilferings, and a thorough deadening of the moral sense. Countries where the wage-rate is low, and where the peasant is disinclined to move on the chance of bettering himself, seem to be those in which the feeling is strongest, and the Scotchman, who has always had a harder struggle for existence than his Southern neighbour, is, in spite of his superior self-reliance, habitually more frugal than the Englishman. On the other hand, countries where life is easy, and where splendid chances are numerous—such countries as California and parts of Australia have been for a generation—may possess a free-handed, speculative race of countrymen—miners, and even yeomen—with none of the economical characteristics of the European peasant. The greater frugality of the country population is therefore due to its circumstances and its needs, and the comparative lavishness of town life is chiefly noticeable in cities where wealth circulates freely, and where chances are numerous. There is reason to suppose, accordingly, that this

[1] "There has been much declamation against the materialism of cities . . . but there is a more terrible plague in the materialism of villages, which petrifies millions of human beings, killing all noble ambition in them, and confining them within the circle of a mechanical, brutal, and gloomy existence. . . . For the covetous villager there is no moral law, or religion, or clear notion of right. Under his hypocritical frankness is concealed a sombre arithmetic, which, for acuteness and perspicacity, surpasses all that the cleverest mathematicians have devised. A villager who is enamoured of coppers, and dreams of changing them into silver, to convert them later on into gold, is the most ignoble beast conceivable; for he has all the man's malicious and subtle imaginings, and a terrible persistency of aim."—Galdos, *Marianela*, pp. 41, 42.

advantage of the city over the country is not in its nature permanent. If we can assume a form of State Socialism which monopolised investment, taxed accumulated wealth heavily, and secured the labouring man work on equal terms wherever he lived, the reasons for the frugality of the villager would to a great extent disappear. Even if we assume the changes effected to be much less noticeable, a closing up of the outlets for emigration would deprive a large class in cities and in some country districts of the opening and chances to which they now trust in place of economy, and a severe competition of highly-developed countries, one with another, might easily reduce wages. The motives for frugality would become imperative, and the "Père Grandet" of French romance would have his counterpart in every London court.

Mr. Ticknor, as reported, put the case against a national debt as if it were only dangerous when it was held by the foreign creditor. On that assumption, the English, French, and United States debts, which are chiefly held in their respective countries, would be no serious evil. It seems more reasonable to consider whether a community that has anticipated its future progress to any great extent is not always in some peril. Such an inquiry will, of course, be independent of the question whether the debt was not contracted on reasonable grounds, or perhaps unavoidable. National existence would be regarded by most reasonable men as worth paying for, and when a statesman, by a nice calculation of chances, raises his country from being a second-rate state into the position of a first-class power, at the cost, it may be, of less than a year's income, the world does not censure his policy as extravagant. The peaceable acquisition of a State like Alaska by purchase is even less open to criticism. The cost of slave emancipation to Great Britain has always been considered a reasonable charge, and we now know that if the United States had emancipated the blacks in the Southern States at double their market value, instead of freeing them by war, it would have been an extremely sound bargain. The debts contracted for the purchase of a telegraph system, or for the construction of railways or water-works, are generally allowed to be right in principle. As a rule, we may perhaps say that a community is only censured when it charges current expenses or unproductive investments, such as fortifications, to posterity. Indeed, it is sometimes held, that as fortifications are a provision against future as well as immediate dangers, part of the expenditure on them may fairly be charged to the generation that will reap the advantage. Altogether, a State is practically justified for borrowing wherever it is a question of permanent acquisition or improvement; but an administration is not at present allowed to speculate on the chances of the market as a syndicate, a merchant, or a private adventurer might.

Under the influence of these ideas the growth of national debts has been very rapid. Russia, France, Italy, Spain, and such South American States as have enjoyed credit of any kind, have been the most flagrant instances of free-borrowing, while England, Holland, and the United States are the only countries that show an inclination to reduce their funded debts. It is customary to assume that the wealth of a prosperous country increases almost as rapidly as its indebtedness. For instance, if it be shown that France owed £911,000,000 in 1882 against £140,000,000 in 1820, it is retorted that the wealth of France has increased from £1,520,000,000 to £9,070,000,000 between 1815 and 1882.[1] Again, in the case of an undeveloped country, like one of the Australian colonies, where the money borrowed has not been squandered, as in the Argentine Confederation, but spent in reproductive works, it is usual to point to the railways and State lands as valuable assets. Then, again, the competition of money-seeking investment is so great that a large number of States can borrow at 3, $3\frac{1}{2}$, 4, or, at most, $4\frac{1}{2}$ per cent, where they anciently borrowed at 5 or 6. In this way the charges of old debts have been very sensibly reduced in several countries. Indeed, taking the money-market as a test, it may be said that Russia, Turkey, certain South American States, and Portugal are the only countries where national credit has been seriously impaired by borrowing, and even among these the decline is sometimes due to the fact that the country has drawn too largely in quite recent times upon its credit. The debt of Russia, if it could be kept stationary, or nearly so, for a few years, is not excessive for its growing population and immense natural resources.[2] What financiers fear is, that the money lent is employed in preparations for war that mean waste if peace is maintained, and that may mean incalculable loss if war is resorted to. Generally, the feeling seems to be, that every country has possibilities of great industrial development; that the necessity of maintaining national credit is understood

---

[1] "National Wealth of France compared with other Countries," by Fournier de Flaix, *Statistical Journal*, xlix. pp. 186-200.

[2] It is roughly about £5 a head, of which a fourth is nominally covered by debts from railways and municipalities. In the Netherlands the debt is £20 a head, and in New Zealand nearly £60.

by all but barbarous communities, and as a corollary, that there is no particular reason to be alarmed at the great increase of national indebtedness throughout the world.

There are, perhaps, some considerations on the other side. An increase of indebtedness is of its nature permanent; an increase of prosperity is not only not certain to last, but is practically certain to be reduced now and again by bad years. It means that money has been laid by and invested in remunerative enterprises, such as factories, ships, railways, houses, or the reclamation of land. Obviously, if population increases slowly, or is stationary, the development of wealth at constantly increasing rates cannot continue. A point may be reached when further production becomes increasingly difficult, and when families spend their surplus incomes more and more in articles of ostentation and comfort, because investments are less and less remunerative. Six or eight years of great depression, attended with the closing of factories, the throwing of land out of tillage, and the working of half the railways at a loss, would tell very seriously upon the capacity of even a prosperous country to meet its engagements. As for the supposed guarantees of a debt, they are all more or less visionary. In a time of great depression the State must resume its customs' duties or its mines, if it has pledged them, and its lands and its railways may be unsaleable at any depreciation. The only real guarantee of a debt is national character. The financial world requires to feel assured that under any possible form of government the importance of maintaining the national credit will be regarded as paramount to every other consideration. It is among the solid advances of practical morality that this is so much better understood than was once the case. Countries like Spain and Greece and the Argentine Confederation, that made no effort to pay their debts fifty years ago, have begun to learn by experience, though still in a halting and imperfect manner, that repudiation is far too costly a luxury to be indulged in.

Nevertheless, there seem to be two possibilities in the future that may reasonably inspire a little anxiety. One is, that States over-confident in the future may encumber themselves with obligations which it will scarcely be possible to discharge by any sacrifice. Let us suppose, for instance, that England tries an experiment in State Socialism, and buys up the land in Great Britain to distribute it again to small tenants by issuing a $2\frac{3}{4}$ per cent stock. We may assume, further, that the operation is carried out skilfully; that the landowner gets a sufficient, but not a fancy value for his land; and that the State may reasonably expect, if existing values are maintained, to lose nothing by the transaction, and even to gain ultimately, if farming by small occupiers proves a success, as great authorities have contended that it is bound to do. All of course depends upon this latter consideration. Now, it is at least conceivable that even though the small farmer gets more out of the land than the great landowner did, the farmer may yet fail to pay expenses, because the foreign market may be shut against his produce, and the home market may have diminished. For instance, the English coal-measures may have begun to fall off,[1] or countries like

---

[1] The probability of this has constantly been prophesied, notably by the late Mr. Jevons; but the alarm seems to have subsided, because the measures are more extensive than was at first supposed, and can be worked profitably at greater depths than was thought possible. Still, they are not inexhaustible, and their value might be depreciated before they were worked out by the opening up of mines elsewhere.

China and the United States may produce so cheaply as to drive English goods out of the market. In that case the English taxpayer, who has paid £1,600,000,000, let us say, for the land, and has created the money by charging himself with interest to the amount of £44,000,000, may find himself every year losing £10,000,000 or £12,000,000 upon his purchase. It will not be easy to make up this deficit by increased taxation. A property-tax would fall largely upon the very class who are by hypothesis unable to pay rent. An income-tax, if it were severe, would drive the large class of Englishmen who have invested their savings in foreign countries to make their homes abroad. Confiscation of Church lands, large as the estates of the Church are on paper, would bring in very little, till the compensation due to actual incumbents had been paid off, and would be very unpopular in the country if money, heretofore spent in the parishes, was diverted to the Treasury for the benefit of non-resident fund-holders. Put it how we may, it is difficult to suppose that the pressure upon the taxpayer in such a case as has been assumed might not be very severe and long-continued.

Now, in such a crisis, it is difficult to believe—and this is the second danger—that the taxpayer might not be sorely tempted to draw a distinction between debts due to a foreign creditor and obligations incurred to fellow-countrymen. Forty years ago, a very able student of political economy proposed to declare the National Debt a 3 per cent annuity terminable at the end of a hundred years.[1] A great part of the National Debt had been contracted for what the writer regarded as immoral purposes; a great part had been raised in the most wasteful way; and the difference

[1] Professor F. Newman.

in price between 3 per cent stock and an annuity, only determined at the end of a century, was so small as scarcely to deserve consideration when the great relief the nation would sustain was taken into account. The fact that this proposal, though it came at a time of great national depression, was received with indifference or indignation, may be taken as evidence that the commercial instinct and sense of national honour were perfectly sound in the England of that day. It may seem unreasonable to assume that the world will ever have a lower standard of good faith in the matter of indebtedness than it had forty years ago. Still, it is well to remember that even good moral purpose may break down under an impossible burden. The American States, which Sydney Smith lashed so wholesomely for repudiation, had more to say for themselves than their English creditor was disposed to see. Pennsylvania was threatened with an exodus of taxpayers if it raised money enough to provide the interest it owed. An English Government, in the hypothetical case put, might have to face the same possibility. It would probably argue that it was better for the English fund-holder to lose a part of his interest than to be paid in whole for a time by loans that would soon culminate in general bankruptcy; that if the State has a right to impose a five shillings in the pound income-tax, it may reasonably reduce incomes by five shillings in the pound; and, finally, perhaps that the fund-holder had been over-paid in the first settlement, and would receive his substantial dues on a smaller dividend. It is unnecessary to point out what is sophistical in these arguments. They cannot be called inconceivable, for every country that has repudiated has used some of them by turns, and the only question is, whether an English-speaking people would ever come to adopt them. What is to be feared is, that if national debts continue to increase on the assumption that general prosperity is bound to advance in the future as it has done in the past, a great many communities are bound to have recourse to repudiation when bad times come, though the form of bankruptcy may be artfully disguised. A sweeping succession duty would be an insidious and very practicable form of relieving the State from unpleasant obligations.

Englishmen are perhaps apt to rely too much on the precedent of integrity which has been maintained in England for two centuries. Over-indebtedness, leading to bankruptcy and to ruin or heavy temporary complications, has been a common feature of state-life throughout history. The decline of the Roman Empire was undoubtedly hastened by the heavy indebtedness of the cities,—an indebtedness which was often occasioned by their engaging in great public works. The Mississippi scheme of Law, which plunged France in bankruptcy, was an attempt to apply the most daring principles of modern finance under the administration of a thoroughly corrupt court. France was bankrupt again at the time of the Revolution, and the resource of confiscating the Church lands and many private estates was perfectly valueless. The American colonies were mostly impecunious or worse under English rule. Spain has a long record of insolvencies. Even England has never paid her full bill for the glory of the French wars under Edward III., and has witnessed the spectacle of a Lord Chancellor suspending payment of debts, because the Crown was insolvent, not much more than two centuries ago.[1] Nay, there are still men living who

[1] In 1672, under Charles II.—Lingard, vol. xii. pp. 18, 19.

can remember the time when the Bank of England was relieved by law from the obligation to give gold for its notes. When a State undertakes enterprises beyond its strength, it always does it at the risk of bankruptcy, whatever its good intentions may be. The question is, whether the tendency to State Socialism may not be a tendency also to the running up of large debts.

Two consequences seem to follow inevitably upon repudiation of any kind. The one is that the private as well as the public standard of honour will be lowered. Individuals do not as a rule profess to be more moral than the Government and the law, especially in countries where the State is highly organised. The other is, that the class ruined by repudiation is likely to be that class which is essentially conservative of tradition, of refinement, of all the passive elements of character. In such a case as has been assumed, the aristocracy, deprived of power and prestige by the forcible purchase of their landed property, would be reduced to insignificance by the resumption of a large part of the compensation first awarded them.

The general purport of the argument has been in agreement with Mr. Ticknor's predictions, though it is rather more optimistic than Mr. Ticknor would perhaps have agreed to. That standing armies are likely to increase seems probable. What we have to say, on the other hand, is, that wars need not necessarily increase in proportion, and that the training of a soldier may prove a valuable adjunct to the primary school. That cities will increase more and more upon country districts seems inevitable; and it has to be admitted that the life of the poor in an overgrown town is stunted and etiolated : neither physically sound nor morally complete. On the other hand, science and

State Socialism may gradually improve the condition of the dweller in towns, and the reaction against town life may lead to changes that will make existence in the country more tolerable. That nations will plunge deeper and deeper into indebtedness as the State becomes more and more industrial seems not unlikely. The worst to be apprehended from this will be its effect upon national character. Whether we are changing in the direction of a higher or of a lower morality is, therefore, the point that is most really at issue.

CHAPTER IV

SOME ADVANTAGES OF AN ENHANCED NATIONAL FEELING

The future of society depends very much on the perpetuity of national feeling.—Patriotism is generally regarded as an accidental and not very high altruism.—In antiquity it was largely alloyed with self-interest and the municipal feeling.—Patriotism is now the filial feeling to a mother country; the acknowledgment that we owe duties to our fellowmen, and cannot adequately perform them to the human race.—A nation from its richer memories and larger life ought to command more devoted allegiance than a city.—The rival feeling of personal loyalty is now disappearing, and need not be regretted.—The Church has incidentally done good work for society in vindicating the limits within which thought and morals ought to be independent of the State.—On the other hand, the attempt of the State to force morality upon the immoral will was never more than partially successful, and ended by provoking general revolt.—The State, which restrains immorality only when it becomes dangerous to society, has practically done more than the Church to enforce the moral law.—Sacrilege has ceased since it has been treated only as a secular offence.—The substitution of restraint by moderate laws and public opinion for ecclesiastical censures and punishments has not been visibly unfavourable to sexual purity.—The hypocritical formalism of modern society is not so dangerous to individuality as pressure by a Church inquisition. Moreover, under the Church rich offenders escaped, and these are now the most severely restrained.—The Church relieved poverty in a casual and ineffective way, and from a wrong motive, the idea that the alms-giver would be benefited. The State relieves it in a way better calculated to preserve self-respect in the poor, and from the higher motive, that every member of the community who will work is entitled to live.—Both systems have been only partially effective; but the Church system was a complete failure, while the State system, under all disadvantages, has reduced pauperism till it is a comparatively small feature of society.—Though the

CH. IV *SOME ADVANTAGES OF NATIONAL FEELING* 181

Church has in some respects and in some times and places mitigated slavery, slave emancipation has been a triumph of secular statesmanship.—The Mediæval Church has been overpraised for its services to learning. Its real object always was to save the soul, not to inform the mind.—The great extension of primary education in modern times is an achievement of secular statesmanship, and has been repeatedly and violently opposed by the Churches.—The State has superseded the Church in its hold on popular imagination by the great benefits it assures its members.—In some instances the morality of the State is higher than that of the Churches; for instance, in the treatment of women and children and dumb animals.—The feeling of the industrial classes for industrial organisations is not likely to supersede national feeling, and industry is likely to be restricted within national limits.—The nation is bound to remain the unit of political society, because the interests and feelings of different races and countries are too discordant to be harmonised under a central Government.—The modern State does incomparably more for men and women than ancient forms of society attempted, and ought to inspire deeper reverence and love.—In return for its services it is entitled to demand a more complete surrender of selfish personal interests.

THE argument thus far has attempted to show that what we now call the higher races will not only not spread over the world, but are likely to be restricted to a portion only of the countries lying in the Temperate Zone; that under the pressure which will be increasingly felt as outlets to trade and energy are closed, State Socialism will be resorted to as the most effective means of securing labour from want; that great armies will need to be maintained; that the population of cities will grow in number year by year; and that in proportion as the State's sphere of activity is increased will the indebtedness of the State increase also in every civilised country. Whether this condition of things will be good, tolerable, or bad, must depend very much on the spirit in which the community takes it. If we compare the description in Thucydides of the state of Athens during the Peloponnesian war and that in Synesius of a Roman provincial city, surrounded and sometimes blockaded by barbarians, we shall see that the great difference lies in the temper of the men rather than in the circumstances of the time.[1] If the people of Athens had not been quickened with the inspiration of empire, if they had stooped to count heads or ships, they would have acquiesced in the secondary place which was all their leading families were disposed to claim for them. As it was, they staked their existence upon a splendid adventure, and though they eventually failed, crowded centuries of glorious life into the achievements of two generations. Had the people of Ptolemais been led and inspired as the Athenians were, they might have made their city a stronghold of civilisation; and what is true of Ptolemais is true, of course, in a much higher degree of the Roman Empire. It fell to pieces, not because its administrators were always inefficient, or its armies weak, or its finances and mechanical resources inferior to those of the nations which overpowered it, but because there was really no sense of national life in the community. Unless the general feeling in a people is to regard individual existence and fortunes as of no practical account in comparison with the existence and self-respect of the body politic, the disintegrating forces of time will always be stronger in the long run than any given organisation.

Now patriotism, or the readiness to make sacrifices for fatherland, is a very peculiar virtue. It is generally treated as a mere phase of altruism, and is more praised

[1] Synesius, *Epistolae*, civ. It may be admitted that Ptolemais was never as populous as Athens in its best days, though Procopius speaks of the African town as having been anciently prosperous and well-peopled (*De Aedif.* vi. 2); but if Athens was the more powerful, it was assailed by more formidable enemies. The great difference is the measureless inferiority of the Roman governor of Ptolemais, Phryx Johannes, to Pericles.

by poets and orators than taken into account by moralists. For instance, Kant strikes at the root of patriotism by denying that the country has any original and natural right to claim obedience from its citizens,[1] and theologians and writers on ethics commonly hold that patriotism is dangerously apt to be a misleading force, diverting men from their obedience to a higher law, such as the recognition of Papal authority, or of the supreme dictates of morality. Mr. Lowell—surely a patriot of very rare and high type—has laid it down that our true country is that ideal realm which we represent to ourselves under the names of religion, duty, and the like. Mr. Lowell adds: "That it is an abuse of language to call a certain portion of land, much more certain personages, elevated for the time being to high station, our country."[2] Now it is obvious that a view of this kind may be reconciled with conduct which appears to the world to be dictated by national sentiment. For instance, when America was rent in twain by the War of Liberation, Mr. Lowell lent

[1] Kant no doubt conditions this principle by saying that the independence of other men, which is inalienable to humanity, must not be exercised so as to encroach on the independence of others (*Rechts-Lehre*, Band iii. SS. 38, 39). At the same time he recognises the right of the citizen to emigrate " Der Unterthan (auch als Bürger betrachtet) hat das Recht der Auswanderung," Band iii. S. 174. Mr. Sidgwick observes, " the duties of patriotism are difficult to formulate," and goes on to remark, that " whether a citizen is at any time morally bound to more than certain legally or constitutionally determined duties does not now seem to be clear ; nor, again, whether he can rightfully abrogate these altogether by voluntary expatriation " (*The Methods of Ethics*, pp. 223, 224). The question is certainly not a simple one ; but if thousands of citizens, who have supported a policy of lavish expenditure, leave the country when the burden of taxation becomes unpleasant, the very existence of the State may be threatened. No moralist will defend this extreme case ; but is there no duty upon the sons of men who ran into debt for the general good, as they not unreasonably conceived it, to take the consequences of their fathers' mistakes upon themselves?

[2] *Biglow Papers*, note to No. III.

his powerful assistance to the cause of nationality, and though all that he did might have been justified on cosmopolitan grounds—such as abhorrence of slavery, or the desire to see the experiment of free institutions worked out fairly upon a great continent—the fact remains, that the transcendentalist was fighting in the ranks with men who cared chiefly for the national flag, and that, except for the momentum of numbers and energy which these men gave, the cause of general civilisation could not have triumphed. It is, of course, theoretically conceivable, though it is surely very improbable, that the human race may gradually be educated into the cosmopolitan conception of duty. Capital, we are often told, has no sentiment. It is determined in its choice of a home by no other considerations than those of gain and security. Accordingly, manufactures are freely transplanted from England to Belgium, or America, or India, without regard to the interests of the English people, the merchant navy of a State entering upon a war is transferred without delay to a neutral flag, and it constantly happens that a belligerent power is supplied with arms or food or money from its enemy.[1] It may be asked, whether the average citizen will not at some future date be careless

---

[1] Two remarkable instances of this may be quoted from the history of the great war with France when feeling on both sides was strained to the uttermost. Rothschild having to transmit £800,000 to the Duke of Wellington, sent it through France (*Life of Buxton*, p. 289). Bourrienne, being ordered to provide 16,000 military cloaks, 37,000 jackets, and 200,000 pairs of shoes for the French army before the campaign of Eylau, procured them from England through a Hamburg house (*Mémoires de Bourrienne*, tome vii. chap. xx). In the first case, Frenchmen smuggled eight tons of gold through France to supply the needs of an army fighting against their own countrymen. In the second instance, whole factories in England must have been employed upon what—in the case of the jackets and cloaks, at least—every one knew to be military equipments for the use of the enemy.

of local and temporary interests. The man who emigrates undoubtedly shows, by the act of renouncing his native country, that he thinks himself entitled to carry his labour to the market where it is best paid without regard to any claims that England or Germany may have on him. Practically, he is often justified in contending that he will be more useful to his countrymen in his new dwelling-place than at home. A day may come, however, when a man who leaves an old and indebted State will be like the partner who peremptorily withdraws from an embarrassed firm. In other words, if it is right for States to assume large obligations, it can only be so because they have a reasonable certainty that successive generations of citizens will accept the responsibility of that indebtedness. Therefore, unless we regard the State as merely the casual aggregation of persons who find it to their advantage to live in a certain part of the earth, we must assume that there is, or ought to be, a virtue of patriotism, which will bind the Englishman to England, and the Frenchman to France in some special and not easily dissoluble way.

The difficulty is to separate patriotism, as we know it, from infinite base alloys of interest, personal feeling, or vanity, and to define its exact place in the moral code. The patriotism of Greek statesmen and heroes seems to have been a very mixed quantity. It was undoubtedly leavened—and very largely so—by self-interest. It was not as easy then as it has been in modern times to transfer nationality. The circle of possible friends was smaller even for a man of patrician birth; the isolation of exile was intolerable; the trust placed by his new protectors in the deserter more suspicious and exacting. Demaratos, Pausanias, Themistocles, Aristeides, Alcibiades are conspicuous instances of the false position in which a man disowned by his fellow-citizens found himself; while Englishmen like the Dukes of Berwick and Ormond, or Lord Bolingbroke; Frenchmen like Dumouriez, Moreau, and Pozzo di Borgo, enjoyed consideration, at least, in their new homes, and the full confidence of the Courts that protected them. Mr. Symonds has explained at length an element of Greek patriotism, so-called, that has often been misconceived—the personal attachment that bound together the companies in the Sacred Band of Thebes.[1] When it became possible for Greeks to prosper in Alexandria and Antioch and Rome, and when the peculiar feeling of the Sacred Band came to be out of date, the Greek ceased to be a patriot. So it was with Rome also, and we may say naturally and excusably. The old feeling for Rome as a sacred city, which sustained its people during the Punic Wars, seems to have passed away by the time of Sylla; and national feeling in the days of Cicero, Augustus, and Trajan, was little more than the desire of an aristocracy for caste ascendency, the contempt of Italians for conquered races, and a feeling in the higher circles of society that life was only desirable in Rome. We can scarcely give the name of patriotism to the devotion of a tribe to its chief, or to the bitter hatred of one race for another; and these feelings come out predominantly in the history of the Middle Ages. The gentlemen of Aquitaine, who so largely contributed to win the battle of Poitiers, were fighting against what we should now consider France, and were certainly not fighting for England, but for an English king, who had

---

[1] *Contemporary Review*, September 1890, pp. 415-417. Sir George Cox has demurred by anticipation to Mr. Symonds's view, but practically admits the fact.—*General History of Greece*, p. 574.

claims upon their allegiance, and whom they renounced when his yoke proved burdensome. Nevertheless, it is probable that the terrible French and English wars did actually lead to a great development of the spirit of nationality as we understand it, and so to a larger conception of patriotism. Still, both in England and in France, centuries passed before the duty to the laws or to Fatherland was recognised as more important than loyalty to the sovereign.

It may be admitted that a great many various motives contribute to form even a modern patriot. Still, it is not very difficult to express a popular idea of the limitations of the modern feeling. Patriotism is now the feeling that binds together people who are of the same race, or who at least inhabit the same country, so that they shall try to preserve the body politic as it exists, and recover for it what it has lost, or acquire what seems naturally to belong to it. It seeks within the country to procure the establishment of the best possible order. It enjoins the sacrifice of property, liberty, or life for the attainment of these objects. It favours the existence of whatever is peculiar and local; of a distinctive literature, manners, dress, and character. When it conceives the common country to be weak, it tries to discard every foreign element as dangerous; and when it is conscious of its strength, it tries to assimilate what is best from abroad. The fierce pride of the Englishmen in Algiers, who went back into captivity sooner than acknowledge that they owed their liberty to the King of France, is now out of date;[1] but the general rule, that no man can receive distinctions except from the head of his country, is expressed in law and approved by opinion. Stated in this way, patriotism seems to be based on the

[1] *Siècle de Louis XIV.* chap. 14.

reasonable acknowledgment of two facts in our nature: that we owe a duty to our fellowmen, and that we cannot adequately perform it to the race at large. In the American War of Liberation, to which reference has been made, there was a Southern general of high moral character (Stonewall Jackson), who, though he was a believer in State rights, was not a believer in slavery. He found it impossible to dissever the two causes, and he elected, as most will think, pardonably, to fight for the good of the State, which he clearly apprehended, against the abstract and transcendental rights of humanity. Such problems are constantly occurring; and no community can allow its citizens to take part against itself on the ground that they belong to an ideal realm of religion, duty, and the like. If a body of English officers, for instance, feeling strongly that our intervention in Egypt was immoral, had fought at Tel-el-Kebir against their countrymen, they would have been shot by martial law if they were taken, and no public opinion, however hostile to England, would have condemned the execution. Practically, it would seem, therefore, as far as our imperfect moral sense can see, there is an obligation upon every citizen not actively to injure the State he belongs to, which no man is allowed to disregard. If he finds the State attacking what he thinks a true religion, or violating the rights of labour, or waging an iniquitous war, he is bound to oppose its action by civic means; and if he fails in this, he is by modern practice allowed to renounce his citizenship. If, however, he does not take this extreme step, he commits himself to supporting the policy of the State, though he disapproves of it, and is not blamed for assisting to carry it to a successful issue.

In some important particulars, a lofty feeling of

patriotism has become more possible now than it ever was in past centuries. The physical law, that the greater mass attracts more powerfully than the smaller, holds good in the moral world, and attachment to a great country is bound, other things being equal, to be more dignified and generous than attachment to a city, though the city may have been Athens or Rome. No doubt there were certain great periods in the life of antiquity when the Athenian was merged in the Hellene, fighting for the whole west against eastern barbarians, and when the cause of Rome against Carthage was practically the cause of Italy. These, accordingly, were the ideal times, when men rose above their natural level. A modern nation, however, if it has a past of any kind worth remembering, is likely to have survived greater struggles than any Greek city, to have ampler records of heroism, and an incomparably more varied life. A great country, of which it can be said that

> One half her soil has walked the rest,
> In poets, heroes, martyrs, sages,

is one in which the religion of the soil can scarcely be dissevered from national life. Of course it is essential to the perpetuity of this sentiment that the nation should be homogeneous. The Turks have not inherited the fame of Justinian and his generals by over-running their empire; and if by some industrial migration Germans, Polish Jews, and other even more alien races were to supersede the English labourer to any great extent, the new England would be weaker than the old by all the links of tradition. Practically, however, the case of the Turks, who have camped in Europe without absorbing or being absorbed, is exceptional; and a nation, as a rule, is too large to be swamped by an industrial immigration, as cities have now and again been. We may therefore reckon the substitution of the nation for the city in political organisation as one circumstance that is favourable to the growth of an enlightened patriotism. For intensity, nothing probably surpasses the municipal feeling, as it has existed in cities that were just powerful and dignified enough to appeal to sentiment.

The substitution of attachment to the State, the country, the fatherland, for the feeling of personal loyalty must also be regarded as a distinct moral gain. Such a sentiment as that which led Jacobites and non-Jurors to fight for a line of sovereigns whose triumph in their own estimation was bound to be dangerous to Church and law, or at least to abstain from recognising a better order, and to estrange themselves from all interest in their country's struggles, all wish to see that country triumph, must be regarded as among the most lamentable of delusions. It was possible for the sovereign in times when this feeling prevailed to be sincerely patriotic. A king, like Charles II., who cared first for his pleasures, and next for power as a means for promoting these, and who valued neither the well-being nor the honour of his country, has been the rare exception in England. Perhaps Louis XV.—as selfish, as immoral, and less able—is his only counterpart in France. But loyalists like Strafford, who would have employed half-savage Irish troops against his own countrymen; like the Scotch Jacobites, who invited a French invasion; like the French émigrés, who were willing to serve indifferently in English, Austrian, or Prussian ranks, provided they fought against the cause approved by their countrymen—are unhappily only typical instances of what the loyalist must logically become.

In a few cases the want of nobler feeling has been redeemed by an unselfish devotion, which asked for no private gain, and shrunk at no sacrifices. Habitually, the loyalist in exile has either calculated that he was on the side which would win ultimately, or has been so completely demoralised by life outside of his countrymen, as to have lost every trace of disinterested public feeling when he returned in triumph. Of the Cavaliers who lived to see the Restoration, and of the *émigrés* who returned to France, it may be said pretty generally that they acted as if they had not intended to serve the lost cause for nothing. The Cavaliers, indeed, though they asked for a great deal, got comparatively little, because many of their estates had been sold in the open market, and because the Presbyterians enjoyed the credit of having brought the King back.[1] The French *émigrés*, whose offence against their country had been more serious, came back to find their debts and encumbrances sponged out,[2] to get a compensation of £40,000,000, and to have something like a monopoly of office and promotion for fifteen years. It can scarcely be matter of regret that a feeling which so constantly

---

[1] *Autobiography of Sir John Bramston*, p. 117. Clarendon gives an instance where Lord Lovelace, having sold an estate below its value to Bulstrode Whitelocke, refused to complete the title unless he was paid an additional sum; but even in this strong case, Lord Lovelace seems to have prevailed only through legal technicalities (*Clarendon's Life*, s. 281). Mrs. Hutchinson says that her husband saved the estates of many gentlemen of his county by getting himself appointed sequestrator.—*Memoirs of Colonel Hutchinson*, pp. 326, 327.

[2] "The emigration and the laws of 1793 by depriving them" (the grand seigneurs) "of their estates, set them free from their creditors" (Madame de Rémusat's *Memoirs*, vol. ii. p. 414). "The whole mass of confiscated land, not now in possession of the families to whom it belonged in 1793, or of those to whom those families have sold it, would not amount to the value of property lost by confiscation in Ireland by the single family of Fitzgerald."—Lord Holland's *Foreign Reminiscences*, p. 281, published in 1850.

passed into the merest self-seeking is disappearing from the domain of public life.

Even those who most feel what a gain it has been that religious considerations should be ceasing to balance secular in the estimation of citizens, will regard the old fanaticism for Churches very differently from the irrational sentiment of loyalty in its more extravagant forms. It may be presumptuous for a man to believe that the Church he was born in, or has passed over to, represents the final results of thought on the most difficult matters of speculation, and that God will punish to all eternity those who, through perversity, or it may be for want of spiritual light, refuse to accept the truth when it is put before them. Still, most men will admit that there must be one way of conceiving the relations of God to man which is truer than any other at any given time, and that to apprehend this rightly ought to be of supreme importance. Even if we assume blank materialism to be the gospel of the future, it must be useful to apprehend it distinctly, that we may clear our minds of dreams and human inventions. Still more, if we believe in any form of religion that teaches a higher law than the State prescribes, and is able to enforce it by a sanction that is not of this world, must the benefit of Church authority appear incontestable. It is well to remember that secular society has revolted not only against obsolete faiths,—for many forms of Christianity appear to men in general as rational as unbelief; not only against a corrupt clergy,—for the clergy have not always been corrupt, and, to take a single instance, were both learned and zealous in England when the great Rebellion descended upon them;[1] but

---

[1] "All confess there never was a more learned clergy," said Selden of the Caroline divines.—Selden's *Table-Talk*, p. 134.

against the persistent efforts of religious organisations to enforce common morality at the expense of individual liberty. Let it be borne in mind, also, that the Church in western Europe has perpetually represented a dualism that was of the highest value for freedom of thought. Sir Thomas More died on the scaffold, not because he disputed the right of Parliament to make Anne Boleyn Queen, or to settle the crown upon her children, but because he denied that the ultimate power to determine religious controversy could be vested in the head of the State.[1] It is probable that he misinterpreted the intentions of his contemporaries; but it is certain that after the lapse of three centuries and a half, when the secular power is far stronger than it was, it claims nothing in any civilised State that Sir Thomas More would have denied it. Except for the protest of men like Sir Thomas More, Henry VIII. might have made the State supreme in England, as it actually is in Russia. Take again modern times. That marriage should be treated by the State as a civil contract, and that primary education should be given on secular lines, are principles now very generally accepted. They seem to many men worth fighting for, worth dying for. Nevertheless, although their acceptance has been delayed by the opposition of the Churches, it may surely be contended

[1] More declared openly that he believed Parliament could make a private person king, and told his friends in confidence that he had freely remonstrated with the King about relaxing the Statute of Præmunire.—Roper's *Life of More*, pp. 66, 80, 81. The Act of Uniformity, as Mr. Child has pointed out, drew up "all manner of spiritual authority" into the Crown, and practically gave the King the power of defining doctrine. —Child's *Church and State under the Tudors*, pp. 66, 67. Still, it is probably to be assumed that Henry never contemplated using these extreme powers to their logical extent. He and his successors always acted with the advice of the bishops, who presented the same mixture of pliancy and independence in Church matters that the Parliaments displayed in matters temporal.

O

that the gain resulting from a marriage-law controversy or a Kultur-Kampf infinitely outweighs its inconveniences to an administration. Few, indeed, are the journalists and thinkers on the Continent who can speak and write against a government measure with the freedom which is tolerated in the meanest priest. Lacordaire was silenced for calling Louis Napoleon a tyrant, but he submitted only because his Church was subservient to the usurper, and where he was simply ordered to change the form of his work, a lay journalist would have been imprisoned or sent to Cayenne. A few years later, the French clergy were freely comparing the head of the State to Pontius Pilate, and suffered no annoyance.

It is one thing, however, to feel that the Churches have been useful in past time as a counterpoise to autocracy, and quite another to wish that their authority should be maintained. As a rule, the Churches are in their very essence opposed to liberty of thought and conduct; while the State is gradually tending to become more and more tolerant of each. It has been noticed above that the law of life which the Churches seek to impose has been found intolerable. Two familiar instances will show what is meant. Every thoughtful student of history is aware that the Protestant Reformation was attended with a general dissolution of morals in those countries which did not provide adequately for the maintenance of ecclesiastical law.[1] The old Church discipline was relaxed or swept away; and while even

---

[1] "Of the following general facts I hold superfluous proof (1) that after the religious revolution in Protestant Germany, there began and long prevailed a fearful dissolution of morals; (2) that of this moral corruption there were two principal foci — Wittenberg and Hesse." — *Discussions on Philosophy*, by Sir W. Hamilton, pp, 497-499, note. Compare Ranke, *Gesch. der Deutschen Reformation*, Band v. SS. 435-437.

the best men, such as Luther, found themselves at sea on such a question as polygamy, the illiterate and lax plunged into every kind of vicious extravagance. We see Luther perpetually grappling with the problem, why sin was bolder and prayer less earnest since the Gospel had come into the world.[1] Yet it does not appear difficult to understand that when the drunkard, the fornicator, or the adulterer was no longer liable to be summoned into the Dean's Court, and was not punishable at common law, there was bound to be an interval of decline before a sound public opinion had time to form and make itself felt. The great success of Calvinism in the latter half of the century is probably due very much to the fact that Calvin's rigorous discipline kept his Church free from scandal. The Calvinistic model was accordingly adopted in England, and the English diocesan courts combined the old Catholic rigour against ecclesiastical offences with the Calvinistic zeal against moral frailty. After a fair trial, lasting for about two generations, the whole nation rose up in arms against the inquisition domiciled in every archdeaconry.[2] The revolt, however, had two sides. It was supported by

[1] "As the cold is greater and quicker in winter when the days get longer and the sun comes nearer to us,—so also is the wickedness of man greater, that is, more apparent, and breaks strongly forth when the Gospel is preached." The lady doctor says to him, "Doctor, how is it, that in Popery we prayed so fervently, earnestly, and often; but now is our prayer quite cold; nay, we do not often pray?" The doctor answers thereto, and said: "The devil is always urging on his servants, who are untiring and laborious in service of their god; but the Holy Ghost teaches and advises us how to pray rightly; yet we are so icy cold and slack in prayer that it will not come out."—Luther's *Tisch-Reden*, Band i. S. 226; Band ii. S. 233.

[2] See vols. xxi. and xxxiv. of the *Surtees Society Publications*, containing the Acts of the High Commission Court within the Diocese of Durham, 1560-1591, and 1626-1639. We find the offences varying from adultery, blasphemy, and insults to the clergy, to clandestine marriages and nonconformity. Fines, sometimes as high as £3000, penance, and imprisonment were the penalties.

worldly men who wished not to be meddled with, and by Puritans, who approved highly of the principle of interference, but desired to keep it in their own hands, and to use it against social gaiety as well as against faulty living. The result was that at the Restoration there was a general and strong reaction against the exercise of Church authority in any shape. It was not extinguished suddenly; but it had to content itself more and more with obscure offenders, till it became an anomaly and ridiculous. Like most abuses in England, it has remained on the Statute Book long after it had died out in practice. Less than fifty years ago an Englishman could be punished for not attending church or a registered chapel on Sunday;[1] and later still the Ecclesiastical Court retained the theoretical right to punish him for incest and incontinence. Indeed, these were in England the only courts taking cognisance of such offences, except as private injuries; yet even this has not tended to the preservation of their use or influence. The modern State habitually prefers to legislate on secular principles for such offences against morality—incest, unnatural vice, seduction, and the like —as it finds it desirable not to tolerate.

Now the practical effect of this change is, that where the Church has always aimed at substituting a perfect rule of thought and life for liberty of opinion and moral conduct, the State has never attempted to do more than to protect its own existence against the excesses of liberty.

---

[1] Homersham Cox, *Institutions of English Society*, p. 463, note. The penalties incurred for non-attendance at church under 1 Eliz. c. 2, § 14, and 3 Jac. I. § 14, were repealed by the 9th and 10th Victoria, c. 59, § 1. I believe they were last put in force against men suspected of poaching. The law of sacrilege was abolished by 24 and 25 Victoria, c. 96, § 50. Breaking into a church, however, is more heavily punished than breaking into other buildings.—Stephen's *Blackstone*, vol. iv. pp. 203, 204.

The Church and the State may each punish the publication of blasphemy, but the Church does it because it is an offence against God, and because the individual ought not to blaspheme; while the State only considers that licentious attacks upon convictions which are sacred to some of its subjects are an offence to good feeling, and an incentive to disorder, or a cause of undesirable acrimony. The Church punishes sexual immorality as dishonouring to the libertine, and the State, as a rule, only meddles with it when advantage is taken of the young and weak, or when there is likely to be a public scandal. The Church denounces Sunday traffic as a breach of the fourth commandment, and the State only proscribes it as an encroachment on necessary rest. The Church almost invariably regards the marriage-tie as indissoluble, or nearly so; and the State, where it is not influenced by the Church, habitually allows divorce in a great number of cases. It would seem, in all these particular instances, as if the State was deliberately substituting a lower law for a higher. Practically, however, secular society will bear comparison, even on these points where it is least exacting, with any State that was governed by the Church in old days, taking even the times that were best for Church discipline. In the first place, it has never been possible to maintain the religious ideal. Now and again history records with admiration how some saintly prelate or confessor has reproved a monarch for flagrant immorality. The Bishop of Soissons, for instance, compelled Louis XV. to dismiss Mdme. de Château-Roux and her sister for a few days, as the price of receiving the sacraments. Unhappily, this brilliant instance of a great duty bravely discharged, and the fact that thirty years later the Abbé of Beauvais denounced the same king to his face, are very insufficient offsets to the general toleration which the Church extended to the vilest debauchee in Christendom. There is no occasion to suppose that the Popes or the rulers of the French hierarchy were indifferent to the scandals of Versailles and of the Œil-de-Bœuf. What influenced them in remaining apathetic—in not excommunicating the king and his mistresses—was the fear lest the Church should lose the support of royal authority; and this or a meaner motive has been equally operative with the Anglican clergy, who ought to have admonished George IV., and with the French clergy under the Second Empire. It may be said that the case taken of a sovereign and his court is exceptional. It is exceptional only in the fact that the infamy is conspicuous. How many English clergymen in the last three centuries have dared to denounce a large landowner for drunken or immoral habits? If they have done so, it has been at the risk of a civil suit for defamation of character, with a fair chance that their bishop would disapprove their zeal, and with the certainty that their parochial work would be heavily hindered, that opposition to them would be fomented, and that the alms of the richest contributor would be withdrawn. Even during the short rule of the Puritans, which was strict enough to provoke a reaction of unbridled licentiousness, there is evidence that powerful offenders—a Martyn or a Wentworth—were never meddled with.[1] In the struggle to repress irrepressible human nature, the Churches have always been worsted, and their defeats have necessarily been disgraceful.

[1] Clarendon goes so far as to say that Cromwell was well pleased to see Cavaliers and Presbyterians notorious for "scandalous lives," "luxury and voluptuousness."—*Clarendon's Life,* c. 37.

Even, however, if the Church ideal could be maintained, it would be at the cost of something better than the formal abstinence from evil,—of human liberty. If we can conceive a generation that abstained from saying what it thought for fear of Church censures; that was sober, moral, and cleanly-mouthed, not because it regarded vice as evil, but because it feared fine, imprisonment, or disgrace; that talked with the tongue of By-ends, while within was all uncleanness, we should have the picture of a society more hopelessly corrupt than the world has ever yet seen. The sons of such men would be born, suckled, and bred in lies; would inherit the lust of the flesh, the craven spirit, and the tortuous intellect. In vindicating for every man the right to think mistakenly, to speak foolishly, and to live within limits riotously, the State has vindicated also the right to believe on conviction, to denounce error fearlessly, and to lead sweet and wholesome lives, untainted by Pharisaism, and not degraded by the reproach of a profitable conformity. When we measure the actual results of liberty, we find surely that they are good, even in the domain where liberty is accounted most dangerous. The offence of sacrilege is so peculiar by its nature, that what appears revolting profanity to the Conservative may seem nothing more than a splendid iconoclasm to the Reformer. In ages when there has been a religion established by law, the policy of those who assailed it has invariably been to show their contempt for it and lessen it in popular estimation by acts of public indignity. Not to mention the early Christians, who, it may be said, could not compromise with such flagrant errors as those of Paganism, we find that Protestantism, even in England, which has been conspicuously temperate, carried on its war against the

Established Church by acts that must have been profoundly offensive to every pious person who retained his ancestral faith. Thus, for instance, we find as early as the days of Wycliffe that a gentleman of Wiltshire, who had received the sacramental bread from his parish priest, took it home and lunched upon it with wine, oysters, and onions.[1] Under Henry VIII. and Queen Mary, acts which we can only designate as deliberate outrages upon the Church of the majority, were extremely common. Sometimes it was a crucifix—the symbol to ordinary men of their Lord's death and suffering—that was carried off and burned or broken up; sometimes a cat in priest's robes was hanged, or the priest parodied behind his back while he was officiating in the sacred mysteries; very constantly the consecrated bread of the Eucharist was ostentatiously seized and trampled under foot, or given for food to a dog.[2] In short, the more hotheaded of the English Reformers were guilty of deliberate acts which it is possible a Hell-fire Club would have shrunk from two centuries later;[3] and though the intemperance of the Reformers was palliated by the sincerity of their convictions, and their readiness to seal them with their blood, it is certain that much which they did would be punished in any civilised State as sacrilege. No

---

[1] Walsingham's *Historia Anglicana*, vol. i. pp. 450, 451.

[2] See Maitland's chapters on the Ribalds of the Reformation, and specially pp. 242, 252, 254, and 291, 293.—Maitland's *Reformation in England*.

[3] The worst acts imputed to the monks of Medmenham—who may appropriately be termed a Hell-fire Club—are, I believe, the invocation of the devil by Lord Sandwich, the giving the sacrament to a dog by the same worthy, and a picture in which a naked Venus was represented as "mater sanctorum," excesses which were meant to be private, and acts, however scandalous, which were probably much less offensive to the apathetic religion of those times than the acts of the reforming ribalds to the more pious among their countrymen.—Rae's *Wilkes, Sheridan, and Fox*, pp. 13, 134; Dilke's *Papers of a Critic*, vol. ii. p. 233.

administration, however, finds it necessary in these days to protect the convictions of its citizens from deliberate insult, except in the rare cases where the Church is practically stronger than the State, and where the war of faiths is carried on under something like the old conditions. To all appearance the liberty granted might with safety be greater than it is. The line of demarcation between the late Dr. Matthew Arnold comparing the Trinity to three Lord Shaftesburys,[1] and the late Mr. Bradlaugh editing a comparison of it to a monkey with three tails,[2] is rather one of literary style than of reverence; and it is difficult to see why the two offenders were so differently punished. Meanwhile, it is instructive to notice that these two sallies of irreverence, and a few lines by Mr. Swinburne, are all that represent the sacrilegious spirit in Englishmen who have taken any noticeable place among their countrymen during the last fifty years, though the temper of the times is believed to be sceptical, and even aggressively irreligious.

It would be easy to give plausible grounds for supposing that the absence of Church control, though it always led to excesses when it first ceased, has in the long run been attended with advantage to sexual purity. There are certain patent facts which give colour to this supposition. England has not seen for two centuries such a Court as that which Hamilton described in the *Memoirs of Grammont*, and whose tone was reflected in Wycherley's comedies. The days when the wits of the *Rolliad* made it their inexhaustible joke against Pitt that he led a cleanly life, seem as far off as the days of Charles II., and it is popularly assumed now that public

[1] *Literature and Dogma*, pp. 306, 307.
[2] In my first edition I mistakenly charged Mr. Bradlaugh with the authorship of a comparison which he only gave publicity to.

opinion demands absolute decorum from a leading man. Nelson, who intrigued with his friend's wife; Wellington, who was certainly not irreproachable; and Warren Hastings, who purchased a divorced wife from a needy foreigner, would scarcely be permitted now to save the Empire. A similar change, though not quite so strongly accentuated, may be noticed everywhere. The French nation has always been taxed with a disposition to regard immorality as inevitable and venial, and so long as it is not carried to excess, nothing more than one of "such wild tricks as gentlemen will have."[1] Readers of Rabelais, of Brantôme, of Bussy Rabutin, of Duclos, of Voltaire, and of Champfort, find it difficult to believe that there was a moral French society between Francis I. and Louis XVI. The best observers tell us that, at present, provincial life in France is as pure as it is anywhere, and that Paris would not be perceptibly worse than any other great city if it was not the favourite resort of profligate and wealthy Bohemians from every part.[2] It is probably true to say that the rich men, who give a tone to society, are everywhere more liable to suffer from a social scandal, and consequently more anxious to avoid it, than they have been in any previous part of the world's history. It is also true that girls and young women are better protected by law than they have ever been, and that the disposition to protect them is only kept from going further than it does by practical difficulties. The old Poor-Law of England, for instance, which threw the whole cost of an illegiti-

---

[1] "The French, even when practically chaste in their own lives, regard adultery in the male sex, at least, with a sort of amusement, not unmingled with admiration."—Hamerton's *French and English*, p. 232.

[2] Hamerton's *French and English*, pp. 206-232, and Hamerton's *Round my House*, pp. 178-181.

mate birth upon the father, has been discarded, because it was found to deprive women of a desirable reason for self-restraint.[1] Therefore, it is perhaps correct to say that the substitution of secular for clerical influence, of moderate laws and the restraint of public opinion for ecclesiastical censures and punishments, has not been visibly unfavourable to correctness of life in the sexes. More than this it might be hazardous to affirm at present. The great sin of great cities does not seem to be on the decrease; and temporary, or it may be permanent but irregular unions, in which the women and the children are not safeguarded as in marriage, seem to have increased of late years in undesirable proportions, especially in Catholic countries.[2] Above all, we have to remember that what Goethe said of humanity—that "it is always advancing, but in spiral lines"—is eminently true of the ascetic principle in morals. The times of Charles I. and of the Commonwealth appeared to establish a tradition of austerity, and scarcely any one could have anticipated the deluge of depravity that overwhelmed England after the Restoration. It is certain that the literature, the art, and the tone of wealthy society in France were demoralised by the libertinage in high places of the Second Empire.

It may be asked whether the mechanical pressure exerted by public opinion in modern society is not just as destructive of vigorous individuality as Church authority could have been. Under the old system, a sceptic bowed to the consecrated wafer, though he did not believe in the Real Presence, and abstained from sacrilegious words and acts, because he was afraid of

[1] This was the emphatic opinion of the Poor-Law Commissioners, pp. 346, 347.
[2] France and the South and Central American Republics are the countries specially alluded to.—See Nelson's *Central America*, p. 51.

being imprisoned or burned. In the nineteenth century he attends church, repeats a creed which he believes to be outworn, and lets his children be taught from a book which he regards as a collection of old wife's fables, because he knows that violently to repudiate the faith of the majority will injure him in society and in his profession. Under the old system, a libertine abstained from seducing his neighbour's wife for fear of being fined in the Dean's Court, and made to do public penance; at present, he is afraid of an action at law, of some social disrepute, and of political ruin. Are not the conformity and the morality no better than an organised hypocrisy? And where is the gain in having discarded the ecclesiastical system? The gain, it may be admitted, is not complete or unalloyed. Nevertheless, in matters of religion, it may surely be said that the tolerance of secular society is distinctly greater than that of Church courts influenced by professional feeling as well as by conviction. Probably, even now, there is essential truth in the description of English society which a German cynic gave thirty years ago. "A man in England may be an atheist, but he must belong to the Church of the atheists." What is dreaded is not so much the reproach of wrong belief, or of unbelief, as the awkwardness—the indecency, so to speak—of isolation. Even so, have the prophets of unpopular doctrines—a Colenso, a Herbert Spencer, or a Renan—suffered anything comparable to the treatment of a Latimer or a Du Bourg, a Servetus or a Giordano Bruno? Is it not the case, too, that where the penalty exacted is small, and almost fanciful, a man does not feel degraded by submitting to it as he does by an imperious demand upon his allegiance? Many a man is a formalist because he will not fritter away his life in the worry of a fight for his small and half-formulated doubts, who would show something of the old spirit if he were called upon to turn Protestant, being Catholic; or, being Protestant, to worship the Host. In the case of morality, another difference between ancient and modern times has to be remembered. Anciently it was the rich offender for whom the laws were spiders' webs, which he could break through at pleasure. At present, it is the prince, the statesman, or the man in society, who is marked down for a flagrant offence against morals, while the mechanic escapes unobserved. We may surely say that a condition of society which exacts a severer rule of life from the rich than from the poor, is to that extent healthy and full of promise, and better than the old practice of the Churches.

While it is apparent that society has lost nothing by transferring the correctional functions of the old Churches in certain matters of religious and moral obligation to the secular law-giver, it is demonstrable that it has gained very much since the State has vindicated its supreme right to deal with such matters as pauperism, the rights of labour, and popular education. All these are issues in which the Church has failed from having a low ideal, as well as from inherent ineffectiveness. Take, for instance, pauperism. It is probable that no Church has ever possessed the wealth requisite for coping with national indigence after discharging the other duties that were justly demanded of it. From the very nature of Church endowments, it is habitually the wealthy parts of a country that are best supplied, and national interests and needs are inevitably sacrificed to local and family considerations. Thus we find in England of the Middle Ages that, in all Cumberland and Lancashire, with an area of more than 2,000,000 acres, there were only seventeen religious houses; and in East Hampshire, in a district that measured fifty miles by twenty, there was not a single foundation from which the poor could be relieved. On the other hand, wealthy counties, like Norfolk and Lincolnshire, were studded with rich houses at easy distances from one another.[1] To them that had was given. But this inherent defect in the Church system, that it has always been local and parochial, rather than national, is very far from being its worse fault. Charity in the Churches is inculcated as a religious duty profitable to the person who practices it. It occasionally blesses him that gives, and it habitually demoralises and degrades him who takes. The condition of receiving Church doles has always been to need them at the moment; and the question of deserving them is most frequently treated as of very minor importance. Nothing like an attempt to give work, or even to test by work on any large scale, has ever been attempted, as a rule, by religious benefactors. Now it may freely be admitted that secular methods of dealing with pauperism have often been foolish and bad. The English Poor-Law system, as competent observers found it in 1834, was so administered as to promote inefficiency in men and immorality in women. Still the spirit of all English legislation on this subject is in its intentions sound and liberal. What lies at the bottom of every Poor-Law Act is the feeling that every man born into the body politic is bound to work, and must have work found for him if he cannot find it for himself, on the ground that every man is responsible for the support of his family—parents or children. Whether the State is to organise public works, and provide an insurance fund against sickness

[1] Pearson's *Historical Maps*, pp. 61, 62.

or old age, or whether it is best to leave these matters as much as possible to private initiative, are questions that need not be discussed here. What is important to notice is, that the promiscuous alms-giving which the Churches have habitually encouraged is discontinued, or even punished, in the most civilised communities; that secular legislation compels wealth to contribute to the support of industry; and that we seem slowly but surely to be approaching a time when no man shall need bread, except by his own fault, and when no woman shall have to purchase her children's bread by her own shame.

It must be borne in mind that it does not necessarily follow because a bad system is abolished that a better is immediately substituted. The dissolution of the English monasteries was followed by a great debasement of the English coinage, by the confiscation of the Guild lands, which were the English artisan's benefit funds, and by arbitrary legislation which proposed to fix the labourer's wages below his needs. Therefore it is no wonder if the transition to the secular system of relief was not generally welcomed. The change from the old order had been complicated in an unnecessary and mischievous manner. So again, the enclosure of common lands in a later century, and the one-sided legislation in matters of trade—the sweeping away of all safeguards for workmen—were aggravations of the poverty that is bound to exist. Every country has passed through a phase when the nobles succeeding to the Church have been even less regardful of the industrial class. None the less is it on the whole true, that pauperism has declined over the greater part of the world since the Church ceased to dispense charity, and that the right of the labourer to work has come to receive universal recognition. Moreover, it is at least noticeable that in the Middle Ages the leaders of a Jacquerie were as hostile to the Church as to the State.[1] The Primate of England was beheaded by Tyler's followers, and the Convent of St. Albans terrorised by sympathisers with Tyler; the Bishop of Salisbury was beheaded by sympathisers with Cade, and in either movement Church officials were obliged to hide for their lives. It can scarcely be supposed, therefore, that the poor were conscious of profiting to any great extent by Church alms. As a fact, we know that lawless vagabondage and extreme destitution in great cities were features of every period of the Middle Ages. The tendency of the representatives of labour in modern times is to give increased power to the State, and to attain their ends by influencing its councils. It may prove that the expectation of obtaining relief through the State has been a fallacious one. Meanwhile, that the vagrant poverty of our large communities has been considerably reduced can hardly be doubted. The English poor-rate in Charles II.'s time amounted to little less than half the entire revenue of the Crown,[2] and the paupers and beggars in 1696 were estimated at more than one-fifth of the population. They are now one-thirtieth. Two years later (1698) Fletcher of Saltoun declared that in Scotland, which had then a population of about a million, there were 200,000 persons begging from door to door, and that "in all times there have been about 100,000 of those

---

[1] The confession of Jack Straw says: "We would have destroyed all the beneficed clergy, bishops, monks, canons, and the rectors of churches off the face of the earth."—*Walsingham*, vol. ii. p. 10. Even if we take this confession to be a forgery, it must be assumed to represent in an exaggerated form the views held by the insurgents.

[2] Macaulay's *History of England*, vol. i. pp. 437, 438.

vagabonds, who have lived without any regard or subjection either to the laws of the land, or even those of God and nature."[1] Scotland has now about 100,000 paupers to a population of 4,000,000. It seems on the whole fair to say, that the Church system of relieving poverty was neither effective nor popular, and entailed great demoralisation; and, on the other hand, that though the State blundered for centuries in its methods, it has already achieved an appreciable measure of success, and has raised the character of the working-man, while it has mitigated distress. It is the more remarkable that this should be the case as the action of the State in every country was for a long time trammelled or misdirected by the prejudices or interests of a wealthy class.

Next in importance to the recognition of the right of the labourer to be assured employment, is the right of the labourer to sell his work at the best possible price. In early times it was a more imperative necessity for the State to see that labour was not withheld than to secure its proper recognition. Leaving out of account, therefore, those remote ages in which whole populations were sold in the slave market, till the slave superseded the free labourer in many parts of the civilised world, we find two forms of personal bondage existing in modern or comparatively modern times —serfdom and slavery. The serf, owing duty to an estate rather than to a lord, could not be separated from wife and children, and practically has always been able to work for himself. His position, though far from perfect, has not necessarily, except at times, been so bad as to demand the interposition of the Churches, which are not charged primarily with the care of

[1] Fletcher's *Second Discourse on the Affairs of Scotland*, pp. 100, 101.

man's material needs. This, however, cannot be said of slavery. It has habitually been so cruel that the weaker races, like Caribs and other American Indians, have died out or declined under it, and even so strong a race as the negro could not maintain itself in the West Indian Islands under British rule.[1] Again, slavery has been the fertile cause of sexual immorality, the master practically doing as he pleased with his female slaves, even to the extent of taking married women from their husbands. Lastly, the slave system was inherently regardless of family ties, so that even in the Southern States Virginia was a mere breeding-place, out of which the members of one household were sold into every part of the country. Now it is true that an exceptional churchman, like Las Casas, has now and again denounced slavery in unsparing terms, or has even devoted his life to a crusade against it. It may also be claimed for some particular Churches that they have in their corporate capacity done a good deal to improve the position of the slave. The Roman Catholic Church, for instance, has habitually treated black and white as equals before the altar, and the Independent Smith, the Wesleyan Shrewsbury, and the Baptist Underhill did good work in exposing the cruelties of the Demerara, Jamaica, and Barbadoes planters. Habitually, however, in countries where slavery was established, the Churches have acquiesced in it as the natural order of things, have perhaps vindicated its divine original, have thrown in their weight against its abolition, and have not even protested solemnly that the marriage-tie was sacred, or

---

[1] Between 1817-1822 and 1827-1832, in an average term of twelve years, the slaves registered in the West India Islands diminished in a population of 558,194 by 60,219 wear and tear, and exclusive of manumissions.—"Parliamentary Papers," quoted in Appendix to *Memoirs of Buxton.* Compare M. Lewis's *Journal,* pp. 50, 140, 141.

that religious instruction ought to be imparted. In the latter days of North American slavery, an opinion that religious negroes were more tricky and idle than others became prevalent, and led to the withdrawal of religious teaching on many estates—the Churches making no protest.[1] Now it may be granted that the Churches were not called upon to denounce the unrighteousness of the sin of slavery while it was tolerated by the State. Bishops and pastors have to take the world as they find it in many matters, and the great majority in a slave State are likely to have been honestly in favour of an institution with which they were familiar from childhood. Still, even moderate men have always accounted it a blot on the great Christian sects, that in their desire not to lose their influence over the propertied classes they have habitually refrained from inculcating humanity, purity, and regard for family ties, except in a very general and abstract way. At any rate, the credit of abolishing the slave-trade, of freeing the slave by war in the United States, and by legal reforms in other countries, has been left essentially to secular politicians. The negro race is not that which has profited most by the abolition of slavery. The white labourer is even a greater gainer by the fact that he is no longer forced to compete with the products of unremunerated toil, and a disgrace that was reflected on all manual labour has been removed. The industrial classes have to thank the State everywhere for this reform, and, to say the least, owe no gratitude to the Churches.

In this matter of slavery, and in the cognate question of the right of workmen to unite in Trades-Unions that they may raise the rate of wages, what we have to

---

[1] See Olmsted's *Journeys in the Cotton Kingdom*, vol. ii. pp. 212-229, and Kemble's *Journal of Residence on a Georgian Plantation*, pp. 342, 346.

notice is the fact that the State is everywhere doing work which the Churches will not or cannot do, and where it has the same object as the Churches, habitually employs a more reasonable method. Another emphatic instance of this difference is seen in the treatment of education by the two great organisations. The mediæval Church, often unwarrantably abused for defects which belonged to the age, has as often been extravagantly over-praised for its supposed services to learning. The broad fact is, that its services were to a large extent accidental, and that when it was best performing its own functions, it was hostile to letters. Accidentally it was the interest of men who had a taste for study to take the tonsure, and so secure themselves a maintenance, protection, and, if they were in a monastery, the command of a few books. The true purpose of the Church, however, as conceived by the best of its own sons, was not to inform the mind but to save the soul; and to take a single conspicuous instance, the Franciscan revival of religion in the thirteenth century was aimed at the pride of intellect as much as at the lust of the flesh. "The habit and one little book," satisfied the founder of the order;[1] and his disciples improved upon his teaching. There is not a more pathetic history in the records of literature than that of Roger Bacon, who, having as he believed the secret of all knowledge, was constrained to sacrifice the labours of forty years, his superiors strictly forbidding him to write or communicate his thoughts.[2] Now in this particular instance a Pope interposed to procure for Bacon the liberty of bequeathing his results

---

[1] Milman's *History of Latin Christianity*, vol. iv. p. 265, note. "He despised and prohibited human learning," p. 275.

[2] Bacon's superiors threatened to confiscate his book and impose a severe fast on him if he communicated anything that he wrote to the outside world.—*Opus Tertium*, cap. ii.

to posterity; and we have to remember that the secular clergy as a body had no tradition of opposition to learning, and that the Benedictines in particular have a splendid record—chiefly it is true for later times—of devotion to studies bearing upon ecclesiastical matters. Still, the broad fact remains, that the Church of the Middle Ages did not of set purpose promote learning of a secular kind beyond what was necessary for the vulgar needs of life; and that when there was a revival of learning, the scholars and the clergy were soon at feud. Bishop Pecock, for instance, was disgraced for teaching that faith rested upon reason; Reuchlin was fiercely attacked for studying Hebrew; and Ramus silenced for attacking the old logic. It fared no better with the precursors of scientific anatomy and the founders of astronomical science. Looking back, it is easy for us to say that the Church was unwise in its policy of attacking the new learning, which was certain to establish itself; yet this view is not indisputable. If the Church could have silenced a handful of scholars and scientific men, it would probably be the Universal Church at this day. If its rulers believed that the life of men beyond the grave was more important to them than their present enlightenment, they were justified in putting free inquiry down by the axe and by the stake.

After three centuries the opposition of all the Christian Churches to education not directed by themselves is as marked as it ever was. It is not now a question of the liberty to publish treatises that will only be read in the first instance by a highly educated minority, but of opening the gates of knowledge to every child. To the politician of western Europe, of America, or Australia, the question presents itself as a very simple one. The educated workman can use his powers more efficiently than the uneducated; the educated soldier is more than a match for the drilled barbarian, other things being equal; and there is, as a rule, less crime in an educated community.[1] Sound schools of every kind are therefore not a mere luxury or convenience but a condition of national existence. Practically, the statesman in every country would gladly enlist the clergy on the side of education if he could do it by concessions that were not destructive of his purpose. Practically, the clergy in every country demand the control of the schools; and while they are willing to teach the elements of knowledge, desire above all to send out the scholars entrusted to them saturated with a superficial and gross theology. The battle, of course, varies in different countries. In parts of South America the clergy have succeeded in keeping the schools in their own hands, and these are among the most backward States on that continent; in Belgium they would compound for the liberty to drive out a teacher they dislike, and to interfere as they choose in school hours; in England they are united in dislike of Board or quasi-secular schools, and aspire to prohibit any improvements that may make these dangerously attractive. In Holland they have actually succeeded in securing a return to pure denominationalism. In Ontario the Church of Rome, in the first instance, procured an exceptional right for those of its members who were not within a certain distance of a Catholic school to remain uneducated;[2] and the Protest-

---

[1] My impression is that the great causes of crime are want and congenital predisposition. Education has a tendency to reduce want and to inspire a keener fear of consequences. More perhaps cannot be claimed for it.

[2] Catholics in Ontario cannot be compelled to attend any school, unless they reside in a separate school section, *i.e.* in a section in which there is a school of their own denomination.—School Act of 1871, § 3.

ants later on have retaliated by introducing an expurgated Bible, compiled by order of the Minister of Education, into the mixed schools. In Victoria, Catholics and Protestant ministers agreeing to oppose secular teaching, are divided among themselves what is to be substituted. On the whole, however, it is probably correct to say, that the Churches everywhere distrust and oppose any educational system which they do not themselves administer or cannot meddle in freely; and that the State everywhere finds it impossible to leave the schools to the Churches. That experiment has in fact been tried in every country and has failed in all. In England it was so absolute a mockery that in 1838 an impostor or lunatic succeeded in passing himself off as the Messiah, almost under the shadow of Canterbury Cathedral, and in a county where Church influence ought to have been predominant. A year later the Archbishop of Canterbury carried an address to the Queen, protesting against grants in aid to any but Church schools. In Victoria, after twenty years of subsidies to the denominational system, it was found that thirty per cent of the children had no school teaching provided for them,[1] and that about forty per cent of the schools established had no religious instruction given in them at all.[2] In France the favour shown to the Church under the Second Empire led to a complete paralysis of school-teaching, and in the day of trial France with one-third of its population illiterate was no

---

[1] Within a year after the passing of the Victorian Education Act, 1872, the school-attendance had increased from 68,436 children to 99,536.

[2] In the evidence taken before Mr. Higinbotham's Commission (1866) the Inspector-General testified, that in 39 out of 100 schools visited no religious instruction at all was given, while in three schools only was religious instruction given by the clergyman. Almost every witness spoke more or less to the same effect.

match for Germany with her soldiers, one and all, educated up to the highest point compatible with their station in life. No doubt, secular education has also been advocated in France on moral grounds; and M. Paul Bert unquestionably showed good reason for believing that the doctrines taught in Catholic seminaries are still very much those which Pascal dissected in the *Provincial Letters*.[1] The great reason, however, why secular education has been adopted generally in France, and specially in Paris, has been because the Church showed itself apathetic and unsuccessful as a disseminator of any knowledge that did not bear upon religion and obedience to the Church.

It may freely be admitted that the Church has not always been to blame for its deficiencies. It has been impossible to entrust it with that compulsory power, without which a school system can never be universally successful. It has never disposed—in modern times— of such enormous funds as the State can raise by a local rate or a tax. Its worst sins of omission belong to periods when statesmen also were careless how the children of the poor grew up. There is some truth in what the advocates of the clerical party say, when they contend that education without moral training is only putting weapons into the hands of criminals, and that to enlarge the mental horizon of many thousands, who can never struggle out of their actual low level, is only to increase misery and unrest. Even those who believe with De Maistre, that the moral man can only be formed upon his mother's knee;[2] even those who are convinced

---

[1] Paul Bert. Speech of July 5, 1879, and *La Morale des Jésuites*.

[2] "Ce qu'on appelle l'homme, c'est à dire, l'homme moral, est peut-être formé à dix ans; et s'il ne l'a pas été sur les genoux de sa mère, ce sera toujours un grand malheur."—*Soirées de St. Pétersbourg*, Troisième Entretien.

by the teaching of history, that the character cannot suffer because the mind is cleared, may admit that no great experiment is so absolutely successful at once as to make cavil impossible. Still, when all abatements have been made, the success achieved by the secular system is enormous. It is now the State everywhere which is fascinating every family by proffering the *bâton de maréchal* to its children, as it forces upon them an education that will fit them to rise to wealth and dignity. More and more the State is endeavouring to do this work costlessly, or at the smallest possible cost to the parent. Can we wonder if all the world over it is superseding the Church in its hold on popular imagination. It is still true that the peasant's son may rise to be Bishop, Cardinal, or Pope; but it is no longer true—even proximately—that the secular lottery offers only blanks to the poor man's son. In the United States, where primary education was well developed before the higher education had struck roots, every avenue of success is not only theoretically but practically open to the son of the poorest labourer; he may be head of department, general, judge, or president. Every State in the civilised world is approximating to this model. Every Church is proportionately weaker in the capacity to stir the democratic fibre.

It would be easy, if we pursued the comparison of State and Church ideals, to show that the State has taken the larger, more liberal, and more tender view of the relations of the weak to the strong. The Church undoubtedly forbade infanticide, but it has habitually left children under the parental control, even when this was capricious or intolerably severe. It is the State that has interposed to prevent the child's strength from being overtaxed, and to insist that it shall receive proper education. The Churches from all time have treated the wife as the handmaid of the husband; bound to submit to ill-treatment, to spoliation, and to unfaithfulness at his hands, with none or with the slightest possible redress. The State has insensibly remodelled its customs till a woman in every civilised country can own property, can live apart from her husband, and in certain cases can retain the guardianship of her children. In these instances the State has done little more than many excellent though not typical churchmen have always desired to see done. In one remarkable particular, secular politicians deserve the credit of having discerned and successfully applied a new principle in morality—the duty of tenderness to the brute creation. No doubt it has always been natural for good men to feel compassion for everything that is capable of suffering; but even men like St. Anselm and St. Francis,[1] who felt this instinctively, never raised it to the rank of a religious obligation. In one remarkable instance—the opposition to vivisection for scientific purposes—the reformers have proceeded on the transcendental ground that humanity at large has no right to purchase relief from its own suffering by torturing the helpless. The question is not whether all these changes are maturely thought out and administered with the wisest possible limitations. The broad fact can hardly be disputed that secular civilisation, "the wisdom and the wit of this world,"[2] is informed with a moral purpose, and is steadily working out what we may call the Christian law of life, though it

---

[1] Eadmer, *Vita Anselmi*, lib. ii. cap. iii. §§ 27, 28; Milman's *Latin Christianity*, vol. iv. p. 269.
[2] *Sermons by Dean Church*, p. 120.

respects human liberty so profoundly that it shivers and shrinks back repeatedly before it ventures to step within the sphere of spiritual activity. The advocates of Church authority and of individual lawlessness unite to denounce as violations of freedom every fresh act of that impassive, ever-dilating power which rends asunder the unrighteous contract between employer and servant, between landlord and tenant, which protects the child from degradation and rescues the woman from misuse; but the trust of citizens in the justice of human society grows stronger as the powers of the State are enlarged. The love of an Englishman for his country in old days might be little more than love for the land in which men of his own tongue governed themselves and kept their homes from the foreign enemy. He might be at the mercy of corrupt officials, governed by harsh laws, weighted by oppressive taxation, and without the possibility of rising in any service but that of the Church. The love of any man speaking the English tongue for his country is now for a land that can give him ampler protection than his fathers ever dreamed of, that invests him with the prestige of a dominant race, that adjusts his public burdens so as to be least onerous, that gives him the right to assist in making the laws, that protects him against his own weakness, and offers him the means to start on equal terms in the race for honour or wealth. Merely the dream of what a country might be has transformed ignorant men, serving forcibly in the hostile ranks, into heroes who fell where they stood sooner than drive back the army of liberation; and has transfigured prosaic women into heroines, who gave son after son to the national cause. Is it wonderful if the prodigies of Hungarian and Italian heroism have been more than matched in America, where there was a country of noble memories with a settled government and wise liberties to maintain?

Only two causes seem likely to interfere with the growth of national feeling. On the one hand, the great body of the citizens may be more interested in industrial organisations stretching over the whole earth; and on the other hand, the dream of a few thinkers, that we shall rise beyond the nation as we have risen beyond the family, the tribe, and the province, may come to be realised. The first is the more immediate danger. It is possible to suppose the great body of artisans, for instance, taking a supreme interest in the claims of the various trades, and attaching only a secondary importance to the different countries in which individual members happen to live. Something of this kind is discernible at present. If we can assume that it will extend, it might conceivably happen that a whole labouring population would decide to repudiate burdens of purely national concern, and would migrate freely from the State, if they were outvoted, sooner than submit to any inconvenient pressure. That a man should be first a Trades-Unionist, and only in the second place an Englishman or Australian, would not be in itself more remarkable than the spectacle, which has often been witnessed, of men who were first Catholics and only Englishmen or Frenchmen when the claims of the Church were satisfied. It is difficult to conceive, however, that men will ever attach themselves as devotedly to a Trades-Union, wise and dignified though it may be, as they did in times past to the Church, which gave them a great deal in this world, and promised them everything in the next. It must be borne in mind, too, that while the State professes to reconcile or adjust conflicting interests, no trades organisation has ever been able to make itself more than sectional. The claims of one body of workers are habitually opposed to the needs of others, so that they can only unite, now and again, on some very general ground, like the limitation of the hours of work. It may be added that there is a great and not unreasonable jealousy among the workmen of every country lest they should be swamped by the immigration of competitors. This feeling is likely to become stronger as times go on, as America and Australia fill up, and as it becomes increasingly clear that there is no great field for the employment of whites in the Tropical Zone. It may, indeed, be hoped by optimists that in the far future the comity of nations will be so far extended as to make it increasingly easy for individuals to change their country; but it can hardly be expected that the United States, to take the most important instance, will continue to find land and labour for several hundred thousand emigrants yearly. It is needless to say, however, that if population in England and Germany continues to increase at its present rate, an emigration of a million will mean no more thirty years hence than half a million meant thirty years ago. Practically, then, the Trades-Unions of the future are likely to become not more international in their character, but more exclusively national. Each will try to secure the best possible terms for itself in its own country; each will protect itself against competition from outside; and as a consequence the mass of men will have to abide in the land where they are born, and to make the best of it.

These considerations apply partly to the cosmopolitan theory. It will have to contend with the narrower feeling that is bound to prevail, when men no longer look upon the world as full of possible homes for them. There are, of course, some who dream that the whole human race will be united into one grand federation. Visions of this sort, if they are ever realised, can only be so in so distant a future that it is scarcely worth while to discuss them. It may be observed, however, that there seem to be certain limits to national growth which no policy however imperial can transcend. It is fashionable to lament the infatuation of the British counsels that severed the connection of the American colonies with Great Britain; and no one at this day would care to defend George III., or Grenville, or Lord North. None the less it may be doubted whether the colonies could have borne the strain of the French war in which England engaged a few years later; and more generally, whether England has not done better for herself in India, Africa, and Australia, from having an absolutely free hand. At this moment Australia and England are united in a manner that gratifies sentiment and interest, and entails no particular obligation on either party to the union. The Australian colonies are protected to some extent by the prestige of imperial power, and attract English capital rather more freely than they would do if they were independent. England gets the repute of Empire, and the advantage that trade follows the flag, and the certainty that, in the case of another Indian Mutiny, she could call up thousands to her standard from an adjoining continent, whereas, if the colonies were independent, the Irish element would be actively sympathising with whatever was hostile to Great Britain. If, however, the dream of some English theorists were accomplished, so that Australia exchanged a very satisfactory form of self-government for representation in an imperial senate, the loss to the great dependency would be incalculable.

The best men would be taken away to a distant country, would lose touch of their own proper countrymen, and even if they clearly saw what was good for Australia, would be perpetually compelled to compromise and accept what was best for the Empire. The result would be an angry separation in a very short term of years. Nevertheless, the interests of Australia and Great Britain would be incomparably more easy to reconcile in a British Parliament than the interests of the whole world in a general council. Putting aside the union of the human race as chimerical, is it possible to conceive even the Germanic race—including Germany, Scandinavia, and Holland, with the British Empire and the United States—combining for such simple purposes as the preservation of the world's peace, or to procure Free Trade, or a common system of Protection? Yet these people have a common origin, cognate tongues, to a great extent a common religion, and might conceivably arrange their commercial interests so as not to clash violently. The difficulty is that each would feel it was surrendering more than it gave. The citizen of California would object to being taxed that a Russian attack on Herat might be repulsed; and the Australian would not care to guarantee Alsace and Lorraine. The chances are as great that some powers which are now unwieldy will be broken up, as that others will increase their boundaries; and that any but a compact dominion will be kept together under a centralised form of government seems difficult to believe. The best we can hope is, that the federal principle will be developed, and that international arbitration will become more and more practicable.

Dr. Matthew Arnold circulated a story that a catechism used in French schools, after enumerating the various benefits of civic society, asks the question, "Who gives you all this?" and makes answer, "the State." Mr. Hamerton has shown that this story is substantially incorrect, and that all that can be said is, that in a single manual, which teachers are allowed but not obliged to use, something of this sort may perhaps be found with the words "the country" in place of "the State."[1] It is surely permissible to inquire whether teaching of this sort, instead of being ridiculed as superficial, denounced as irreligious, or condemned for placing the Commonwealth in a place of honour that belongs to the parents, ought not to be enforced in every school. A child, whose parents do their duty by it in a spirit of tenderness, is never likely to be insensible in after-life of what it has owed them. It is useful, no doubt, to inculcate filial reverence at schools, but it is really taught in homes. On the other hand, the more general teaching, that all good things come from God, ought not to exclude the obvious fact that God works upon human society through the agency of men and women, that is, through parents, and through the civil power. Whatever may have been the case in old days, a child's obligations to the State are now infinite. The State watches over the infant life from birth; provides that the growing child is not stunted by excessive toil, is properly clothed and fed, and is so educated as to have a fair start in life; it assures the adult against starvation, protects him from foreign enemies, from tyrannical employers, and from the criminal classes that prey upon property; it secures him liberty of thought and faith, and it offers him the means of safe and easy insurance against illness or death.[2] It is constantly

---

[1] Hamerton's *French and English*, pp. 194-196.

[2] Of course, no one State does all this; but the exceptions are so trifling that it has seemed not misleading to speak generally.

endeavouring to extend the sphere of its beneficent energies. It is no doubt true that though all this is attempted, there are many inadequacies in the political scheme, and that myriads of human beings lead lives of unbroken toil or horrible destitution. Still the broad fact remains that human co-operation for political ends is yearly becoming more fruitful of good purpose, more sympathetic, and more successful in its attempts to relieve want; and that every child growing up towards citizenship ought to understand the incalculable debt which it owes to the brotherhood of man. Neither is it merely material benefits with which a great country endows its citizens. The countrymen of Chatham and Wellington, of Washington and Lincoln, of Joan of Arc and Gambetta,—in short, the citizens of every historic State,—are richer by great deeds that have formed the national character, by winged words that have passed into current speech, by the example of lives and labours consecrated to the service of the Commonwealth. The religion of the State is surely as worthy of reverence as any creed of the Churches, and ought to grow in intensity year by year.

It is the note of every true religion, however, that if it promises great good, it demands proportionate sacrifices. In days when to be an Englishman meant little more than to be safe from Spain and the Inquisition, and to be allowed to live in the land where a man's fathers had made their homes, even these benefits appeared so transcendently important by the side of what was possible in France and the Low Countries, that Englishmen of every degree seemed to quicken to an electric spark of heroism. The sailors and explorers achieved impossible adventures; the poets and thinkers were of more than mortal stature. The new England which does incomparably more for its people than the Elizabethan England did, commands less and indeed scarcely any gratitude, because the Englishman has a choice of fatherlands in which he may preserve the English nationality. He transfers himself without a pang to America or Australia. If, however, the world is filling up, as seems probable; if great migrations of toilers are bound to become impossible at no very distant date, the mass of men will have to regard the country they are born in as their home for life, and will be attached to it by interest as well as by sentiment. It seems not quite visionary to suppose that a day will come when service of some sort will be exacted from every man under pain of social discredit, or legal liabilities, as military service is now exacted from every able-bodied man on the Continent; when the immigration of aliens will be restrained within reasonable limits, when wealthy men will be forced by public opinion to give money for national endowments as freely as they did in the Middle Ages;, and when the doctrine that men can divest themselves of obligations to their country by leaving it will seem extravagant. In that case, the spirit of uncalculating devotion to the common cause, which even in our own days has changed the face of half Europe and rescued society from dissolution in North America, will become a steady principle of action, deserving to be accounted a faith, and lifting all who feel it into a higher life.

CHAPTER V

THE DECLINE OF THE FAMILY

The religion of the family will gradually die out as the religion of the State becomes more and more absorbing.—The power of the head of the family was anciently autocratic over the lives, property, and self-respect of the members.—The right of private war or of the blood-feud has been abolished.—The rights of fathers and husbands over the lives of children and wives have been abolished, or nearly so.—The ancient rule of secular legislation, which the Churches have copied, was that marriage was indissoluble.—The State has done its best to maintain this principle down to quite recent times.—Christianity, however, has made this important change, that it does not tolerate the libertinage which was the old compensation for the restrictions of marriage.—The old marriage of suitability was not more mercenary in its essence than the marriage of inclination. The essential difference between the two is, that the one makes family considerations the matter of vital importance, and the other only desires to satisfy individual caprice.—Nevertheless, changes in modern society have made the indissoluble marriage bear so heavily upon women that it is impossible to maintain it.—That the tie between husband and wife should come to be easily variable, instead of permanent, is bound to make the tie between parents and children weaker.—Moreover, the right of parents to use their children's labour has been found to work so badly, that the State is interposing everywhere to limit work and make education compulsory.—As parents are losing their rights over children, children are losing the sense of duty and obligation to their parents.—These changes in the conjugal and parental relations are working in the direction of individualism, and may be for good as well as for evil.—The family, however, is the natural provision for the conservation of character, and the consequences may be undesirable if we destroy pride in the past, responsibility for the present, and care for the future.—The changed relations of master and servant are also taking away a small and occasional but efficient safeguard of family feeling.—The tradition of a fixed family home has been destroyed.

IT has been argued that the religion of the country is likely to become a deeper and more serious feeling as the sphere of State action increases, as the State shows itself more beneficent in its aims than a good king, more effectively moral than the Churches, and more comprehensive and human than King or Church, aristocratic caste or guild of associated workmen. On the other hand, it seems possible that not only loyalty and faith and class or clan feeling will be merged in the new power, but that what we may call the religion of the family will gradually die out. In a certain sense, of course, the family must always remain the unit of the State. The union of men and women, even if we leave children out of the question, is so important in its effects upon character, that on its influence for good or evil must the condition of society very largely depend. When, however, we bear in mind that for many centuries the head of the family has exercised more or less autocratic powers under his own roof, and that infinitely various forms of virtue and vice, strength and foible, have been developed in consequence, the importance of any great changes that tend to exalt the State and emancipate the individual at the expense of the family will become apparent. What is perhaps most curious is, that the State has always been tender of family rights; and that in all its encroachments upon parental or conjugal authority, or upon family feeling, it has simply obeyed an irresistible necessity.

The powers of the family or its members have, of course, varied enormously in different ages. The right of the parents to deal as they would with the newly-born babe has been recognised more or less in all but Christian and Mahommedan communities.[1] Children were as freely exposed in the old Greek and Roman world and among

---

[1] Muir's *Life of Mahomet*, vol. i. p. cclxi. note, and iv. 228, 221; *The Koran*, Sura xvii. 31; vi. 137, 141. Compare 81, 8.

the Norsemen as they are in modern China.¹ There was no limitation to this right, which belonged absolutely to the head of the family. In the case of the wife, or of children who had been acknowledged, the father had the rights of the magistrate; that is, he could not legitimately put to death, except for a grave and appropriate cause; but there was no recognised tribunal to which an appeal from his sentence would lie. These excessive powers over life imply an absolute authority over the person and property. The husband could lend his wife to a friend,² or choose a husband for his daughter and a wife for his son. He could make his children labour as he chose, and might neglect their education as he would. Neither wife nor children could possess property. He could adopt a stranger to share his children's inheritance. This, of course, is the extreme type of the family as it existed in the laws of Athens and Rome.³ Extreme as it is, it has coloured all but the most modern legislation, except in the parts relating to life and death. So completely are we at variance with ancient morality on that score, that Rousseau is considered infamous for having allowed the State to care for his children; and Philip II. and Peter the Great are generally reprobated

---

¹ Coulanges, *Cité Antique*, p. 101. Compare Grimm, "Das erste und aelteste Recht des Vaters aeussert sich gleich bei der Geburt des Kindes; er kann es aufnehmen oder aussetzen."—*Deutsche Rechts-Alterthümer*, S. 455.

² See the remarkable story in Plutarch, that Quintus Hortensius applied to Cato the Younger for the loan of his daughter, who was already married to Bibulus, and was finally gratified with the loan of Cato's wife, Martia, her father having been consulted. The loan, however, took the form of a gift for life, Martia being formally married to Hortensius, though, being left a widow, she married Cato again. Hortensius, it is said, had no object but to be connected with Cato's family.

³ See generally on this subject the chapter on "L'Autorité dans la famille," in the *Cité Antique*, by Coulanges, and Hearn's *Aryan Household*, chap. iv. § 3.

for having, as is supposed, ordered the death of sons
whom they not unreasonably regarded as a menace to
the highest good of the country.[1] On the other hand,
as late as the thirteenth century the Church Courts in
England ruled that a husband could transfer his wife to
another man for a period determinable at the recipient's
pleasure.[2] The right of selling a ward's marriage was
among the most profitable incidents of feudal tenure;
and the ward was so far better off than the natural
child, that a guardian was bound to choose the husband
in her own rank. In England it is probably correct to
say that the consent of the parties has always been the
first thing considered, and the consent of the parents
nothing more than a necessary formality, without which
the marriage of minors could not be valid. As, however, a girl of seven might be betrothed in mediæval
England,[3] and as down to a later time the marriages of
mere children were still common, the parental authority
was practically absolute; and to marry without the consent of the parents was regarded as an outrage upon

[1] Motley seems to incline to the belief that Philip contrived his son's
death (*Rise of Dutch Republic*, p. 403). Ranke and Sir W. Stirling-Maxwell
describe the death as natural, but mention the charges against Philip
(*Spanish Empire*, p. 34, and *Life of Don John*, i. pp. 74, 75). The
essential point is, that Philip has generally been believed guilty. As
regards Peter the Great, Coxe decides against Peter (*Northern Tour*, vol.
ii. pp. 308-315). Kelly takes it as proved (*History of Russia*, chap. xxvii.)
Oustrialoff, of course, accepts the official story, that the Tsarevitch died of
apoplexy (*Hist. of Russia*, ii. p. 84); and Schuyler apparently thinks
that he died of the consequences of torture, while it was still doubtful if
Peter would carry the sentence of death into execution (*Peter the Great*,
vol. ii. pp. 431-433).

[2] See John Comoy's grant of his wife: "Noveritis me tradidisse et
dimisisse spontaneâ voluntate meâ domino Gul. Paynell militi Margaretam
uxorem meam . . . et concedo quod praedicta Margareta sit et maneat
cum praedicto Gulielmo pro voluntate ipsius Gulielmi."—*Rot. Parl.* vol. i.
p. 146.

[3] "All persons who had completed their seventh year were held
competent to contract espousals."—Reeve's *History of English Law*, vol.
iv. p. 53.

decency. In France, the consent of the parents was anciently regarded as the most necessary point, and the consent of the parties rather as a desirable accessory. It is still impossible for a Frenchman to marry without the permission of his father, or, if his father be dead, of his mother, unless he resorts to the extremity of the legal process known as "a respectful summons." The French father may apply to have his child imprisoned for a term not exceeding six months; but this power, which is subject to revision of the Court, is practically no more than the right of the English father to ask that his child may be sent to a reformatory. In either case, the right of imprisonment which the father could formerly exercise has been transformed into a right to move the civil power without the intervention of the public prosecutor. As for the right of the parent to transfer his child to strangers who will adopt it, to leave it uneducated, or to put it to sordid or excessive toil during the years of growth, the first of these still exists everywhere, and the second and third have only been encroached upon in quite recent times. In France, however, a child parted with by its parents to a stranger appears to retain a claim upon the parental inheritance which cannot be set aside by a will.[1] In France, therefore, and in countries with French law, the power of the head of the family to distribute the property he has inherited or acquired has been set aside for political considerations.

The effect of this primitive legislation, though it aimed only at giving the family a religious chief and the State a person responsible for the acts of children or kinsmen, was naturally to invest relationship with very

[1] This applies even to a child who has been adopted into another family: "L'adopté restera dans sa famille naturelle, et conservera tous ses droits."—*Code Civile*, livre i. tit. viii. s. 348.

solemn obligations. The family that was a little church and a little jurisdiction within itself, that had at one time a worship of its ancestors, and that was always more closely bound to its members than to the city or the State, came naturally in many cases to be a law to itself. The blood-feud is a striking instance of the obligations which the family feeling might involve. In days when a man owed his existence in the first instance to himself, and only in a very secondary manner to the State, it was very important not only that his sons should be able to speak with the enemy in the gate, but that they should be resolute to leave no wrong done unavenged. The result, however, was of questionable value. The old Greek adage that "a man is a fool if he kills the father and leaves the children alive," expresses what was bound actually to happen. Families were not kept from quarrels by the knowledge that a feud would be one of extermination; but whichever was the weaker or was surprised was wiped out.[1] Accordingly the first great step in constructing political society has always been to substitute the arbitration of the State for the blood-feud. Cursory observers are often struck by the apparent barbarism of a tariff which assesses the exact value of injuries to the person; but such legislation really shows that the family is being merged in the nation. It was proof of considerable civilisation that Horatius was tried for killing his sister. Anciently, the offence would only have been against his father; and as it was, Horatius was acquitted when his father accepted the responsibility of the act.[2] It is perhaps true that the blood-feud to some extent softened

---

[1] Thus Flosi, who reluctantly took up the blood-feud against Njal's family, was careful not to leave a survivor, old enough to bear arms, out of thirty people.—Dasent's *Story of Burnt Njal*, pp. 124, 171.

[2] Livy, i. 27.

the spirit of revenge by systematising it. Modern sentiment, in spite of the influences of Christianity, recoils a little from Jimena marrying the Cid, whose hands are red with her father's blood. Corneille justifies the action by duty to the King and a secret passion for Rodrigo. The old story, however, is entirely consistent with the spirit of primitive times. Rodrigo shows that Jimena has no cause for complaint, as he killed her father in fair fight and to satisfy the blood-feud, and because he is willing to make the injury done good. "I killed a man, and I give you a man."[1] As, however, such compositions were not often possible, the State found it desirable to interpose habitually, and has gradually adopted the rule that vengeance belongs only to the State; that the individual must never use force except in strict self-defence; and that he may not even omit his revenge—that is, accept atonement or composition—in any but trifling cases, as every offence is committed primarily against the body politic.

The right of the father over the lives of his children, and the right of the husband over the life of his wife, are now practically obsolete. The first is so repugnant to modern feeling that even a novelist scarcely dares to conceive a situation in which it occurs. In *Serge Panin* a mother-in-law kills the son-in-law who has made her daughter miserable, brought dishonour upon his name, and is too cowardly to die by his own hand; but it may be doubted if modern sentiment would have tolerated this lawless justice upon a nearer relative. The case of the wife is a little different. There is a survival of old custom, atrophied or nearly so by disuse, in the doctrine of our law-books, which justifies the

[1] "Maté á tu padre, Jimena . . . Para vengar cierto agravio. Maté hombre, y hombre doy."—*Romancero del Cid*, xi. p. 7.

slaying of an adulteress taken *en flagrant délit*, so far as to hold the avenging husband free of the highest guilt, and only liable for manslaughter.[1] This relic of custom has been so far modified by judicial interpretations that a man is only allowed the benefit of it when he acts literally in the moment of wrath, and it is becoming less safe for him, year by year, to punish faithlessness by death. The modern explanation of this toleration of violence is that the provocation has been intolerable, but it seems more reasonable to regard it as a survival of that old feeling which Calderon has expressed in one of the most powerful of his plays, where "the physician of his own honour," a man who has murdered his wife, knowing her to be innocent, for no reason but that she is the object of a dishonourable love, is publicly praised by the King, and rewarded with marriage to another noble lady, who takes his hand, knowing it, as she herself admits, to be "bathed in blood."[2] Calderon exhibits the feeling that the wife's chastity was due to her husband rather than herself in its most extravagant form; while modern English practice has very nearly reached the point when adultery is only punishable as the breach of a very solemn contract, by which the man has suffered loss as husband and father. It will be noted that the husband's rights were given to him to safeguard the family; and as the worship of ancestors, the family name, and the succession to property have never been regarded as liable to suffer by the husband's adultery, he has never been punishable; though his wife has been allowed the relief of a judicial separation or of divorce, the redress

---

[1] *Blackstone,* book iv. chap. 14.
[2] *Gutierre da la mano á Lenora.* — *Lenora.* "Mas mira que va bañada En sangre, Leonor."—*Lenora.* "Cura con ella Mi vida, en estando mala." —*El Medico de su Honra. Jornada III.*

permitted to her varying in different countries. So again, the life of the male head of the family has been regarded as peculiarly sacred. It is scarcely more than a hundred years since the penalty in England for a wife who murdered her husband was to be drawn and burned;[1] but the husband who murdered his wife was only hanged. The ancient jurisprudence of France was equally severe for crimes against the head of the family, though it was usual to exchange the extreme penalty of burning alive for beheading in the case of well-born women.

Both those who attack and those who defend the indissolubility of the marriage-tie are apt to think that the engagement which man and woman take to remain united "till death us do part" expresses an obligation created by Christianity. This view is the very reverse of fact. The highest civilisations of the old Pagan world had derived or instinctively adopted the theory that marriage was for all time. This was especially true of Rome, where an extravagant tradition said that there was no divorce for five centuries;[2] and of Germany, where Tacitus tells us that a woman had one husband as she had one body and one life.[3] The very exceptions to the rule show that the law aimed at maintaining a general principle with the smallest possible concession to human weakness. Christian Churches evade the recognition of divorce by declaring that there has been no marriage if the man is incapable of founding a family. Athenian law permitted the woman in this case to have

[1] It was changed to drawing and hanging in 1790.—30 George III. cap. 48.
[2] Ramsay's *Roman Antiquities*, p. 252.
[3] *Taciti Germania*, cap. 19. Grimm, however, modifies this by showing that divorce was allowed for sterility, adultery, pronounced incompatibility, and persistent desertion.—*Rechts-Alterthümer*, SS. 453, 454.

a lover in the family she had married into, but shrunk from declaring the marriage ceremony to be void.[1] On the other hand, if the woman was sterile, Roman law allowed her to be repudiated, that the family might not be extinguished, and worship to the family gods cease.[2] It has been a difficulty of all times that men may sometimes be unavoidably kept away from their families by being captives in a strange land, though of late this inconvenience is scarcely felt. In Roman law marriage was dissolved by captivity, because the assumption was that the loss of freedom would be permanent, and the captive accordingly ceased to belong to his proper State. If, however, the wife did not take advantage of her liberty to marry again, the husband who was ransomed or escaped might resume her when he resumed his citizenship. It is remarkable that English customary law has recognised this exception to the indissolubility of marriage, so that a wife whose husband has been absent for seven years and cannot be heard of is not punished if she contracts a second marriage,[3] though she is still liable to be resumed by the first husband, which the Roman matron was not ;—a liability which seems degrading to self-respect. Human nature has always shown itself impatient of conjugal restraints, and whatever laws the State may enact are always certain to be evaded by a large class. Roman legislation, however, was on the whole less easily foiled than that of the Latin Church. The substitute for divorce in the later and laxer times of Rome was not a dissolution of the religious marriage, but a form of concubinage under contract regulated by law and approved by

---

[1] Plutarch's *Solon*.

[2] This is said to have been the reason of the first divorce in Rome, that of Carvilius Ruga.—*Val. Max.* lib. ii. cap. i.

[3] This right is recognised and confirmed by 1 Jac. I. cap. ii.

fashion. The substitute in the Middle Ages was to discover that the marriage was invalid, as having been contracted within the prohibited degrees of affinity, and without a proper dispensation.[1] The Roman custom which forbade the union of all direct ascendants or descendants, whether by blood, adoption, or marriage,[2] did not allow of these demoralising evasions, and must be regarded as the outcome of higher sanitary science and stricter ethical practice.

On the whole, it is probably correct to say that every healthy society has endeavoured, in its best times at least, to treat marriage as indissoluble, and that when breaches of this practice have occurred, it has been through the irregular passions of powerful and wealthy men seeking to mould the law to their own wishes, or through the growth of a Bohemian and vagabond class. Christianity came into the world at a time when the old religious marriage was beginning to be found burdensome, and adopted the view which the most religiously-minded men of the time would instinctively take. The scandals of the Ecclesiastical Courts are only proof that the Church put itself into a thoroughly false position when it claimed the perilous office of determining under what circumstances the marriage-tie might be dissolved. It is noticeable that in England the change to secular society effected at the Reformation was attended with an infinitely greater rigour in matters affecting marriage. The early Reformers would no doubt have legalised divorce under conditions of absolute equality for both sexes;[3] but under Elizabeth a

[1] This immoral practice was swept away at the Reformation by 32 Hen. VIII. cap. 38.
[2] This was done by the Lex Julia et Papia Poppaea, A.D. 9.—Ramsay's *Roman Antiquities*, p. 249.
[3] The "Reformatio Legum Ecclesiasticarum," drawn up by Cranmer,

theory came in that divorce was never to be permitted, and the only relaxation was when divorce by Act of Parliament was allowed. This, however, was only granted for a single cause, and was so costly as to be practically very rare. It is noticeable that in France also, after the liberty of divorce had been introduced at the Revolution, regulated by Napoleon, and practised for five and twenty years, it was abrogated without much difficulty by a reactionary but still secular government, and has only lately been restored. Summing up, it seems probable that from the earliest times of civilisation the indissolubility of marriage has appeared to be desirable, and has been promoted by the State for civil reasons, quite as strongly as it has been enjoined by traditional religions for reasons of faith that are in some instances outgrown, so as to be now scarcely intelligible except to scholars.

While, however, the difference between ancient and comparatively modern times as to the institution of marriage may seem small, there has been one enormous difference introduced by Christianity—the idea of purity. Of course, no powerful society has ever existed without a moral code of some kind. In Rome it was unchaste for a woman to commit adultery, because if a bastard were born into the family he could not continue the family worship; it was unchaste for a man to marry a barbarian,[1] or to intrigue with a matron, and

Haddon, and Cheke, proposed to give divorce if the marriage had been brought about by force or fear, if either partner was unfaithful, and if there was irreconcilable enmity between them.— Reeve's *History of English Law*, vol. iv. pp. 546-548.

[1] "Sequiturque nefas, Ægyptia conjux" (*Aeneid* viii. 688). So, too, Horace speaks of the soldier of Crassus as dishonoured by a barbarian wife (*Odes*, III. v.) Forbiger remarks that the expression in Virgil, "crime against heaven," is not at all too strong for the marriage with a foreigner, "which Roman law forbade," or perhaps rather stigmatised as improper (*injustum*).

it was unchaste to commit acts that are now heavily punished in every Christian country. On the other hand, there is no reason to suppose that a man who intrigued with public women or with slaves was considered unchaste unless he did it in a scandalous way,[1] or was held to have given his wife some special cause of complaint. That the Germanic standard was higher than the Roman is probable; but unless we assume that the Germans and Norsemen were very soon corrupted we know that their practice was not very different.[2] To put it briefly, the ancient marriage was based on suitability of family connections and fortunes rather than on inclination, and as love had not been in the contract the husband was easily pardoned if he allowed himself some license outside the house, provided he rendered his wife all proper respect under the common roof. This *mariage de convenance* has lasted down to our own days on parts of the Continent, and the liberty enjoyed by the Roman husband has been more or less freely claimed by husbands everywhere; but the tolerance of old custom is becoming a thing of the past. It no doubt lingers in our laws. As a rule, the husband can divorce the wife for a single act of misconduct, while the husband must either be guilty of systematic misconduct, as in Victoria, or of some additional offence, such as protracted desertion,

---

[1] To take two familiar instances, Plutarch appears to blame Cato the Censor for making a slave his mistress in the house where his daughter-in-law was living; but Pompey's attachment to the courtezan Flora is spoken of as rather creditable to him than otherwise. Valerius Maximus pretty well indicates the boundary line of Roman continence when he praises "frugalitas" as "ab *immoderato* Veneris usu aversa."—Lib. ii. c. 5.

[2] M. Henri Martin says, for instance, of the Frank Princes (c. 500-550): "Jetés par la conquête au milieu d'une civilisation corrompue, ils ne faisaient guère avec elle qu'un échange de vices, prenant ses raffinements sensuels, et lui communiquant leur brutalité."—*Hist. de France*, tome ii. p. 12.

as in Scotland, or of cruelty, as in England, if the wife is to be absolutely released. The husband in England can claim damages from the man who has ruined his family life, but the woman can claim none from the rival who has supplanted her. The law, therefore, having the threads of obsolete theory woven into its woof, has been various and uncertain in the changes that it has admitted. Still, it can hardly be doubted that as the conception of their eternal tutelage has been dispersed, and women have come to be regarded as more or less the equals of men—at least as deserving equality before the law—men are held more strictly to account in matters of conjugal morality. In other words, the primitive marriage of suitability, the marriage which aimed first at constituting the conditions for a new family, and which only regarded inclination in the second place, is being superseded everywhere by marriages that are supposed to be based upon love, and only not disallowed by the judgment. It stands to reason that conjugal fidelity enters into the contract far more than it anciently did on the man's side.

It cannot be supposed that a system which has endured and been approved through so many centuries as the *mariage de convenance* has witnessed is immoral in its essence, and the gravity of the change which is now overthrowing it cannot easily be over-estimated. Englishmen are apt to think of it as a system under which girls of fifteen, just fresh from the convent, are married to worn-out debauchees of sixty, and it is of course a system under which this abuse is possible, just as under the English system of liberty a girl in her teens may run away with her father's groom, and a young man of one and twenty tie himself for life to a courtezan. We must look at typical instances of the

French system to understand what it has really been, and how many of the noblest and best women in a country distinguished for its women have entered upon congenial lives in this manner. In its practical rendering by the best people the *mariage de convenance* has always meant the marriage in which the conditions of family happiness were based upon high character, suitability of circumstances, and, if possible, old family friendships. St. Simon tells us that when he first thought of marrying he fixed upon the daughter of an old friend, though he had never so much as seen the lady, because his veneration for the father's character led him to believe that he could not go wrong in choosing from such a stock.[1] Mdme. de Sévigné's daughter, Mdme. de Grignan, tells us of a betrothal which was arranged after this fashion: "The fathers at the fireside were talking over the perfections of their children (a son and daughter respectively), when M. de St. Aignan said, 'We ought to bring together two persons so worthy of one another.' 'I am willing,' said Sanguin; 'shake hands on it.'"[2] These no doubt are instances from the old régime and from the aristocratic class; but if we take the *bourgeoisie* at the time just preceding the Revolution, we shall find very much the same course of procedure, though the parental authority is perhaps a little less marked. Mdme. Roland tells us that most of her suitors proposed for her to her parents, before they

[1] St. Simon adds, that when he found the eldest daughter otherwise arranged for, he proposed to wait till a younger sister should be of age to marry.—*Mémoires de St. Simon*, tome i. c. viii. Lord Burleigh in the Precepts addressed to his son goes on the same lines as St. Simon. In choosing a wife, he directs Robert Cecil to "enquire diligently of her disposition, and how her parents have been inclined in their youth."

[2] *Lettres de Mdme. de Sévigné*, December 22, 1677.

had even been admitted to the house. In her case, as her father had forfeited the right to control her actions, the decision was practically left in her own hands, and she decided to marry a man twice her age, whose character she could sincerely respect. She considered marriage, as she tells us, "an austere union, a partnership in which the wife, as a rule, takes upon herself to provide for the happiness of both."[1] Knowing that her attachment for M. Roland was based upon esteem rather than love, she guarded herself against possible heartaches by sharing her husband's labours and pleasures, so as to leave herself no time for irregular fancies. Mr. Hamerton tells us that even now there are many persons in France who deliberately prefer the marriage based upon suitability of position and character to the marriage of mere inclination. "I remember," he says, "being much amused by the indignation of a very beautiful young French lady about a rumour that she had been wedded for love. She reiterated her assurance that it was a baseless fabrication, that her husband had only seen her once before her betrothal, and then quite formally in the presence of other people, and that their marriage had been entirely one of *convenance*. In short, she repelled the idea of love as if it had been a disgraceful and unmerited imputation."[2] Mr. Hamerton, however, goes on to explain that dowerless girls constantly receive good offers in France. Everywhere, of course, rational people will not entangle themselves in the obligation to support a family till they can see a fair prospect of being able to do it. Therefore, even where the assumption is that all marriages are of inclination,

---

[1] *Mémoires de Mdme. Roland*, pp. 129, 192-194.
[2] Hamerton's *French and English*, p. 357.

some are sure to have been partly determined by money considerations, while some will be purely mercenary. Where the marriage, supposed to be of inclination, has really been made for the sake of settlements, the fact that a young man or a young girl has acted from mere calculation in such a matter is perhaps rather more repulsive to sentiment than if the marriage had been treated of by the heads of the families from first to last as essentially a matter of business; and, on the other hand, where a marriage of suitability becomes almost instantly a marriage of affection, as is said to be very often the case, there seems no reason why such an alliance should be rated as in any way lower than the love marriage.

However, it is idle to argue with the master of many legions, or to say anything against a change that has been the almost inevitable result of circumstances, and that expresses the settled impulse of the Germanic race. The marriage of inclination is now the only avowed one in the greater part of the civilised world, and is rapidly supplanting the marriage of suitability in France. Writers like George Sand and Ibsen are only apologists for a revolution already made. In proportion as women are emancipated, do they claim a freedom which is desired rather as a relief to ennui than as an offset to masculine libertinage. Some changes have made the marriage yoke more difficult to bear than it was. One is, that desertion is increasingly common since emigration has become a habit with the working-classes. Another is, that the felon, who was formerly hanged without mercy, is now released periodically, and can resume full marital rights over his wife's person and property, where the law has not been altered to meet his case. A third probably is, that the duty to children is less felt since the State has charged itself with the care of seeing that they are not positively starved or allowed to run wild. A fourth is, that partly from experience, and partly through the influence of modern notions of heredity, a wife knows that her husband's license is a wrong inflicted upon her own children.[1] They only receive divided tenderness, and succeed to a diminished estate; they inherit depravity, if they do not inherit disease. A fifth is, that the legislator has found it convenient everywhere to relieve the married woman from tutelage in certain important particulars; to make her responsible for her acts, capable of bearing witness against her husband, and able to own property in her own right. A sixth is, that the religious sanctions of marriage are less regarded since society has become increasingly secular. A seventh is, that as the whole conditions of industry have changed, a wife's work is less important to her husband, and the unprotected woman is more easily able to earn a living for herself. To stay at home and spin wool, or sew, would often be very unthrifty conduct in a modern wife, who can make more out of doors as a laundress, a charwoman, a factory operative, or an employee in a shop. To all these causes of change we may add, that the law for very shame is relaxing the old harshness which was part of a logical theory. The woman who separates from her husband can now keep her children, so far as is consistent with their own good; and cannot be tortured, as was once possible, by having to renounce the privileges she bought with maternity if she will not live with a depraved and uncongenial husband. Last of all, the barbarous suit for restitution of conjugal rights,

---

[1] M. de Pressensé put this argument very powerfully in the debates that led to giving the liberty of divorce in France.

that practical reduction of marriage to what George Sand has cynically called it, "the right at Common Law to outrage a woman," has been nullified even in conservative England.

So overwhelmingly strong are these reasons, that many even of those who regard divorce with horror and alarm are constrained to support it as a requirement of justice. They feel, too, that it is idle to talk about the sanctity of home-life being impaired where the home has had no sanctity; and that to keep men and women, who are in a false position, miserable and in a condition that inclines to immorality, is a heavy price to pay for the peace of mind of those who, having no discomfort themselves, take a pleasure in thinking that the marriage-bond is indissoluble. On the other hand, even those who regard divorce as desirable and right in itself without regard to cases of extreme hardship, must admit that the transformation of an union for life, determined by many reasons besides inclination into a partnership during good conduct,—very widely interpreted,—or it may be even during pleasure, is a change that cannot fail to be fraught with eventful consequences. Those who have advocated the marriage of inclination have found a strong argument for it in the fact that, even if the dream of compatibility has proved delusive and short, the mere fact that husband and wife came together of their own accord deprives them of the right to murmur, and interests their pride in the maintenance of the marriage-bond. Perhaps this argument tells more forcibly in countries where the two systems are in operation. The experience of those American States in which divorce is extremely easy appears to show that wherever unions are dissoluble a certain percentage of people will dissolve them. On the other hand, it seems certain that as the thought of family duties disappears more and more from marriage, as it comes more and more to be legalised concubinage, in which legal formalities are employed only to guarantee the wife's self-respect and assure her social position, the whole condition of home-life will be changed. It is not improbable that in many cases husband and wife, who are not very sure of themselves, will refrain from complicating their relations by having children. They will thus be always ready to quit one another, and the mere fact that they so hold themselves in readiness, will in many cases bring about a separation. Even where they have a family, the feeling is apt to be less tender to the children, who were not the first thought in marriage, but only an inevitable incident, so to speak, than is the case in countries where the perpetuation of a family, the constitution of a home, have been the first thought. Foreign observers of England have constantly commented on the disposition of those who can afford to send their children away from home to school;[1] and on the settled principle that married couples are not to live with either father-in-law.[2] The good effects of these customs are seen in the readiness with which the Englishman becomes a citizen of the world, making his home wherever he goes. Yet something may be said for that French intimacy of parental tenderness, which makes a mother

---

[1] "The want of natural affection in the English displays itself specially in their conduct towards their children, for having kept them at home till they arrive at the age of seven or nine years at the utmost, every one, however rich he may be, puts away his children into the houses of others."—*Italian Relation of England*, c. 1500. Compare M. Taine in the nineteenth century : " Il n'y a pas en Angleterre de séparation profonde entre la vie de l'enfant, et celle de l'homme fait," and " un père, une mère, est bien moins que chez nous au courant des sentiments de sa fille, des affaires ou des plaisirs de son fils."—*Notes sur l'Angleterre*, pp. 122, 123, 141.

[2] *Ibid.*

the confidante of her mature son in all his follies and his plans, which so consecrates filial piety that it is the one virtue which it is not permitted to smile at, and which so glorifies the family surroundings that the emigrant, however prosperous, always wanders back at last to the village in which his race is settled. It will be very marvellous if the present cordial relations of parents and children in France survive marriages of inclination, and their correlative, the law making marriage dissoluble.

Till very lately the law was careful not to interfere between parents and children. It was held that the parents, so long as they cared for the lives of their offspring, had an absolute right to decide how they should be brought up. The single exception in England to this rule has been in the case of heirs to property whose future social condition might be impaired if they were left in the hands of an immoral or atheistic parent.[1] It was under the operation of this principle that Shelley was deprived of his children, and there seems no reason for supposing that the law was not administered with perfect fairness in that particular case. Indeed, there has been a more complete instance of its application in later times, when daughters were taken from a mother's guardianship and transferred to their father's care, because the odium attaching to their mother's opinions might affect their prospects in marriage.[2] The anomaly which the English law embodied was too monstrous to endure. On the one hand, any child not entitled to property was left absolutely in the

[1] In the case of *Wellesley* v. *The Duke of Beaufort* it was stated, however, that in reality the jurisdiction of the Court was over all the children in the realm, and was only not exercised in all cases because it was not all children who possessed an estate which required the protection of the Court.
[2] The case of *Besant* v. *Besant*.

hands of a parent who might be brutal and immoral, who was often careless and lax. A girl—to take the strongest and most probable case of wrong—might be brought up ignorant of the most rudimentary knowledge, a Pagan in faith, without sufficient food or clothing, without the common decencies of life in her home, and might be forced to drudge in the fields, or at a loom from her tenderest years. As she grew older, the law did not safeguard her in any efficient way from being forced to earn money by prostitution, though it never of course actually sanctioned this. That the great nations of the world are as good as they are, shows that parents have for the most part treasured the honour of the family in a rude but sufficient fashion. On the other hand, that every country has been scourged with a criminal class that defied punishment and Church restraints is conclusive proof that in many families the parents have been untrustworthy guardians of their children's characters. It has, however, been the healths and the minds of children that have suffered most under the enormous powers delegated to the family. Most of the labour to which the young can be put is either brutalising or unhealthy. Work in isolation, such as tending sheep or scaring birds, is apt to make the brain torpid; the work in gangs, while it endured, was actually demoralising; and for children, who need fresh air and exercise, work over a loom or in a stifling room can only be carried on at the cost of vitality. Nevertheless, the necessity for the parent to make money by his children's earnings has habitually been so great that he has used his authority simply to compel labour. The State has interposed in the last resort, and not without many misgivings, because the interests of its future men and women—their health and mental equipment—were bound to be more important to it than the maintenance of parental authority. The State is limiting the hours of work for children in every country, and it is compelling their attendance at school.

There have been many lamentations from those who think that the father is best left alone, and that a State system cannot be adapted to various capacities, as wise parents would adapt their training; and from those who think that schools cannot teach morality in that religious form which they believe to be the best. Without examining these arguments at length, it may be observed that the State has never attempted the costly and litigious work of national education in wantonness or from a light heart, but invariably because it conceived that it had no alternative. Neither has it wrested education out of the hands of individuals, for private and endowed schools have never been the majority; but out of the hands of the Churches, which have generally been strong enough to exclude competition, and not rich or enlightened enough to use their monopoly well. However, the purpose of this argument is not to defend the change to State education, but to point out that, wherever it is introduced, it necessarily transforms the position of the children. For certain hours of the day they are working under the civil law, and very possibly against the wish of their parents. They grow up better educated than father or mother, and know that they are not indebted to them for their schooling. As they become adults, they understand more and more that the State has only exacted from them a labour profitable to themselves, while their parents are taking advantage of their tender years to confiscate the proceeds of their industry. The child in an old society knew that his father had not cast him into the streets as a foundling, had not sold him as a slave or given him away, and had provided him with food, clothing, and education out of parental tenderness. The child in a modern society knows that the parent has done little more for him than the law and public opinion exact, and draws the conclusion, very often not unreasonably, that he has no great cause to be grateful. Our modern practice is so far from being an anomalous growth of new theories that it has been exceeded in some respects by old statutory provisions. The law at one time directed the parish overseers of the poor to apprentice children, whose parents could not support them, to such among the richer parishioners as seemed capable of the burden, and these had to bear it till the apprentices were of age. Neither could the parishioner so burdened refuse to receive the child assigned to him, though he might appeal to a higher court if he was taxed beyond his means or out of his turn.[1] It will be seen that the old law was pretty exactly one of parochial socialism. The peculiar feature about it is not that it provided for the children of needy parents—for some such provision is unavoidable—but that it took the child from the control of its natural parents and practically transferred it to an artificial family. To this day the State holds—and holds, we may say, unavoidably—that pauperism suspends family ties. Husband and wife are separated from their children and from one another in the workhouse. In the boarding-out system, which is now generally adopted, and with the best results, it is a rule not to assign the child to its natural parent. Unless we are prepared to maintain that the State is bound to care for the physical well-being of the young, but may let their

[1] Stat. 5. Eliz. c iv. ; 8 and 9 Will. & Mary c. 90.

minds lie fallow, we must surely admit that the case for compulsory education is as strong as for poor-relief to orphans and the children of destitute or vicious parents. In one respect it is, of course, incomparably stronger, for the percentage of parents who will allow a child to starve is undoubtedly much smaller than that of parents who will allow it to grow up wild or absorbed in mechanical drudgery.

It may be noticed in passing that where the State limits conjugal rights or parental authority, it gives as much to individualism as it takes from the head of the family. In fact, most changes in the law affecting the family system have come from the need felt by statesmen to modify a power that interfered with State necessities, and from the readiness of citizens to abandon a burdensome obligation. The English husband can no longer compel his wife to return to him, or squander her estate, or deprive her of her children, or inflict on her the moderate correction Dr. Marmaduke Coghill approved of,[1] or the restraint of her liberty which Blackstone expressly allows.[2] On the other hand, he can more or less easily divest himself of all responsibility for her debts or misconduct, and in great part of the civilised world finds it reasonably easy to obtain a divorce. The result, good or bad, is to give man and woman immensely increased freedom of action, the power to draw back from a contract that was once irrevocable, and that was one of the most noticeable conservative forces, and the right to make a fresh start in life. Only

---

[1] Dr. Marmaduke Coghill, Judge of the Prerogative Court in Ireland, ruled, c. 1700, that a husband might give his wife moderate correction with a little cane or switch. Swift alludes to his being jilted in consequence.—*Letters to Stella*, July 1, 1711.

[2] "The Courts of Law will still permit a husband to restrain a wife of her liberty, in case of any gross misbehaviour."—Blackstone's *Commentaries*, book i. chap. xv.

a man of exceptional energy can change his profession or trade once fairly entered upon in an old society, but in a new society a man goes on experimenting till he finds the career in which he works best, and this facility of change has a great effect in promoting individualism. Something like this will be the condition of the married couple who feel that they are not absolutely committed by one unfortunate mistake. Whether the losses may not more than overbalance the gains—whether the frequent changes of object that make the intellect subtle and versatile may not make the affections callous and insincere, whether the Germans were not partly right in saying that there should be only one marriage for one life—may be matter for serious consideration; but the one point seems evident—that individualism is bound to gain as family obligations are weakened. So again with the duty to children. It is conceivable, and perhaps probable, that in many countries the parents will retain and deserve by increased tenderness a great deal of that authority over their children which was anciently given them by law. The instinct of parental love is so intimately associated with our nature that we cannot imagine it will ever die out; and Plato's conception of a commonwealth, in which the children are to be taken at birth from the mother and brought up by the State, is inconceivable, for the twofold reason that the State has never assumed duties which were not forced upon it, and that parents generally would be opposed to any such surrender. Still it is conceivable that, as parents lose their proprietary and administrative rights over children, an increasing number will be inclined to shift all responsibility upon the State. We may imagine the State *crèche*, and the State doctor, and the State school, supplemented, it may be, by State meals, and the child, already drilled by the State, passing out from school into the State workshop. To whatever extent all this takes place, it will increase the parent's freedom, will relieve the mother from the incessant watchfulness which a household now entails, and will set the father free to work less or to choose more congenial work. Here again it is easy to see that there may be good and evil in the change. Mrs. Grote has hinted at a common opinion, most often left unexpressed, that a man of genius is wise to take a mistress rather than a wife, in order that he may live for his art and not for his family;[1] and Mr. Hamerton in a more temperate argument has pointed out that " the married man never goes, or hardly ever goes, on the same intellectual lines which he would have followed if he had remained a bachelor."[2] Now, some of the cases Mr. Hamerton puts—where a man having married a rich wife, sacrifices his career to her wishes, or where, having married an extravagant wife, he toils for her luxury—are cases that only concern a few persons. But the need of providing for children is a constant source of excessive toil and impoverishment. If fathers generally come to feel this obligation less and less, it will certainly leave them freer to consider their own pleasures, or, it may be, their own capacity for good work. They will lose what is sometimes a wholesome discipline; they will be relieved from what is often a burden heavy to bear.

Now, when we have discarded all that was temporary in the old system of family relations—the need of defence against enemies, the obligation of a common

---

[1] Grote's *Life of Ary Scheffer*, p. 49. Cf. p. 91.
[2] Hamerton, *The Intellectual Life*. Part vii. letter v.

family worship, and the pledges for good behaviour exacted by the State—there remains something indescribably holy and serious in the conception of the household. It might be better for society in one way that a father should never feel bound to pay his adult son's debts, or the son his father's, but the moral gain of such examples, which are still fortunately very frequent, is incalculable. It is certain that pride of family has often been unreasonable, even where the ancestors were men who had served their country with distinction; and where the boast is to descend from a king's harlot, or through a long line of close-fisted fox-hunters, it can only be regarded as a very sad example of human weakness. On the other hand, if there be any truth in scientific doctrines of heredity, the descendants of ancestors who have an honourable record of integrity, of labour, it may be even of splendid public service, are surely entitled to pride themselves on their pedigree. The possibilities of atavism may determine a man to follow the line in which an ancestor distinguished himself. Neither is it easily possible to overrate the influence exercised by family traditions—however vague and unintelligent—upon a sympathetic character. Other things being equal, the member of one of those families, in which all the men have been brave and the women pure, starts with a better chance of blameless life than the child whose best hope is that its family record may not be remembered against it. No one will assume that the impairment of the old family system, the growth of the democratic feeling against titles, or the increasing disposition to treat wealth as the only title to consideration, will ever altogether extinguish the pride of descent. The instance of America shows how deeply rooted the feeling is, even in a new and democratic society. The real value of family feeling is not, however, so much based upon recognition of the past as upon forethought for the future. Whatever else science teaches us, it teaches that the family with its inherited taints of greed or lust, its quick impulses or cautious movements, its sublimated or impaired brain power, its noble or sordid proclivities, is the one indestructible factor in human society. We may destroy its vantage-ground of privilege and consideration, but, however debilitated, it will remain. No change affecting it can be other than far-reaching. The man who has not shrunk from dishonouring his ancestors has often recoiled from the prospect of bringing infamy upon his children. In proportion as the family bonds are weakened, as the tie uniting husband and wife is more and more capricious, as the relations of the children to the parent become more and more temporary, will the religion of household life gradually disappear. Certain imperishable instincts will maintain the semblance of the old relations, and it need not be apprehended that any large portion of society will either decline upon concubinage, or abandon children generally to the care of the State. What we have rather to look forward to is a state of things in which marriages will be contracted without reflection, and broken up without scruple, in which children will be cared for when they are young with, it may be, even more tenderness than of old, but with incomparably less anxiety to fit them for the moral obligations of life, and in which the claim of parents to be obeyed will cease with the children's need of support. Family life will be a gracious and decorative incident in the system of such a society; but the family, as a constituent part of the State, as the matrix in which character is moulded, will lose its importance as the clan and the city have done.

The relations of master and servant, of master and apprentice, of employer and employed, have in past time presented what we may call bastard forms of family life, and which have been recognised as such by custom and law. One of them, the relation of master and apprentice, has long ago been shorn of its old significance. The others are being unavoidably changed. As large establishments are superseding small in every department of industry, the personal relation between employer and man tends to become weaker; and the "hand," as a rule, looks more to his Trades-Union for support and help than to his nominal paymaster. In domestic service it has become a principle with servants' unions in large cities that no one is to remain in the same place for more than a limited time. It may be safely said of these changes that they have not been without cause, and have mostly been either good or unavoidable. With all allowance for the habits of a ruder time, it is difficult for a student of our old literature to believe that servants were ever really better treated than they have been in the present century; except where they corresponded to the class of what are now called "lady-helps," like the Mercer whom Samuel Pepys played music with and took to parties, and whom his wife did not scruple to thrash when she thought punishment deserved.[1] Swift's notices of servants represent the Irish servants as distinctly worse than they are now, and the English servants as decidedly less to be trusted.[2] It would be

---

[1] Pepys's *Diary*, vol. ii. p. 450 ; vol. iii. p. 26.
[2] See Swift's *Sermon on the Causes of the Wretched Condition of Ireland*, and his *Rules that Concern all Servants*.

easy to quote evidence from novelists like Fielding to the same effect. Nevertheless it may be freely admitted that there was a reasonable percentage of cases till very lately in which servants remained in the same family all their lives, identified themselves with its fortunes, and shared its affections and hopes. Thousands of persons still living can remember how the family servant—often, it may be, exercising a self-assertion that was almost tyrannical—was yet an important part of the surroundings that made home lovable. Such servants are now bound to disappear, and are said to be disappearing even in France; and the compensation for their extinction has in a broad sense been more than adequate. The whole class is, as a rule, better housed and better fed, and gets better wages. All that need be here noted is that the class which goes out to service is apt to lose its own family ties, without, as was formerly the case to some extent at least, acquiring new ones; and that the family which employs servants is now contracting only for so much labour, and not only does not expect the attachment which it may conceivably deserve, but knows that it cannot retain its employees except at the cost to them of professional ostracism. The change is one that will be very differently felt in different households. There have always been many in which the servant was never naturalised. For those, however, in which the relations of high and low were gracious and cordial, the transition to a state in which the house is little more than an inn, owned and worked by the occupants, cannot fail to be an impairment of the completeness of family life.

Neither can it be doubted that, as the habit of emigration to colonies has weakened national feeling for a time, England being regarded as only one out of many countries belonging to the Englishman, so the abandonment of their country homes by many families that were identified with them for centuries has weakened one of the mainsprings of family feeling. Squireens and yeomanry have been bought out, or have left, because they found themselves overshadowed by rich neighbours with whom it was impossible to compete, and whom it was not pleasant to defer to. Associations have been destroyed that can never be renewed. Even, however, if all the representatives of the old families could be replaced, England and half a dozen modern countries are getting so crowded that their populations are forced to live for the most part in towns. Some of the disadvantages of this change have already been considered. It need only be noticed here that it is bound to destroy the religion of the homestead; and though that may only be a gross form of human weakness which induces men to linger where the cradle of the race was laid, where generation after generation has been committed to consecrated dust, where the very meadows and woods are instinct with memories of ancestral life, we are so constituted that our very weakness will sometimes lend intensity to our loves. May it be that as husband and wife, parent and children, master and servant, family and home lose more and more of their ancient and intense significance, the old imperfect feelings will be transmuted into love for fatherland.

CHAPTER VI

THE DECAY OF CHARACTER

The question postulated is whether the changes that increase the influence of the State may not diminish the sphere of individual energy.—The inquiry is complicated by the consideration that a strong motive—such as the love of power or fame—may stimulate energy, even where circumstances are most unfavourable, as in ancient Athens.—Moreover, the Church and Army develop individuality in some ways, though they crush it in others.—Religious influence has been stronger than ethical in past times. What then will be the result if the State takes the place of the Church in organising society, and if science supersedes it in criticism of the past and in divination of the future?—A tendency to disbelieve in the miraculous may leave unaffected the faith that there is a moral government and foreordering of the world.—It need not therefore destroy a temperate belief in the efficacy of prayer.—The belief in a future state is likely to be less positively held.—These changes, though they may leave religion in society as an appreciable element, are bound to impair its influence over the masses, which was once great and good.—The austere tradition of Puritan family life, with its strength and its shortcomings, has gone for ever, and is replaced by a sensuous, genial, and fibreless society.—Women are bound to be profoundly influenced by the changes that are making them more and more like men, as they are exempted from tutelage, encouraged to stand alone, and induced to occupy themselves with pursuits hitherto esteemed masculine.—State education and State military service are bound to render the intellect more mechanical and to sap the energy that is developed by competition.—The right of public meeting is likely to be limited in the future, and this will interfere with the power to give instantaneous body and form to new thoughts by the contagion of popular feeling.—The immigration of aliens in large numbers is likely to be restricted everywhere, as also the right of individuals to practise their professions or trades in a foreign country.—This will add enormously to the power an administration now has over those who criticise or oppose it. Exile will mean ruin.—It is anticipated by some that the future has in reserve for us great scientific discoveries which will at least elevate the mind, and which may perhaps reconcile reason and faith.—This is to assume that doctrines which aim at spiritualising the character can be reduced to the condition of problems that satisfy the intellect. They would lose all that is distinctive in the process. The most that can be said is, that religion will gain when its teaching does not outrage possibility, and science by learning that it is not all-sufficient.—Beyond this there is reason to suppose that science has done her greatest and most suggestive work. There is nothing now left for her but to fill in details.—Certain forms of literature, such as the epic, the drama, the pastoral, and the satire appear to be already exhausted.—The real genius of the age takes a lyrical form, and is feeble and incongruous when it attempts any other.—Moreover, life has been toned down, so that there is much less wealth of strong incident and effective situation than was the case anciently. —Again, when work has been perfectly done the artist does not care to attempt it again, and the world will not tolerate reproductions. Topics are being exhausted.—This, however, will tell after a time even more against lyrical poetry, because the single mood or situation is less capable of variety than the human character.—The novel is not likely to replace poetry for work of the highest kind. History, however, which is perpetually accumulating fresh material, may furnish practically inexhaustible material to minds of the highest order.—Criticism has only recently begun to exist. It is likely to exercise a growing influence over all matters of science as observation and thought are accumulated.—While, however, there is a comparative certainty about the judgments of science, the criticism of taste is apt to be very variable, as if fixed canons could not be applied with precision to living men.—Criticism generally errs by being too eulogistic, or, at least, disproportionately eulogistic.—As, however, it is likely that the classical and best models will be discarded as contemporary literature grows upon us, criticism will suffer, because its standards will be impaired.— Although the results of science admit of being communicated in good style, science is passing so much into the hands of experts that its familiar interpretation will cease to be needed.—Oratory is likely to be reduced more and more to debating and to the skilful enhancement of commonplace. — It seems probable that as the special correspondent is superseding the traveller, so journalism will absorb more and more of the world's practical intellect; even the abstract thinker finding it advantageous to communicate his ideas through a newspaper with large circulation. — But the journalist writes for the day, and his best work is only of ephemeral value.—It is conceivable that the duration of life will be prolonged, and that the chances of health will be enormously increased by scientific improvements. It would seem as if this ought to increase self-confidence and energy. — A world predominantly of old people will be a world of more stable political order and greater efficiency of exact thought.—On the other hand, it will be a world with less adventure and energy, less brightness and hope.—Neither will ambition be so powerful a motive of action as when a single man—Caesar or Chatham—could initiate and carry out a policy of his own.—Again, it is possible that the most important and sensational changes have already been effected. —Fame is perhaps a little less capricious than of old ; but it is less valuable from being more widely distributed.—This will be especially true of literary fame, as some kinds of literature are dying out, and the competition in those that survive will elicit many candidates for distinction.—The limitations imposed by State Socialism on private enterprise are never likely to be so far-reaching as to preclude money-making and destroy the passion for wealth.— Wealth, however, will be valued as the source of power and ostentation, not as the means of founding a family.—We are realising our highest dreams, and they mean a more stable and equable order, less aspiration, and less energy.—The decay of vital power in the race does not mean that it will become extinct ; but that it will gradually lose interest in all but the day's needs.—It is inspiriting to remember that the world has passed through stormy times before, and has been depressed, and yet the results have been better than expectation. As we can trace advance hitherto, why should it not be continued in the future ?—The faith in progress is based upon an assumption as to the Divine purpose in creation, which is not only gratuitous, but opposed to facts.—All that can be said is, that if we are passing into the old age of humanity we may at least bear the burden laid upon us with dignity.

So far an attempt has been made to show that the races of the world are approaching a stationary condition as regards territorial limits between Aryan and others, what we call the higher being confined for practical purposes to a part of the Temperate Zone ; that democracy is likely to find its consummation in State Socialism ; and that certain notable influences, such as attachment to a Church, municipal feeling, and even family feeling, are likely to become less and less important as factors in the constitution of society. The great possible motors of action, if these changes actually take place, will be the sense of duty to the State, and the self-reliance of individual character. The patriotic feeling is likely to be enhanced by a sense of the great services which the State will render in the new order; by the habit of military discipline which universal service in the ranks will create; and by the mere fact that as the feelings lose a sufficient object in Church, city, or family, they will tend to concentrate themselves upon the fatherland. It remains to consider what effect the new importance of the State may have upon personal energy and independence of thought. The strength of the State can hardly be more than the sum of strength in its individual members; and it is at least conceivable that we may get political organisations which are more complete than have ever yet been—that is, which attempt more and do more—but which are yet deficient in the spiritual reserve which an older and more imperfect society possessed in the initiative and resource of its members. To take examples from history, let us assume—merely as a hypothesis—that modern society is tending more and more to the form of society that prevailed under the Incas, and that such men as Drake and Frobisher, Clive and Warren Hastings, are likely to become rare and disappear.

The initial perplexity of such an inquiry is, that it is extremely difficult to avoid the conclusion that energy of character may assert itself in certain epochs with apparent disregard of political institutions. Athens in its best time was a country in which the limitations of originality in thought or action were enormous. To be suspected of entertaining new views about religion was dangerous, and impiety was charged against statesmen like Pericles and Alcibiades, philosophers like Anaxagoras and Socrates, as effectively as if they had been statesmen of the seventeenth century in Europe. To be wealthy was to be suspected of peculation, and to be powerful was to invite ostracism. The general charged with the command of an expedition might find his plans disconcerted by omens that disheartened the forces, and was almost certain to be recalled on the smallest check. Scarcely any man was more popular than Nicias, who was religious and liberal, and whom all instinctively felt to be "a safe man"; yet Nicias, having a nervous temperament, is said to have lived in such constant disquietude, that he walked the streets day by day with a hang-dog look.[1] Fortunately, Nicias was the rare exception, and the typical Athenian of those days, as we know him, was a man of reckless political and moral courage, setting his fortunes at stake fearlessly in the incessant contest for political power, going to any extreme against his opponents, and speaking his mind about government or religion without regard to the probability that he might be prosecuted. In fact, to take modern parallels, the freedom of thought resembled that of Paris during the last half-century of the monarchy, and the energy of initiative that of the English statesmen who created the Indian Empire. The most simple explanation is, that the Athenian of those days saw magnificent possibilities of fame and power before him. It was possible, even probable, that Athens might become the queen city of the western world, whose commands would be obeyed from Sicily to the shores of the Euxine. In that case the men who had made Athens would have a harvest of immortal glory, and if they lived to see their work done, would be the most enviable of men, rewarded by praise, wealth, and power. The vision quickened those who beheld it to immortal action.

---

[1] Plutarch's *Life of Nicias.* Plutarch quotes from Phrynichus: "A good citizen ; one who does not walk the streets with a hang-dog look like Nicias."

It would seem, accordingly, that we must start upon any examination into the causes that modify character with the postulate that several and perhaps even many races are inherently energetic; and though they may be depressed for a time by foreign conquest, or by poverty, or by bad government, as the modern Italians were for centuries, it is never safe to predict that they have lost the power to rise again. Another important consideration is, that some institutions which seem to crush originality in one direction, may be found to favour the formation of a strong character in another. The influence of every Church, Christian or otherwise, is to discourage examination of those truths which it teaches as fundamental. It allows the intellect of its followers to be apologetic, explanatory, and, it may be, even complementary, but forbids it at all hazards to be critical. Beyond this, every Church is tempted to compromise with human frailty so long as its own supremacy is recognised. It often, almost habitually, prefers the immoral man, who gives it no trouble, to the moral man, who is always fingering his conscience and doubting how far the Church system is adequate. To a considerable extent, accordingly, the Churches proscribe independence of speculation, and weaken the springs of character by relaxing the moral fibre. On the other hand, every Church has a rule of life which is more ascetic and severe than men in general would naturally adopt, and its demands in this way are commonly in proportion with its shortcomings in other directions. The Catholic Church, for instance, which puts Dante and Darwin into the *Index Expurgatorius*, and which is very gentle to sins of the flesh when it speaks through Jesuit fathers in the confessional, does yet exact severe sacrifices from its members: forbids them to attend the theatre or the racecourse, orders them to fast, regulates the relations of husband and wife, and constrains, where it is obeyed, to a great deal of ceremonial observance. A man who complies with the rules of the Church is tolerably certain to be narrow-minded and deficient in his apprehension of independent morality; but he ought to have acquired habits of self-denial, which will partly make up for what he has lost ethically, and which will even fit him to think better, within certain limitations, if he can be trained to think at all. The Army, again, is and is intended to be a great school for extinguishing self-assertion. The ideal soldier is one who obeys orders mechanically without considering whether they are wise or right. Nevertheless, military discipline is generally regarded as elevating to moral character; the man who will suffer privation and face death at the call of duty gaining, as a rule, more by this than he loses by sacrificing the habit to do only what his conscience approves; and this is more markedly the case than ever since the laws of war have been made comparatively moral and regardful of human rights. On the other hand, the soldier is generally found wanting in flexibility when he turns his attention to the business of common life.

Taking now the great principles or motives that have influenced conduct in past times, we may surely assign the highest place to the obligations of morality and religion, which it is not always easy to distinguish from one another. Both agree in telling us to do what we recognise as our duty, because right is right; but the moralist does not care to go beyond the fact that we get our reward in this life in the spiritual elevation which transforms humanity into something higher and better; while the religious teacher, as a rule, tells us that we shall be additionally rewarded or punished by carrying our purified or degraded natures into a new state of existence. The teaching which promises most has undoubtedly had the largest influence in bygone centuries; partly because its propagators were more zealous, and partly because men and women were more fascinated by the vision of a new life without weakness or sorrow, and with the fruition of all knowledge, than by the noble commonplaces of morality. Therefore, if the Churches lose their hold upon society, as they seem to be doing in certain directions, because the State has appropriated many of their functions and is discharging them better, the change will be very momentous, though it may be balanced by gains which will be more than proportionate to the losses. We may conceive, for instance, that a population which has had its intellect quickened in State schools, which has been subjected to discipline in the State army, and which the State has compelled to work, and has tried to keep from excess in drink, may furnish more promising subjects for Christian teaching than the dwellers in great cities, mostly ignorant, often idle and vicious, have contributed hitherto. This, however, is not the anticipation entertained by the Churches in general, and as corporations guided by clever experts are commonly alive to their own interests, the view of religious leaders has to be considered. It is probably correct to say, that thoughtful churchmen conceive the Churches to be losers by all the State improvements which tend to take the relief of poverty into secular hands. Beyond this, they regard with alarm the disinclination of the Civil Government to be bound by religious precedent in such matters as the laws of marriage, the observance of the Lord's day, or the repression of sexual immorality. But what is most dreaded is the growth of an independent and purely secular school of thought,—especially in science and history, whose conclusions may come to influence school teaching, and to permeate society. No religious man doubts that the highest scientific teaching is compatible with ardent religious faith. The names of Herschel, Brewster, Faraday, the Hamiltons, Secchi, St. George Mivart, and in History, of De Tocqueville, Guizot, Palgrave, and Stubbs,—a few names out of a host—are sufficient evidence that a faith as intelligent and as submissive as Pascal's is still possible. None the less, it is instinctively felt that the great mass of men who possess the scientific temperament and training are apt to discard the supernatural element from religion; and that this may lead, not only to a rejection of modern miracles, but to a setting aside of the Incarnation and Ascension of Christ, of that perpetual miracle of the Real Presence, in which Catholics, Anglicans, Lutherans, and the Greek Church believe, and of that other perpetual miracle of the communication of the Holy Ghost in certain solemn moments, or in certain sacerdotal functions, which no Christian Church—except the Unitarian body—has renounced or explained away. It may be, of course, that these fears will be dissipated hereafter, but they certainly exist at present, and seem not unwarranted. There is a story that an Ultramontane speaker in an Austrian Parliament addressed the House with the interrogation: "I suppose we all believe in the Church?" and was met with a shout from the left, "We believe in Darwin." What is apprehended is that the whole world may come to be divided in the same way, and that the disciples of Darwin—or of Darwin's successor—will be the more numerous.

A world without the belief in miracle, and without the belief in a life after death, for which life on earth is a preparation! Such a state of society has never been known yet, though the belief in a future life was not held with unwavering certainty in Hellenic and Roman times. It is not easy to realise all that a complete renunciation of these faiths would imply. It is customary to assume that belief in miracles is already held very guardedly by the great mass of educated Protestants. Almost all these suppose miracles in the ordinary acceptation of the term to have ceased with the Apostolic age. Nevertheless, almost every devout Protestant believes firmly that his own life has been so ordered beforehand for good, that every incident may subserve a moral end. Thomas a Kempis tells us in considering the difficult question of temptations to sin, that "divine wisdom and equity weigh the condition and merits of men, and pre-ordain everything so as to fit in with the salvation of the elect."[1] Luther went even further than this, and declared that temptations were the spiritual discipline of the soul; quoting Archbishop Albert of Mainz for the thought commonly ascribed to himself, that the human heart is like millstones, which grind on themselves if they are not supplied with grist, as an instance that the soul needs struggle to take it out of isolation and keep it from feeding upon itself.[2] Sometimes this doctrine has been so applied as to become trivial, and often so as to become extravagant. An old writer tells the story of a Puritan, who having declared that he should perish eternally as certainly as a glass he threw down was shattered, derived great comfort from observing that the glass lay unbroken on the ground.[3] Mr. Keble suggests in very beautiful

---

[1] *De Imitatione Christi*, lib. i. c. 13, § 6.

[2] Luther's *Tisch-Reden*, iii. c. 26, § 44.

[3] Compare Rousseau, by training a Calvinist, and at the time "demi-Janséniste," throwing a stone at a tree, and deciding, that if it hit, it

verse that the counsels of statesmen may be changed, and the march of armies suspended in order to facilitate the conversion of a single soul.[1] It is probably correct to say that a sane Christianity still contents itself with the limits indicated by Thomas a Kempis. It does not conceive a world in which there are perpetual interpositions, but rather one which has been so exquisitely foreordered, that every event has its moral use and its appropriateness to the special life. There is no departure from the order of nature in the recovery from illness, or the escape from danger, that has often been the cause of a conversion; yet the religious mind, looking at the result, concludes not unnaturally, that Loyola's transformation on a sick bed was as divinely ordered as St. Paul's vision. Accordingly, as long as this belief in the moral government of the world as its supreme purpose is maintained, we may surely say that the belief in miracle survives, though the belief in violations of fixed natural laws may have become obsolete.

So again with the belief in prayer. We are so far from the times when Elisha saw the angels and chariots of fire compassing the city in which he lived to protect it, that such a faith would now appear a hallucination or an imposture. The belief in prayers against drought or rain or against pestilence, and the recourse to days of national humiliation, are dying out. Those who repeat prayers against war, if they do it as more than a mere formality, probably explain it to themselves as a solemn recalling by the nation of its duties to other communities. There is perhaps more real fervour in the prayers offered up for individuals: that the life of a sovereign,

---

would be a sign of his salvation. It hit; and "depuis lors, je n'ai plus douté de mon salut."—*Confessions*, Part I. livre vi.

[1] *Christian Year*, Hymn for All Saints' Day.

a great statesman, or, much more, of a near relation, may be preserved. The reason of the difference, however, lies only in our acuter perception of the uniformity of natural laws in certain cases. We understand that a prayer for rain means a reversal of climatic laws all over the world, and we see how irrational it is to ask that the order of the Universe shall be changed for the sake of a Scotch county, or of a pastoral district in Australia. As well might a Neapolitan Lazzarone pray that his face should be washed for him by the ministration of angels. The inhabitants of every country can modify the climate and enrich the soil if they will only use the intelligence given them at birth, and the Neapolitan may wash himself if he is inclined. On the other hand, the laws of disease are so little understood, and constitutions rally in such remarkable ways, that there seems less impropriety in supposing that Divine sympathy may now and again interpose in cases of this sort in answer to earnest prayer. It may be observed, however, that many of the most profoundly religious persons shrink from petitions of this kind as irreverent and unwise attempts to secure from God what He has already ordered better in another way. Sir Thomas More, who himself prayed earnestly for his daughter's recovery, is said to have regarded the birth of a half-witted son as the answer of an angry Heaven to his wife, who had longed ungovernably for a boy. "Thou hast wearied God with prayers for a man-child, and He has given thee one, who will be always a child."[1] In this case we get a curious combination of the religious and reasoning faculties; a belief that effectual fervent prayer was potent, and could change the purpose of God, and the conviction that such a

[1] Roper's *Life of More*, ed. Singer, p. 169, note 19.

weapon ought not to be employed in a reckless and inconsiderate manner. In proportion as this temperate view has met with acceptance, prayer has ceased to formulate desires, and has come rather to be the expression of the soul's unreserve towards Him who is the last comfort of the comfortless; or it is the inarticulate cry of doubt or pain, "the retreat of the solitary upon the eternal solitude."[1] I have heard Mr. Emerson speak in a lecture of a good man he had known who said that it seemed to him impossible not to be constantly praying, by which probably nothing more was meant than that a sense of being near to the Invisible Presence tempered every wish and animated every thought. Men of this stamp must always be rare, but there seems no reason why they should die out of society. The scientific habit of thought may reject belief in a sympathetic God as unproven and of no demonstrable utility, but cannot affect to regard it as mischievous or provably extravagant.

The belief in a future life, which seems almost instinctive, is yet one of those essential parts of Christianity which it is most difficult to establish with precision, or even to put forward convincingly. It was recommended in the first centuries of our era by the abject misery in which men and women lived. The cities and provinces burdened with debt; the nobles suspected at court, and tracked by informers; the peasantry mostly slaves at the mercy of their lord and of every government official; barbarians rushing in to destroy, or pestilence ravaging; it seemed as if the very perfection of mechanism in the central government

---

[1] *Plotini Enneades*, lib. ix. c. 10. "καὶ οὕτω θεῶν καὶ ἀνθρώπων θείων καὶ εὐδαιμόνων βίος, ἀπαλλαγὴ τῶν ἄλλων τῶν τῇδε, βίος ἀνήδονος τῶν τῇδε, φυγὴ μόνου πρὸς μόνον."

made it all the more an inexorable fatality, crushing out hope and self-respect. Men so wretchedly circumstanced might well deem that there must be a future life to compensate for what was endured below, if they did not regard the whole drama of existence as some wild devil's extravaganza. To this feeling later on was added the perception that such an ultimate triumph of right in this life as Job and David believed in was in no wise to be demonstrated, and that if we looked forward to an exact apportionment for every one according to his deserts, we must believe in some final tribunal where "God at the end compensates, punishes." Circumstances have so completely changed that these arguments have lost much of their weight. Society is better ordered, and men are now happy or miserable in this life very much through their own character and conduct. Again, the enormous difficulties of realising a future state have come to be understood. The argument of Leibnitz that eternal life means the eternal development of character, good or evil,[1] so that the good will always be growing better, the bad always declining upon lower depths, is so appalling to modern sensibility that to many it seems preferable to believe that we have our heaven and hell upon earth. Then again, science counting up the untold myriads of men and women who have passed away noiselessly, and considering how few even now lead a life very much higher than that of brutes, conceives it irrational to suppose that all will be raised again into a higher sphere of existence. There is also a revolt of morality from the doctrine of punishments and rewards. St. Teresa's fine sentiment that she did not fear hell, or hope for heaven, but loved

---

[1] "Il (Sextus) porte toujours avec lui ce qu'il sera."—*Théodicée*. Leibnitz, *Opera*, vol. vi. pp. 359-363.

God for himself alone,[1] is the expression of a thought that has always existed vaguely among men, and that is coming to be more and more recognised as the true motive of action. Nevertheless, those who hold this belief, and who are perhaps purifying religion by holding it, are withdrawing a future life from its place in the moral government of the world. Their gaze, as it were, fixes itself upon the divine life and passion as they were on earth, and refuses to see the heavens opening above.

Now, it can hardly be doubted that these tendencies in modern thought—the tendency to reduce miracle to the recognition of a moral order in the world, the tendency to limit prayer to spiritual aspiration, and the tendency to regard a future life as nothing more than a fanciful and unimportant possibility—are all bound to lessen the influence of religion upon the masses. The traveller who goes into countries where the old faith still lingers in unabated vitality—into parts of the Tyrol, or still more into Russia—is conscious that he has passed into a different moral world. Its ethics, in the acceptation of modern thinkers, are probably worse than those of the civilised west, but it is pervaded with a sense, which the west has lost, of living partly in an unseen world, and with almost entire reference to a life beyond the grave. It can scarcely be doubted that civilisation is at present the winning force, and that while its admirable police will impose a stricter morality everywhere, the scientific spirit which it fosters will dissipate the larger part of traditional religion. It is perhaps correct to say that the religious tone of mind has always been seen at its highest advantage in countries which the secular spirit was already invading

---

[1] Soneto á Cristo crucificado.—*Obras de Santa Teresa*, p. 537.

and conquering. The Catholicism of the French Jansenists, the Protestantism of Puritan times, furnish the most admirable instances of unalloyed Christianity that the world has seen, and their influence elevated the men who were neither Jansenists nor Puritans. Those who judge the religion of England at its best in the seventeenth century by the life of Nicholas Ferrar or of John Bunyan, and who turn to the records of Blaise and Jacqueline Pascal to appreciate the Jansenist, will find that the religious tone of Anglican, Nonconformist, and Catholic was practically indistinguishable. Those who wish to trace what was vulgar and dishonest in the professors of those days will find inimitable portraitures in the *Tartufe* of Molière, which was probably aimed at a mystic or a Jansenist,[1] and in *Hudibras*, which was written by a man who had lived in a Puritan household. It is well to know that there was a bad side, and to remember that the worst men were habitually those who traded upon the success of religion; for the good is so admirable as to induce a

---

[1] There is a tradition that Tartufe was drawn from Roquette, Bishop of Autun, a very ordinary type of the intriguing priest (*Biographie Universelle*, art. "Molière"). Michelet appears to identify Tartufe with Desmarets, an illuminé, and quotes the line:

"Priez Dieu que toujours le ciel vous illumine."

Henri Martin describes him as "l'athée travesti en Jésuite." The only point that Tartufe has in common with the Jesuits is casuistry. "On trouve avec le ciel des accommodements." On the other hand, Louis XIV. would hardly have tolerated an attack on the Jesuits, and Tartufe's ostentation of austerity is incomparably more a Jansenist than a Jesuit trait. The great hatred the clergy generally had for the play appears due to the fact that in the first sketch Tartufe was a clerical confessor (Martin, *Hist. de France*, tome xiii. p. 678). It seems safest, however, to hold that Tartufe was hypocrisy incarnate rather than any particular hypocrite; and we know from Mdme. de Sévigné (*Lettres*, Dec. 1, 1664) that the Chancellor Séguier was described as "la métamorphose de Pierrot en Tartufe."

regret that it was in the very nature of things ephemeral, and carrying in it the seeds of death.

The Puritan household which many of this generation can recall in its latter-day adumbration, was an institution that has a title to be commemorated. The men and women who grew up in a faith that was something more than enthusiasm or passive conviction were penetrated by a sense of the reality of divine law in a way that perhaps is never likely to be reproduced. Habitually abstemious in food, reserved in speech, methodical in act, and possessed with an awful sense of the obligation of physical purity, they carried a certain ungainly erectness into everyday life, and fell readily into line in any great crisis. To him who feels that he is "for ever in the Great Taskmaster's eye" nothing can be trivial, and so it came about that the Puritan approached his small duties with a seriousness that seemed to want grace and proportion; but that earnestness was the secret of a concentration of power, which, when it has been diverted into business, has made Puritans the most successful of speculators and organisers. When the Hebrew faith took possession of a soul that had the Hellenic sense of beauty, it gave the world Milton; when it informed a statesman and soldier of Roman unscrupulousness and ambition, it made Cromwell; and when it tempered the highest speculative originality, it produced a Pascal. The prevailing note in each of these great minds is austerity; and their intellectual counterparts in the modern world are apt to be discriminative and subtle and sympathetic and fibreless. Puritanism is no longer a force in art or letters or statesmanship; and the Puritan tradition of family life is dead, and cannot be revived. The results of that iron drill were obtained at a cost which none who passed through it can forget, or would submit to again, or could endure to see inflicted upon their children. The mother who almost doubted if it was not sin to love the babe that smiled up in her face; the children who spoke with bated breath and were trained to orderly composure on Sundays; the belief of young and old that they lived in a world whose amusements and thoughts were irreverent and grotesque by the side of life with its awful duties, even as laughter above a deathbed would be; the conception of marriage as indissoluble; the recoil from libertinage of thought or of moral tone as from shame and death, are all parts of a system that could only be maintained while the New Testament was believed in as something more than the best possible moral code,—as the actual word of God. Instead of this we have got a new family life, which is infinitely genial, and charming, and natural, which gives free vent to the feelings, and cares liberally for culture and advancement in life. Only the sense of obligation, of duty to God, of living forward into eternity has disappeared. When all is said, the man who orders his life as if it were to end with the grave, or as if his thoughts and works here would not follow him beyond the grave, can scarcely fail to live more in the present than the future. He may have wider perceptions and sympathies and enjoyments than the Puritan, but he will have less self-restraint and will. He will clutch with a fierce avidity at power or wealth, or at the pleasures which are purchased by the possession of power and wealth.

It is likely that this change will affect women even more than men. Hitherto in all countries, but in the Germanic above all, woman has been the moral element in households—the personification of duty and purity in family life. Probably, even now, there are very few men of over fifty who have not grown up believing in the women among whom they lived as devoutly as they believed in God. There might be vice in the highest or the lowest circles, but for men at large it was a presence outside of their homes. It may be the facts of society are still very much the same, but there is a change of tone. The reforms that are removing woman from the perpetual tutelage of husbands and parents are unavoidably constraining her to stand alone in many respects. She is more at liberty to choose her own husband, more free to refuse to marry, more able to shape out an independent career, and has come to possess nearly equal rights over property and over her children. At the same time the old idea that the woman's real function is to be wife and mother exists almost in full force; and the women who wish to compete with men in politics, in the professions, in trade, and to some extent in serious literature, still find that they are kept back by public opinion, though they are no longer restrained by legal difficulties. The result seems to be a conflict of old and new desires. On the one hand are the natural instinct to use beauty and attractiveness in their congenial sphere of conquest, and the practical feeling that in this one domain the woman can draw greater prizes in the lottery of life than the man. In most cases the man who has risen to wealth or eminence can look back upon laborious years, and on times in which he despaired of achieving anything. But a girl of eighteen may become the wife of a duke, a millionaire, or the greatest statesman of the day, by the mere accident of meeting him at a ball, or sitting next him at dinner. Chances of this kind, though known and moderately frequent in all ages, were not numerous enough to demoralise the imaginations of any large number; they are now a perceptible cause of ambition and unrest. On the other hand, the various causes that are driving women to make homes for themselves while they have freed society from the worst feature of conventual life, and from the unattractive celibacy of women, who having failed to marry were supposed to have failed in their careers, are assimilating the thoughts and habits of women to the masculine type. The inquiry now often made why there should be a different law of morality for the two sexes could scarcely have been formulated as lately as a century ago; and it may be questioned if women are not likely to lose something rare and inappreciable if it comes to be recognised that there is no special ideal for wives and daughters. Human nature may probably be trusted to keep its own boundary lines; and the old trick of thought that regards fearlessness in word and act as the true virtue of the man, and sexual purity as that of the woman, will not easily be unlearned. Meanwhile, for the present at least, it seems as if there were an unsettlement of ideas that may lead for a generation or more to much ferment of thought and irregularity of aim and instability of character. The license of some notoriously depraved courts is never likely to be exceeded, or even reached. It is even probable, perhaps, that as women are more and more occupied with serious interests they will be less and less tempted to be frail. What it seems most reasonable to apprehend is, that the old instinctive virtue will be replaced by a calculating common sense, which may easily become a calculating compliance; and that while family life in general will be as inviolable as heretofore, it will lose the sense of religious sanction, and continue to exist only because it is felt to be warranted by a sane estimate of loss and gain.

If these changes ever come to pass, we shall get a world that is mostly secular in its tone, though with a minority who hold a spiritualised faith, and the family, as it loses its influence, will cease to transmit the tradition of a consecrated household life. It remains to be seen whether the new forces that are supplanting the Churches and the family can so elevate individual character as to give it a new reserve of strength in place of what it is losing. What the State does, and does admirably in its way, tends almost entirely to make its citizens more perfect parts of the political machine. Its school-training is bound to be more or less automatic or mechanical; the service in the ranks which it enforces will subdue the will even more than it develops the faculties; and if it organises labour, it is likely to do it on conditions of democratic equality that will maintain as far as possible a dead level among employees. The most that can be said is, that if aristocratic privilege is abolished, and the influence of wealth reduced to a minimum, society will attain to that ideal of the "career open to talents" which has been realised in some critical periods—as under Cromwell and the First Napoleon—with very brilliant results. The best observers of democratic society are, however, apt to accuse it of a jealousy that seems to belong to its very essence—the jealousy lest it should end in constituting an official aristocracy with excessive incomes and powers. It accordingly guards against this by, as far as may be, equalising salaries, distributing powers, and giving promotion by seniority, or by some rude form of rotation; such as the wholesale displacements that occur in America after every triumph of an Opposition. We know by the instances of England and Austria that the opposite principle of selection by fitness—meaning practically selection by favour—may work very badly. That statesmen of ardent patriotism and personal incorruptibility like Pitt and Lord Castlereagh should have allowed two such incompetent commanders as the Duke of York and Lord Chatham to direct great British armies, would be inexplicable if we assumed the consideration of fitness to have entered very much into their combinations. Abercromby, Cornwallis, and Sir John Moore were available when the Royal Duke was taken; Wellesley, Baird, and Hope when Lord Chatham was employed. The Ministers must have known that they were running a fearful risk; but they undoubtedly thought it impossible to pass over officers of high rank till they had been tried and had failed.[1] Therefore it is not very wonderful if the great democracy of the United States acquiesces in a system that puts good and bad on a level in ordinary times, and if it trusts to itself to use extraordinary remedies in the day of danger. It is easier, however, to understand this deplorable system—bad even when the principle of summary changes is abolished—than to justify it as reasonably practical, or to regard it as anything but a danger to administration and to character. In the countries where promotion by merit is now practically unknown, respectable mediocrity and a tame discharge of routine duties have come to be the almost invariable notes of the junior men in the Civil Service. If, therefore, as seems probable, the State is continually extending its control over industry,

---

[1] It may be added that as late as 1808 the Portland Administration intended to put the Duke of York in command of the British army in Spain, passing over Wellington. Fortunately, the newspapers learned what was in the air, and attacked it so violently as to make it impossible. —Greville's *Memoirs*, vol. i. p. 64.

and is taking men more and more into its pay, not only will the stimulus of competition, which has often perhaps been excessive, be removed throughout the services, but the standard of work in all departments is likely to be kept at so low a level that a great school of training for character will be lost. Neither will the State be quickened into emulation of its neighbours if, as seems probable, protective tariffs defend native industry against competition, and reduce interchange within the smallest possible limits.

There are two other ways in which it seems probable that the increased powers which are of necessity claimed by bodies politic will interfere with the free development, or at least with the free expression of religious and political thought. The right of free meeting has commonly been regarded by Englishmen as something like an inherent attribute of citizenship. Even in England, however, it has repeatedly been found necessary to restrain it. In 1795 and 1820 this was done by stringent and unpopular Acts of Parliament, against which public opinion pronounced decisively, and which were, in fact, intended for the moment's need. In 1843 a British Government of scrupulous moderation was compelled to forbid a monster meeting of Irishmen at the Hill of Tara. In 1848 London was filled with troops and special constables, because a monster meeting of Chartists was convened on Kennington Common. Since then there have been repeated occasions when the West End of London has been visited with panic or with riot, because crowds were being addressed in Hyde Park.[1] Therefore, even in England, the right to

---

[1] *E.g.* in 1866, when Mr. Beales headed the Reform demonstration; and in 1884, when 80,000 men met in Hyde Park; and in February 1886, when there were riots.

hold large political meetings is beginning to be questioned or limited, and the right to organise religious processions has been severely abated. On the Continent large meetings in the open air have never had the indulgence of English practice accorded to them,[1] and meetings in rooms are habitually watched by the police. The temptation for any strong party in the State to make a demonstration by showing that it is backed by imposing numbers must always be very great; and, at the same time, demonstrations of this kind may easily be the prelude of civil war. Moreover, politics and religion are intermixed. A large body of Catholic pilgrims may express its convictions in a way that is dangerous to civil order; a procession of Orangemen may provoke a faction fight; and a parade of the Salvation Army is often the occasion of riot. It seems, therefore, to be highly probable that civil society everywhere will adopt a uniform practice, and will forbid large assemblages in the streets or in open spaces, except on occasions of general interest and specified by law. Now it can hardly be said that such a regulation would be any great restraint upon liberty; and yet it is impossible not to feel that it would diminish the influence of the emotional element in human nature. Processions and mass meetings have been instinctively adopted in every country and every age, because they worked upon the imaginations and strengthened convictions or communicated ideas by the contagion of sympathy. The impulse of great change has constantly been derived from demonstrations of this kind. Forbid them, and what administrations will gain in stability will be lost to all the causes that are in an actual minority.

[1] The "loi contre les attroupements" of April 10, 1831, forbids open-air meetings, under penalties going up to two years' imprisonment, and three years' loss of electoral rights.

Incomparably more important than even the right of holding public meetings has been the permission habitually accorded to refugees from one country to become naturalised in another. The right of asylum is perhaps more likely to be extended than withheld. The enthusiasts who make changes are, however, as a rule, not wealthy, and in the rare cases where a rich man is a reformer it is commonly difficult for him to transport his property, unless he has been making provision for the worst with almost unexampled caution. If we take some of the great emigrations, for conscience' sake, during the last three centuries, it is obvious that the Flemings, the French Huguenots, and the Palatines could not have settled in England and Ireland if they had not been allowed to work at the industries they were acquainted with. Similarly, if the Irish Catholics, who swarmed into France and Spain during part of the eighteenth century, had been denied everything but the right to be food for powder, the influx could never have assumed the vast proportions it did. Now there are many signs at present that the employment of aliens is getting to be regarded with disfavour all the world over by professional men and by artisans. Habitually, in the case of the learned professions, the State, influenced by native protectionists, professes to be alarmed lest unqualified persons should trade upon the credulity of the public, and declines to recognise, or only partially recognises, those who have not the hall-marks of its own degrees. The excuse is sometimes exceedingly plausible. Thus, for instance, the Medical Board in Victoria has refused to register a Chinese doctor with a diploma from a medical school in China on the ground that he had not studied anatomy,[1] and the result is that, though the thousands of Chinamen in Victoria are not absolutely debarred the professional aid they naturally believe to be best, the Chinese practitioner cannot legally call himself a doctor, or recover fees. In France there has been a movement against allowing foreign artists to exhibit, and a strike against the employment of foreign models. More reasonably, the enlistment of aliens in the army or navy is getting everywhere to be more and more unusual. The teaching profession has been the constant asylum of exiles. In proportion as the State assumes the direction of this does it confine the service to those who have passed its own special tests, and at this moment an English teacher with the highest certificates cannot obtain the lowest classified post in Victoria unless he submits to a fresh examination, nor conversely can a Victorian in England. Louis Philippe at one period supported himself by teaching mathematics in a Swiss school.[2] Scarcely any public institution would now receive an alien, especially one who, like the Duc de Chartres, was not possessed of a University degree, however competent he might be. Naturally the feeling which asserts itself so strongly among professional men is operative also among handworkers. When labourers are imported, or emigrate out of one country into another, it is generally because they have a lower standard of comfort than the natives whom they will come in competition with, and are

---

[1] In the case of Yee Quock Ping. The Victorian courts upheld this decision of the Medical Board.

[2] He did this in the College of Reichenau, near Coire, in the Grisons, rising every morning at four to do his work, and remaining in the occupation for fifteen months under the name of Corby. He owed his appointment to the patronage of General de Montesquieu.—Stephens, *French Revolution*, vol. ii. p. 509; *Memoirs of Mdme. de Genlis*, vol. iv. p. 180, note by editor.

prepared to work for lower wages. It is urged against them with a good deal of justice, that they displace men who are better citizens and on a higher grade of civilisation than themselves, and also in many cases that they work cheaper because they do slop work. Accordingly the feeling against allowing foreigners to come over in any large numbers is getting to be strong in the Old World, is noticeable in Australia, and is perceptible as a tendency even in the United States. At the same time several States that once encouraged the immigration of foreigners for economical reasons, are now reversing their policy on the ground that only a homogeneous nationality can be safely administered. France is less a home than it was for Germans; Germany is driving out the Poles or forcing them to renounce their language; and Russia is taking very strong steps not only against the Jews, but even against the German colonists in the South, who were anciently invited over by Government agents, and favoured with grants of land.

Now, that nations themselves may lose largely under a system which forbids the infusion of foreign blood is more than probable. Russia could scarcely have emerged from barbarism or become a great power without the aid of men of the most various nationalities;[1] and in England, even if we exclude the descendants of aliens, there is a noticeable list that includes men like the statesman Bentinck, the soldiers Schomburg and Ruvigny, the engineer Brunel, the philologist Max Müller, and the painter Alma Tadema. The greater loss, however, is likely to be on the side of individual liberty. Till lately the restless and

[1] Gordon, Le Fort, Schein, Patkul, Münnich, Villebois, Greig, Elphinstone, Benningsen, Wittgenstein, and Pozzo di Borgo.

energetic man who dissented from the faith or disapproved the government of his country has known that if he is driven into exile he may begin life again in a new country, not indeed without some loss, but without let or hindrance from law. Napoleon himself advised Auguste de Staël to take service in England when he refused, from filial piety, to accept an appointment in France.[1] One of the Roman triumvirs of 1849 earned an honourable living by teaching Italian in Oxford, and no less a man than Garibaldi was glad to take work for a time in a soap-boiling factory in New York. A future Saffi may find that the right to teach at Oxford is confined to Oxford graduates, and a future Garibaldi that he will have to take out his citizenship before he is allowed to do manual labour of any kind in a strange country; it may be even that to take out his citizenship will be as difficult in a good many parts of the world as it is in Switzerland. The inevitable result of all this must be to impose silence upon the men who are inclined to take up arms against abuses in politics or in the social system. The Liberal reformer under a despotism will know that if he escapes being shot or imprisoned he will be starved for want of employment when he is in exile. The man who finds himself ostracised by society, as Godwin and Shelley were, will have to change his name like Godwin,[2] if he has not, like Shelley, private means to fall back upon, and the chance that an unpopular man can disguise himself under an *alias* in his own country is becoming appreciably less as the right to investigate every man's private surroundings is more

---

[1] *Memoirs of Mdme. de Rémusat*, vol. ii. p. 414.
[2] Godwin had to disguise himself under the *alias* of Baldwin when he went into business as a bookseller.

and more conceded to the press. It is quite conceivable that while the laws of every civilised state become increasingly tolerant, the difficulty of changing a fatherland may compel all but the most reckless to refrain from criticising the government, the faith, or the social habits approved by their fellow-citizens. Nor, indeed, is it easy to see why England should accord the old privileges to aliens simply that the expression of thought in France and Germany may be free. Yet that fearlessness of speculation and speech is bound to die out when frank, even unguarded words are more or less certain to involve ruin to a man, and to those he holds dearest, is tolerably certain. Even reserve, even the reputation of thinking have been dangerous under some despotisms. The time may come when all who wish to be safe will render lip-service to the powers that be, and will school their very features into acquiescence, and when that arrives the capacity of feeling strongly will die out.

Happily, the secret force which has acted as a solvent of the old society is to a great extent independent of political combinations. The spirit of scientific inquiry is indeed likely to profit very much by many incidents of the new order. As education is diffused and becomes increasingly secular in its tone, the public that welcomes and can appreciate the results of science is likely to be enlarged. Even on the extreme assumption that State Socialism should discourage practical invention as unfavourable in its immediate results to the labourer, or should starve out inventors by virtually confiscating the proceeds of discovery, there would still be the great domain of abstract science, which is what the minds that chiefly influence progress are most interested about.

When we consider how careless of gain the greatest men of the past have been—from Roger Bacon and Newton to Faraday and Brunel—or, in another department of thought, from Leibnitz and Pascal to Herbert Spencer and Littré, it seems that we need hardly apprehend that philosophy will cease to labour, even though the State, like the old French terrorists, should conceive that it has no need of chemists. On the other hand, there seem to be some strong reasons for expecting that science will do more for us in the future than she has attempted in the past. The first steps, that were the most difficult, have been made, and it looks as if nothing were now needed but to enter in and possess the promised land. In every department of thought there appears to be promise of infinite possibilities. The physiologist dreams of penetrating the mystery of life; the chemist of forming all possible natural combinations in his laboratory from the diamond to sugar; the engineer of extending his triumphs over space. Beyond and above all these there is the vague hope that science may succeed better than religion, either in lifting the veil of the unseen world, or in demonstrating that we need nothing but the seen. Let it be conceded that the fairyland in which our fathers lived has become impossible, and that constituted as we are we find it difficult to believe in anything where we cannot trace the sequence of cause and effect. Even so, a clearer insight into some fragment of the Divine order—something to assure us of eternal sympathy behind eternal power—may mean the bringing back of a faith which was once salutary, and which the world seems poorer for needing.

Unhappily, those who anticipate that science and faith may be reconciled, or that science will give us a new and better religion, seem a little to have underrated the difficulties that have to be overcome before either dream can be realised. It is possible, no doubt, to find theologians who think they can substitute belief in the benevolence of Divine law for belief in a sympathetic and personal God, and who are prepared to discard all that has constituted religion hitherto—belief in miracles, belief in a life beyond the grave, belief in a God who cares for man so that He has put on humanity. It is possible also to find scientific men who assume that religion may be reduced to belief in a great First Cause and the practice of a few ethical principles recommended by long experience. It is doubtful whether even these views, though they converge, could ever meet. Science, with its God in the shape of a plausible hypothesis, and with its shifting lines of morality, could only signal across an impassable gulf to the faith that would regard its purified intuition as the one reality in the world. Outwardly the quietist, who will not pray or wish lest he should be asking of God something that has been better ordered already,[1] is on the same plane as the scientific man, who believes that our acts and thoughts are the exact expression of our antecedents, and cannot be changed. Practically the one man is penetrated with a sense of Divine sympathy, and the other with belief in an order of abstract laws in which sympathy would be irrational and misplaced. Whatever befall the quietist, his obligation to support the burden of life cannot be affected, and his sense of absolute trust in God may even be deepened and purified as he is detached from earth. To the scientific man death by

---

[1] " Wir beten es gescheh', mein Herr und Gott, dein Wille."
" Und sieh, er hat kein Will', er bleibt ein' ewige Stille."
Deutsche Liebe, S. 74.

his own hands seems to be the natural relief from trouble, if he can once assure himself that the balance of probabilities is against his receiving what he deems desirable from life. It is needless to trace the infinite divagations into which even the morality sanctioned by science would stray from religious practice. We must either admit that two theories of religion are equally possible, and to appearance equally good, or we must be content to allow that the Stoic conception of a sublimated humanity, which is the counterfeit of religion that science would naturally adopt, is not to be called religion, though it is very beautiful and grand. Nevertheless it is probable that either system of thought gains in proportion as its teachers succeed in understanding one another. For Christianity it is a great gain to be gradually discarding fables that reduced it to the level of an ordinary mythology. For science the lesson that it does not satisfy every want, cannot teach everything, may be inappreciable.

Of the infinite possibilities of science it becomes those who are not within the sacred portals to speak diffidently. Though the dreams of an Erasmus Darwin or a Tschernischevski[1] may still be far from accomplishment, what has actually been done is so great, and has now and then been so far beyond calculation, that it seems difficult to raise our hopes of practical discoveries too high. It is, however, in the loftiest results of science, its insight into law, that the mind has to look for its noblest satisfaction ; and it is by showing itself to be

[1] Dr. Erasmus Darwin proposed to temper the climate of tropical zones by rigging icebergs up with sails and letting them drift southward. Tschernischevski, in his *What is to be Done?* anticipates the time when the ploughman will go out from his home in a splendid club to set machines going which will relieve him of all work, while he is sheltered by an awning from sun and rain (p. 338).

inexhaustible that science must retain its ascendency. Now, it is surely not unreasonable to surmise that there are limitations in the nature of the universe which must circumscribe the achievements of speculative research. Every astronomer knows that there was only one secret of the universe to be discovered, and that when Newton told it to the world the supreme triumph of astronomy was achieved. Whether Darwin or some one else shall have disclosed the other great mystery of the generation of life, it is none the less certain that all future triumphs will be insignificant by the side of the first luminous hypothesis. Chemistry rests, when all abatements have been made, on the atomic theory, and even if future investigation enables us to forecast with absolute precision what the result of combinations hitherto unattempted will be, so that we can calculate in the study what is now worked out gropingly in the laboratory, that discovery would hardly eclipse the merit of Dalton's contribution to science.[1] So it is in every department of research. Even the greatest men are little more than sagacious interpreters of thought and toil which others have expended obscurely. The discovery of a new metal, a new star, or a new species is now nothing to thrill us with wonder and awe. We know that it has been worked up to by former experiments or is the result of improved instruments, and is no more matter of wonder than that this year's best steamship should make a knot an hour more than was possible five years ago. Then again, not only is science ceasing to be a prophet, but in virtue of her very triumphs, precisely because her thoughts are passing into the life-blood of the world, is

[1] The late Professor H. J. S. Smith was inclined to think this possible and worth working for.

she losing visible influence as a liberal education. It is coming to be matter of history that she has taught us to substitute law for caprice in our conceptions of the Divine will; that she has relegated the belief in secondary causes and the belief in arbitrary interpositions of the First Cause to the lumber-room of fable; that she has given us a broader and intenser view of nature, while she has left us the fairyland of the world's childhood for an appreciable treasure. Other harvests have now been gathered in. The prophet and leader is rapidly becoming a handmaid. Her possibilities can be pretty accurately summed up or forecast in a cyclopædia; and having delivered herself of her one imperishable protest against popular theology, she has no other great moral truth to declare.

If, however, science fails us, we shall be impoverished in that very region of intellectual toil from which alone we have a right to expect exceptional results. Science for many years past has appeared to press the higher imagination into her service, or at least fancy and imagination have seemed to be less rich than they were in their own special department—that of poetry. Nature, as the old logicians used to say, does nothing at a bound; and there has accordingly been a noticeable revival of poetry during the early period of the present century, such as might tempt an optimist to believe that the world had been endowed with a second youth. Goethe, Schiller, and Heine in Germany; Victor Hugo and De Musset in France; Leopardi in Italy; Lermontoff and Puschkin in Russia; and Tegner in Sweden, had for contemporaries in England a marvellous phalanx beginning with Wordsworth, Byron, and Shelley, and ending with Browning and Tennyson. Even if there were a silent fifty years after the last of these great men had produced really great work, it would be rash to infer that the creative faculty had said its last word. Nevertheless, looking back upon the past and counting up what we have lost, it is impossible to feel very sanguine as to the future. Certain kinds of poetry have become impossible; certain others are rapidly being exhausted. Can any one conceive that an epic poem could be written in this age? The epic turned upon the fortunes of society—the dramatic incidents of war or travel—in days when the individual could really incline the balance of a battle or an adventure by his own prowess. Modern war is a series of scientific problems, in which masses are manœuvred and the individual hardly emerges; modern travel, though it may lead us now and again into a wonderland of man-apes or of Herodotean dwarfs, or of deserted cities and Titanic ruins, tells its tale best in prose, and is bound to tell much that cannot be given in a few picturesque strokes. The pastoral is doomed. So far as it had any reality, it was based on contrasts that have ceased to be sharp and interesting, or on a feeling for country life that is now more naturally expressed in a subjective form, such as Wordsworth has employed. The satire as Horace and Juvenal, Dryden, Boileau, and Pope fashioned it has fallen into comparative disuse, and the temper of modern times would scarcely endure the religious vehemence of Juvenal or the vitriolic epigrams of Dryden and Pope. The poetical drama, except in France, has given us nothing for two centuries but pieces for the closet, and in France only Victor Hugo has produced anything for the stage that deserves to be read for its intrinsic worth. Putting aside Shakespeare, whose powers were so godlike and exceptional that it seems unreasonable to draw any argument from them, we may surely say that there are at least six poets of the Elizabethan era, the meanest of whom showed more workmanlike conception of what was needed for dramatic representation of effective plot and situations than is to be found in Shelley, Byron, Browning, and Swinburne, though the least of these is superior in poetic feeling and taste to Beaumont, Webster, and Ford, and to Marlowe in all but two or three passages. There are, in fact, only two classes of poetry in which modern craftsmen have vindicated themselves. One of these is the epic of society of which *Don Juan* is the best instance for light sarcastic workmanship, and *Childe Harold* the most perfect for serious style. In each of these great poems, however, though social subjects are more or less touched upon, the treatment is more purely subjective—more concerned with individual characteristics and feelings—than as they would have been rendered by an old artist handling them. In this particular the story of society, as distinguished from the story of national life, is true to the spirit of its age. Where modern poetry has really discovered a new world, and is unapproachable, has been in its lyrical reproduction of moods and passions. The first part of *Faust*, perhaps altogether the most consummate poem of the last hundred years, derives its singular perfection from the blending of three distinct forms of art in a very exquisite form. There is an epical thought in the background of the piece. The idealist destroying his own past that he may build it up anew reflects the genius of the times when the French Revolution was in the air. Only it was not natural to the poet to conceive an epical movement in an epical form. Then again, there is a dramatic action in the scene where

Faust—a free agent but caught in the devil's meshes—is bringing the Furies into a quiet home. Still, the most effective parts of the so-called drama are the passages of self-questioning monologue or declamation and the purely lyrical pieces. Of course, dramatic and lyrical poetry both deal with the expression of human feeling, and the boundary line between them is often invisible. Still, it is probably correct to say that the drama takes for its principle of organic structure the action of men and women upon one another, while the lyrical poem expresses the feelings of men and women in themselves. Unavoidably, therefore, the dramatist is more popular in his treatment and the lyrical poet more subtle. Othello, thinking out his causes and motives of jealousy as Browning would have depicted him, would have expressed himself in very different words from those which Iago's incisive prompting draws from him.

Now the lyrical work of the present century would seem to be distinctly in advance of any work of that exact kind done heretofore. In the ode, the battle-song, the love-song, and the drinking-song, the poets of the past cannot easily be beaten. These all are lighted up by the glint of social life. On the other hand, if we take the form of poem that hints rather than develops a thought, but hints what it means with precision, and suggests what it would be tedious to express—that form in which Goethe would have been unrivalled if Heine had not come after him,—we find that the passion, the national feeling, the religious doubt, the social cynicism of the present age have been expressed in infinite variety with marvellous wealth of feeling. Discriminate the substance from the form, and we shall see that Milton's *L'Allegro* and *Il Penseroso*—professedly the expression of individual temperament—are yet thronged with pictures of life and its works; while dramas like *Manfred, Luria,* or *Erechtheus* are little more than splendid collections of passages reflecting the subjective moods of the poet. That great poets who were essentially lyrical should constantly have preferred to tell a story in narrative or dramatic form may be ascribed partly to the influence of old association, and partly to the greater variety which is offered by modes of verse that are not in their essence limited to a few stanzas. Even here, however, it may be remarked, that no one, as a rule, tells an old story again without changing its model for the worse if he deviates from the original. The writers of the *Morte d'Arthur* were not craftsmen of the highest order, though they understood how to diversify the rather monotonous tale of chivalrous adventure, and were sometimes capable of fine touches. They possessed, however, an instinct of congruity which kept them from anachronisms of manner and anomalies of ethical feeling. They recoiled from the naked story of Geraint and Enid as inappropriate to knightly times; they conceived Vivien as an overfond woman, not as a *fin-de-siècle* lorette craving for notoriety; and they never dreamed of bringing Arthur to preach morality to the penitent woman who lay before him in tears.

There is perhaps another reason besides a growing failure in the capacity to conceive or work out dramatic situations why the drama in its old form has ceased to be possible, except as a trick or sleight of the imagination. If a change in social relations has made the epic impossible by dwarfing the immediate agency of the individual, a change in manners has robbed the drama of a great deal of its effect. The carnage in *Othello*, though awful and pitiful even to men of that day, was not improbable.

The husband had the notorious right to kill his wife if she were taken in flagrant guilt, and a Southern husband might be assumed to do a little more. Single combat was so frequent and serious that, of authors contemporary with Shakespeare, Ben Jonson had killed two men, and Marlowe was himself killed in a brawl. Jealousy may be as strong a passion now as then; it is said to have transformed the whole nature of one of the noblest writers in France;[1] but it would not in the socially-elevated class lead to prompt and undisguised murder. Take, again, the drama of filial ingratitude. A great French author has treated again the subject of Lear in the most powerful of his works;[2] and the modern Lear is nothing more than a man whom his daughters are ashamed of, having themselves married into a different sphere, and who delights in making unselfish sacrifices for their pleasure. Neither would the tone of modern manners allow the father, who had divested himself of estates and who was repaid with ingratitude, to complain as vociferously as Lear does. The world everywhere is more orderly and reticent than it was, and less suited to theatrical effects. No doubt it is still possible to contrive picturesque situations by choosing topics from ancient history, or from political conspiracies in half-civilised countries, or by descending to life among the criminal classes, or on their fringe. In all these cases, however, the mind of the reader is generally unfamiliar with the order of thought that makes such transgressions of law possible, and in the scenes from actual but low life is apt to be more disgusted by the vulgarity of the surroundings than

---

[1] See the account of P. L. Courier's later life in the *Souvenirs de Soixante Années*, by Delécluze, pp. 248-252.
[2] Balzac in *Le Père Goriot*.

moved to pity or terror by the tragical circumstances of the tale told.

There is, however, another reason, which is perhaps tending to make the drama less possible than it was, and the reason is one which tells, in a less degree, against all poetry. Human nature, various as it is, is only capable after all of a certain number of emotions and acts, and these as the topics of an incessant literature are bound after a time to be exhausted. We may say with absolute certainty that certain subjects are never to be taken again. The tale of Troy, the wanderings of Odysseus, the vision of Heaven and Hell, as Dante saw it, the theme of Paradise Lost, and the story of Faust are familiar instances. Less certainly, we may say that wherever a great dramatist, like Shakespeare or Molière, has left a masterpiece of successful delineation of character, artists will be slow to hazard rivalry and the world to tolerate it. Take, for instance, *Othello*. Such a subject as jealousy cannot, of course, be renounced simply because Shakespeare has treated it, and Webster in *Love's Sacrifice* has given us an innocent wife, a perfidious accuser, and a husband stirred to deadly revenge; but Webster, though it probably did not occur to him that there might be some irreverence in counterfeiting *Othello*, was yet careful, from the different bent of his genius or to avoid the charge of plagiarism, that his conception should be essentially diverse. His husband is no Moor with a sense of incongruity about his marriage; his wife has broken no filial vow, and though she is chaste in body has strayed in thought; and the artificer of ruin is not a man with a grudge against the husband, but a courtier wishing to gain influence. Take again the religious hypocrite as limned in *Tartufe*. Our old literature abounds in caustic satire of the canting Puritan — from Jonson's Zeal-of-the-Land-Busy to Howard's Committee-Men.[1] Nowhere, however, is the sketch so full and particular, and for the world at large—even the English world—it may safely be said that Tartufe is a living original, whom it would be difficult to displace. Now it is in the nature of things that the strongest types and the best adapted for stage purposes should gradually be used up. Effective adaptations of an old subject may still be possible; but it is not writers of the highest capacity who will attempt them, and the reading world, which remembers what has been done before, will never accord more than a secondary recognition to the adaptation. It is not the least merit of Sheridan that he thoroughly understood this, and made his Joseph Surface an original by endowing him with the platitudes of social morality, and suppressing all reference to the religion that Tartufe desecrates. Precisely, however, because these types have been so inimitably sketched is the man who would tread in the same path uncomfortably circumscribed.[2]

Now if there are limits to the conception of human characters, into the making up of which so many elements and motives enter, much more must there be a limit to the expression of feeling and emotion. In Hamlet or Beatrice or Macbeth we pass from one phase of thought

[1] Ben Jonson's *Bartholomew Fair*; Sir R. Howard's *The Committee*. Compare Scrapeall in Shadwell's *Squire of Alsatia*.

[2] Perhaps as strong an instance as any of the way in which later writers are circumscribed by the existence of a recognised type is to be found in the influence exerted by Molière's *Misanthrope*. The character of Alceste has been imitated by Wycherley in the *Plain Dealer*, and by Marivaux in *Les Sincères*. Wycherley in the effort to be original has made his honest man boisterous and brutal, while Marivaux has refined him away into a very ordinary gentleman, who is a little wanting in tact.

to another, and filial sentiment or noble indignation is played off against speculative philosophy, or the woman is shown in sunshine or in storm, or the irresolute man capable of guilt is contrasted with the criminal seared by the enjoyment of power. But the single mood of thought, expressed even in its most various inflections, does not admit of very wide treatment. Browning is not easily surpassed for analysis of motive in thoughtful men; but Browning wrote more at length when he developed a character in dramatic form—in *A Blot in the 'Scutcheon* or *A Soul's Tragedy*—than when he made his subject soliloquise, as in *Andrea del Sarto* and *Cleon* and *Bishop Blougram's Apology*, and it is noticeable that even in these he conceives an imaginary opponent, in order to bring out his thought with greater amplitude. If we turn to Heine, who was more supremely artistic than Browning, we find that he can commonly put the suggestion of sentiment or the touch of observation he desires to express into a dozen or twenty lines. Perhaps it may be added that concision in thought—the power to give the greatest effect with the fewest strokes—is the surest passport to immortality. At any rate, when we consider that the drinking-song and the Cotyttian lyric are now becoming obsolete, that there is presumably less strong passion in the world, and that what there is, is more reticent, that the greatest problems of thought have been hackneyed and made commonplace by discussion, and that a certain trick of workmanlike style is much more generally diffused than it was, it seems difficult to predict that the future of the modern lyric will be as bright as its past. It appears possible to imagine a not very distant time when the student will recoil from every new variation in worse verse of the old themes, as a lover of music closes his ear against familiar melodies ground out on a barrel-organ, and when men gifted with the power to feel and write will be paralysed if they attempt earnest work with the recollection that almost this exact thing has been done before, and has passed into household words or speech.

To some it may seem that the novel, which has been a very potent instrument in supplanting the drama, is never likely to die out, and may in a satisfactory measure take the place of poetry. No one can question that a great amount of very high ability has been spent upon the novel during the present century. Scott and George Eliot, Dickens and Thackeray, Hawthorne and Manzoni, Balzac and Charles de Bernard are only a few in a host of distinguished names. Tried by a rough and popular but fairly good test, these writers have all created types that the world has agreed to accept as very masterly. Scott, though there are signs that he is being forgotten, popularised a conception of Scotch character in its chivalrous capabilities and homely work for which his countrymen owe him a deep debt of gratitude. No other writer has done so much to invest the life of a small community with imperishable interest. Of the other writers mentioned, one—George Eliot—has been almost Shakespearean in the power of putting life into every touch; while Dickens, Thackeray, Balzac, and Manzoni, working more elaborately and at length, have made characters such as Pecksniff and Becky Sharp, Le Père Goriot and Don Abbondio, appreciable additions to the world's repertory of dramatic memories. Of Hawthorne it may safely be said that his idealism was poetical in a very high degree, and yet that one can hardly imagine it expressed intelligibly in verse.

Nevertheless, when all is said it is difficult to conceive the novel taking the place for a new society which poetry has filled for the elder world. If we take the most perfect prose ever written and contrast, let us say, the last chapters of the *Agricola* with the death of Marcellus, Burke's lament on the loss of his son with Milton's sonnet upon his blindness, or Burke's description of the ravage of the Carnatic with Milton's sonnet on the Vaudois, or if we compare De Quincey and Ruskin at their best with Shelley and Keats, we shall surely find that the great poem haunts the memory more certainly than the majestic prose. Neither is this merely for the reason which first suggested verse, because metre and rhythm and alliteration and rhyme are aids to remembrance, but because the limitations poetry exacts are apt to give it concision and simplicity of outline, while its very nature allows it to run riot in ideas and imagery. Now, these reasons will always make the poetical form where it is appropriate more durable and less easy to recast than prose, and it seems more likely that Scott should be superseded than that Homer or Dante should be rewritten. In one way this is to the advantage of the world, which may count upon a perennial supply of novels; but in proportion as it is appreciated will it dishearten the best novel-writers with their work, or induce them to essay other fields of literary enterprise.

While it seems unavoidable that science should come to appear less and less a revelation from God, and that poetry should degenerate into mere literary bric-à-brac, such as the composition of rondels and triolets now is, there are two departments of thought in which it would seem that the human mind may look for compensation—history and criticism. That history will ever be brought to such perfection that we shall be able to forecast the future in more than a very general way is perhaps only a dream. That it may reconstruct the past in a manner that was not even hoped for a century ago seems indisputable. We are getting to understand the constitution of primitive societies by studying primitive man as we still have him in savage communities; we are beginning to comprehend the genesis of agrarian laws, and of laws regulating property of all kinds, as each country develops a school of scientific jurists. When we consider what Gibbon did without the aid of critical editions, with some sources of knowledge sealed to him, and before comparative philology existed, for times of which our records are lamentably imperfect, it seems difficult to set limits to what another Gibbon might achieve under more favourable conditions. Even for English history the work of preparation has only been begun. Were the whole of our public records printed, indexed, and digested, as a small portion has been, the whole history of families, of property, and of administration in England might be given with very few gaps for something like seven hundred years. A book like De Tocqueville's *Ancien Régime*, which forced highly educated men absolutely to recast their notions of a period of history only distant by two generations, is probably still possible for every country in every century of its existence. Now, it may be admitted of Gibbon and of De Tocqueville that, with the instinct of genius, they took two of the greatest subjects available, and, like Newton and Darwin, discovered worlds which are now mapped out and familiar. The Englishman was the first to reconstruct the Roman Empire in a way that men with ordinary political insight might apprehend—the first and perhaps the only one in England to write the true history of the Christian Church.[1] De Tocqueville's work, less colossal in scope but scarcely less astonishing, was to show that what men regarded as an outburst of unexpected forces was only a violent acceleration of orderly change. Still, it may be fairly said that both Gibbon and De Tocqueville have rather opened up new regions to the exploration of others than done anything so absolutely that it cannot be attempted again. Gibbon, to take a single familiar instance, made the first part of Finlay's *Greece*, if not possible, at least better than it could otherwise have been. From Lavergne to Taine and Stephens every succeeding writer on the French Revolution has begun very much where De Tocqueville left off, and has started from the points he has given to make new and fruitful investigations. Considering the vast fields in the past that remained unattempted, that fresh domains are being added in every generation, that the subject-matter is as wide as human nature in all time, and that nothing is so small as to be despised, nothing so great as to be left unessayed by the historian, it may surely be anticipated that history is bound to occupy more and more thought, and to be more clearly and fully understood as time goes on.

The critical faculty, so far as it applies to reasoning, is almost certain to be stronger in an advanced than in a young society, the only apparent exception being when the young society is one of singular acuteness and the old society stagnant for the time. It seems idle to discuss the importance of scientific criticism. It is the

[1] Cardinal Newman has expressed this opinion : " It is melancholy to say it, but the chief, perhaps the only English writer who has any claim to be considered an ecclesiastical historian is Gibbon."—*On the Development of Christian Doctrine*, p. 5.

orderly faculty that is gradually evolving a new world out of chaos; comparative philology in the place of happy or unhappy guesses by good or bad linguists; history in the place of chronicles; and the basis of a positive belief in the place of old cosmogonies or traditions of miracle. Probably few of this generation can appreciate the incalculable debt which even men of this generation have owed to the critic. Professor Agassiz, whom many still living can remember with affection and reverence, was brought up under teachers who held that God had scattered fossils about the world as a test of faith;[1] and an Oxford teacher of the highest local repute at least thirty years later published his belief that the typical vertebra—a column with lateral processes—was multiplied all over the world as a proof of the Crucifixion.[2] A little later an Oxford divine, the accredited head of a great party in the Church, was consulting with an Oxford anatomist to know if it was not possible to point to a whale that might have swallowed Jonah. Now, it is of course demonstrable that a great deal which is false may be believed without substantial injury to the reasoning powers or faith. Machiavel based a work of acute political philosophy on ten books of Livy, which are a repertory of fable, and Sir Matthew Hale combined very sound judgment as a lawyer, and Sir Thomas Browne a rather rational religion with belief in witchcraft. What we have to consider, however, is first whether men like Machiavel would not have been incomparably more useful to society if they had started from the standpoint of Niebuhr and Maine, and next whether for the mass of men such a belief as that in witchcraft, which

---

[1] Professor Agassiz told me this himself.
[2] *Christian Ethics*, by the Rev. W. Sewell.

was harmful even to Hale, is not inexpressibly degrading and fruitful of bad practice. It must be borne in mind also that scientific criticism is very often much more than a mere negation. It is sometimes from the necessity of the case reconstructive, and it is commonly strongest when it supplies something in place of what it takes away. Darwin might have contented himself with showing the difficulties that beset all existing theories of the origin of species, and in that case his work, however valuable, would have been purely negative. As a fact, the mere process of detecting difficulties led him to what he thought an easier solution of the life of the universe, and his theory, true or false, has served to stimulate inquiry, and has at least, we may perhaps say, given a convenient halting-place for speculation. On the whole, whether we regard its positive results or the masculine tone of thought which it stimulates, the spirit of critical analysis in the domain of positive science seems to be that from which we have most to hope in coming centuries.

The criticism of taste is another matter. That there is an absolute canon of beauty seems hardly questionable when we consider that at a distance of more than two thousand years we are still recognising the transcendent excellence of the best Greek artists in style and marble. On the other hand, that any age can consider itself possessed of a true judgment seems a little doubtful when we bear in mind how constantly opinions have varied upon subjects where there ought to be very little difference. There was probably no man of his day better qualified to write sound criticism on the drama as he knew it than Dryden. Dryden tells us that he loved Shakespeare, and he says a great deal about Shakespeare that shows an appreciation unusual for those times, but he confesses that he admired Ben Jonson more, and thought Beaumont and Fletcher superior for the construction of plots, for natural dialogue, for pathos, and for gaiety.[1] Even this might pass, but before he died Dryden declared Congreve to be the equal of Shakespeare.[2] A century later we find Dr. Johnson praising Shakespeare by comparing him with Rowe, and remarking that he had not perhaps produced "one play which if it were now exhibited as the work of a contemporary writer would be heard to the conclusion."[3] Rowe's best piece is an adaptation of Massinger,[4] and if it were true that the audiences which thronged the London theatres to see Shakespeare's plays cared more for Garrick's acting than for the poet, it is certainly proof, as we should esteem it, that the standard of criticism may decline at times. The simple fact seems to be that Shakespeare, though always popular after a fashion, was above the level of his own times; that he survived on the stage because he was less dependent on tricks of style and modes of society than his contemporaries; that Voltaire by his various notices and Garrick by his acting are responsible for a good deal of the dramatist's popularity in the eighteenth century; and that Coleridge and Hazlitt are the first English critics who did him real justice. It is fortunate for the world that Athenian taste was more discriminative of its great poets.

In spite, however, of Lord Beaconsfield's aphorism

[1] *Essay on Dramatic Poetry.*
[2] " Heaven, that but once was prodigal before,
　　To Shakespeare gave as much, she could not give him more."
　　　　　—*Epistle to my dear friend Mr. Congreve.*
[3] Preface to *Shakespeare.*
[4] The *Fair Penitent* is taken wholesale from the *Fatal Dowry*—See Cunningham's *Life of Massinger,* p. 18.

that "critics are writers who have failed,"[1] the fact probably is that literary criticism more often errs by indiscriminate praise than by imperfect recognition. Dryden's panegyric on Congreve is an instance in point, and though we may assume that it was a little coloured by personal friendship, praise so deliberately given in his noblest style by a critic with a reputation to support must be regarded as on the whole a genuine opinion. No one now doubts either that Congreve was very clever or that he is not one of the immortals. Dr. Johnson's *Lives of the Poets* represent an extremely high average of the work done in England during the eighteenth century. Macaulay's limitation that the critic " was undoubtedly an excellent judge of compositions fashioned on his own principles," must be qualified by the recollection that Johnson's principles were substantially those of the age. Now, that Johnson would have put Cowley on a level with Shakespeare or Milton if he had been asked the question, may fairly be doubted, but his praise of the small man is as liberal as what he awards the great, and more appreciative, and he quotes approvingly a sentiment ascribed to Milton, that Spenser, Shakespeare, and Cowley were the three greatest English poets. His praise of Pope's *Iliad* as " the noblest version of poetry which the world has ever seen," will appear strong to those who remember Spenser's *Ruins of Rome*, Fairfax's *Tasso*, and Dryden's *Vergil* and *Juvenal*, but is reasonable by the side of the eulogy on Savage, a deservedly forgotten poetaster, who is praised so that a foreigner reading the two lives would rank him above Gray. It may be admitted that Dr. Johnson was a man of strong prejudices. What, however, are we to say to Dr.

[1] *Lothair*, vol. ii. chap. xxxv.

Matthew Arnold, a modern critic of feeling, of knowledge, and it may even be said of genius, who has extolled Joubert and De Sénancour, men infinitely below his own standard, as if they were great writers? Must we not assume that personal feeling and peculiarities of temperament enter into the criticism of taste to such an extent that no single judgment can be accepted except as the argument of an advocate? May we not also say that though it is always possible to distinguish excellence, it is not always easy to define proportions while a work is yet new? Of two books that deservedly achieved an immediate and great success —Buckle's *History of Civilisation* and Maine's *Ancient Law*—Buckle's was the greatest triumph at the moment and Maine's has been incomparably the more enduring. Again, the critic of style is perhaps peculiarly liable to be overawed by a great reputation. Where the scientific controversialist can advance observation and experiment in proof of his censure, the critic of taste can do little more than assert a damnatory opinion. At this distance of time few would dispute that George Eliot's works after *Middlemarch* exhibit distinct and lamentable falling off in power, but *Daniel Deronda* at least was as vociferously praised as the author's best work had been.[1] Probably only two or three writers in a generation attain such an eminence that criticism is suspended in presence of their works, but these two or three are the very ones who have most influence in moulding a generation, and in whose regard the verdict of a sane judgment is most desirable.

[1] " There have been the strongest expressions of interest," says George Eliot in her Diary; "some persons adhering to the opinion, started during the early numbers, that the book is my best."—*George Eliot's Life*, vol. iii. p. 298. Even M. Schérer hesitated to express, what he evidently felt, that the book was a comparative failure.—*Essays*, p. 60.

On the whole, it seems difficult to suppose that the criticism of taste will be more discriminative, more independent of contemporary fashion, or more original and suggestive than the criticism of the last century has been. Moreover, if, as this argument has attempted to prove, there is likely to be a general decline in the poetic faculty, criticism will have to occupy itself with worse material, for contemporary writers are after all those with whom the age is bound to be most conversant. Whether men of scholarly taste are even likely to hold their ground as society becomes more distinctly industrial in its tone, and if means are taken to prevent the transmission of easy fortunes, may be fairly doubted; but already the men who are conversant with our old literature are comparatively rare, and the scholars who can appreciate an old classic—Sophocles, Catullus, or Dante—are too few to make any impression on thought. As classical studies are gradually eliminated from all but a few schools, they will become rarer still. In the English colonies I have known, the tendency is to tolerate University training as a necessity for professional men, but to regard primary school education, or something only a little above it, as sufficient for all the needs of practical men and men of the world. Indeed, high schools in Australia seem to be maintained chiefly because some people like their children to have the distinction of a rather costly training, because a few others intend to send their sons and daughters into professions, and because a good many find it convenient to keep their children of a certain age away from home during the day. Now, the primary school Reader of commerce and of educational use has been brought to very great perfection by different editors, and contains a fair sample of what children of thirteen or fourteen will be likely to appreciate or ought to understand. It is giving scores of thousands who would have learned nothing under the old régime a knowledge of some good prose and verse, and is educating many whose mental food would otherwise have been Watts and Tupper and Robert Montgomery to an understanding of Campbell and Macaulay and Longfellow. For its special purpose the best work of this kind can hardly be improved upon. Still, there can be little doubt that selections of this kind are coming to be thought all-sufficient, and are displacing the higher English classics, from Shakespeare to Wordsworth, so that these are less and less studied. The probabilities are that two generations hence it will be rare in any civilised country to find an adult who cannot read or write, or who has not a tincture of letters derived from school manuals and completed by newspapers; but that it will be rarer still to find even a wealthy man who knows the classics as Fox knew them, or who is as conversant with the literature of his own land as Canning and Peel were.

It may be argued with some plausibility, that although works of the higher imagination will perhaps cease to be produced, as the field is exhausted, and as the faculty of subtle criticism dies out among the learned and the multitude, the mind will be able to recover in prose even more than it has lost in poetry. It has been assumed that history will take a wider range than ever; it may be supposed that oratory will become more and more an art, as States governed by Parliaments give more and more advantage to fluent speech. Beyond this the example of Mill has shown how much even political economy may be recommended by a faultless setting; and it may be safely said, that no subject however abstruse—in metaphysics or in natural science—is incapable of being enhanced by style. Plato has embalmed discussions of great subtlety and of difficult argument in prose, which the world will not consent to forget; and Buffon produced a voluminous work on natural history, which made the tour of the world, and was known by repute or by fragments in the salon and in the cottage. Probably the instantaneous success of Mr. Darwin's *Origin of Species* was due very much to the admirable simplicity and sustained interest of the narrative, which even the general public could follow sufficiently to understand. In connection with this it must be remembered that style after all can only be dignified or effective if it expresses dignified or effective thought. The decay of poetry has been assumed to be due to the fact that topics are being exhausted, and that the less varied and emotional life we are approaching will not lend itself to energy and colour in description. Unhappily, very much the same may be said of science. Even if the epoch of great discoveries is not exhausted, the new results are almost certain to be less simple, less sensational, more painfully approached by long processes of inquiry, less easy of comprehension to the outside world than the first revelations of astronomy and geology have been. Goethe has remarked that the beginnings of a science are always its most attractive part. The luminous conception, the broad outlines, the strong contrasts of colouring can be indicated from the first; but as inquiry and research proceed, abatements and modifications of the central theory have to be considered, and the attention is wearied with detail. The man of encyclopædic knowledge is being supplanted by the specialist, and the specialist is constantly finding that he cannot narrow his work too much. Darwin from his wonderful powers was capable of both kinds of work; but we may safely say that his monograph on earthworms, though part of a broad theory, would never have stimulated thought as the *Origin of Species* did. It seems probable, at least, that the Buffon and Darwin of the past will be replaced by a cohort of skilful investigators, each taking for the work of his life an exhaustive inquiry into a single species of *Scarabæus* or *Bakterion*. What happens in physical science will have its counterpart in scientific history. The successors of Gibbon, Mr. Finlay, and Mr. Bury, are inevitably less capable of giving pictorial effect to their narrative, because it is more circumstantial and minute. The mere hesitations of a man balancing evidence are against effect in style; and as the scientific spirit takes nothing on trust, it would not allow even a Gibbon in the present day to present his conclusions more or less positively in a flowing narrative.

The experience of free assemblies during the present century does not seem to sanction the hope that there is a great future for oratory. The very marked tendency has been to substitute what is known as debating for the classical form of speech. In other words, appeals to the feelings are very little valued, and statements of fact and the clear exposition of argument very much. It is difficult to say whether much has really been lost by this transformation. The reports of speeches from the best times of the British House of Commons appear to show that Lord Chatham ranted in very overflown language,[1] that Sheridan was chiefly regarded as an

[1] Lord Chesterfield, a very favourable judge of Lord Chatham, put him below Bolingbroke and Mansfield for "undeviating eloquence," but above them for "the strength of thunder and the splendour of lightning." In one place he says that his matter is generally flimsy, and his argu-

exhibition of fireworks, and Burke hardly listened to at all; and that Fox and Pitt were very much speakers of the modern school. On the other hand, there is some reason to suppose that Sheridan's most remarkable effort—the Begum speech—has been so mutilated in the printed version as to be unrecognisable;[1] and the chances are that this applies in great measure to Lord Chatham. Taking the modern oratory in its best form —a clear business-like argument, relieved by pathetic touches or appeals to generous feeling—it may be admitted to be a measurable force. It has been said that no speech ever changed a vote; but even if this be true of Parliament, there remains the fact that some speeches have powerfully influenced national feeling, and that a party is always the weaker for being without orators. Still there are two strong reasons why we may expect a gradual and growing change towards a lower level of eloquence. One is that the art of public speaking is much more generally practised than it was, and that it is difficult for any one with the limitations imposed by the modern preference for debating to tower head and shoulders above the mob of gentlemen who spout with ease. The other is that the great commonplaces of oratory are even more easily exhausted than those of poetry. Patrick Henry carried a House of Assembly with him by asking if they who had cowed

ments often weak."—*Letters*, Feb. 2, 1751. On the other hand, he allowed him the praise of great versatility; "he excelled in the argumentative, as well as the declamatory way."—*Character of Lord Chatham.* Lord Brougham says that he was charged with often passing from the sublime to the ludicrous.—*Statesmen of the time of George III.* And Lord Macaulay says, that "his merit was almost entirely rhetorical," and that "his style was not always in the purest taste."—*Essay on Chatham.* Lord Lytton sums him up: "Others take force from judgment, fancy, thought; Chatham from passion."—*St. Stephen's*, Part I.

[1] Rae's *Wilkes, Sheridan, and Fox*, pp. 218-233.

the British lion were to be afraid of its whelps.[1] So hackneyed an allusion as to the British lion would now only provoke ridicule. We can hardly doubt that allusions to Marathon and Salamis, though still common, were becoming a joke in the time of Aristophanes. That Demosthenes was able to thrill a judicial assembly with them again[2] testifies to his genius, but does not prove that smaller men could have succeeded by playing upon the same thought.

On the whole, it seems probable, that the best work of men able to write good prose will go even more than it already does into the form of general literature—reviews and newspaper articles. Given a much larger reading public than at present—and State schools are bound to provide this,—and a much lower general level of acquirement and taste than the educated classes of the world have possessed for the last century, it seems inevitable that hand-to-mouth work should meet the essential needs of the generation. No one who considers the admirable results achieved by modern leader-writers and correspondents can doubt that a great deal of supremely good literary power is actually used up in this manner. A hundred years ago an Englishman wanting to be informed about the state of the Continent would have found much better material in Clarke's *Travels in Russia, Poland, and Scandinavia*; in Moore's *Travels in France and Germany*; in Beckford's *Letters from Spain*; and in Brydone's *Letters from Sicily*, than the *Times* or the *Courier* would have given him. At present the current statistics of any Continental country are best learned from a gazetteer

---

[1] "Shall we, who have laid the proud British lion at our feet, now be afraid of his whelps?"—Tyler's *Life of Patrick Henry*, p. 260.

[2] Demosthenes, *de Corona*, p. 297.

or a handbook, and its ephemeral politics or excitement from the special correspondent of any great paper. The old-fashioned traveller has to explore some provincial district, like the Carpathians or Bosnia, or to give information not easily obtained about some interesting stratum of society, if he would attract readers. Books of travel are still numerous; but the traveller only makes a reputation when he opens up a field which the correspondent has not attempted; when he is a Burton, a Vambéry, or a Stanley. It may be a century or more before the world at large is Europeanised, and before all its countries are brought under pretty much the same conditions, so that local dialects, costumes, and customs will have disappeared; but every change in this direction is increasing the capacity of the daily press to deal adequately with what the public cares to know. This is perhaps the least noticed instance of the way in which the press supplies a want anciently catered for in a less ephemeral manner; but of course it has supplanted governments for the ascertainment and propagation of authentic news; and its statistical summaries are practically what the commercial world goes by. All this is so completely within the domain of a newspaper that it seems impossible to regret it, or even cavil at it. That significant or interesting facts should be put freshly before the notice of all is bound to be an important factor in progress. It must be remembered, however, that it is not only new facts which are best disseminated through the newspaper or the magazine. Journalism is the most efficient, if not the only real medium through which new thoughts pass into circulation. So popular a measure as Free Trade might perhaps have been carried anyhow, but was carried ten years sooner than it would have been, because the press gave opportunities for discussing it freely. So abstruse an idea as Hare's, of the representation of minorities, would probably be as forgotten by this time as Harrington's theories, if the press had not from time to time revived it for controversy or advocacy. A thinker, like Hobbes or Harrington, would have gained little in immediate notoriety by writing for the *Mercury* of the day; and would have lost everything in permanent consideration. At present, there is no man contemplating any immediate reform, who may not reasonably balance in his own mind whether he will not exert more influence through a newspaper with a large or an influential circulation than through a book. If he is important enough to be assured that the press will discuss his book adequately, or if his subject is too complicated and vast for newspaper articles, he will naturally prefer the less ephemeral form. Cases of another kind are, however, the more numerous, and to a man who feels that his volume, that has cost years of preparation, may probably only get a success of esteem—half a dozen favourable notices and three months of circulating library existence—the temptation to write in the form that is certain to count readers by thousands, and likely to provoke discussion, is very great, even if his motives are purely disinterested. If, like many authors, he lives to some extent by his pen, the attraction of journalism is incomparably stronger. A list of really successful books that have paid nothing or very little to their authors would include some names of distinction, and many of men who might have done reasonably well if they had put their thoughts into an ephemeral form.

Now, that the press, being as it is bound to be a great power in modern society, should be perpetually recruited from the best thinking ability of the day is in itself highly desirable. What we are bound, however, to regard as an offset to the manifest advantages of the free promulgation and discussion of public matters, is the fact that the journalist's work, calculated as it is for the day's needs, is rarely sufficient for anything beyond. In some cases a man employed for a time on the press has also done permanent work, and the reverence attaching to his name has caused the ephemerides to be collected and preserved. Will any one say that the political articles of Coleridge and Heine, even the literary articles of Goethe, were in any way worthy of their genius? To take more modern instances, is Sir Henry Maine likely to be remembered by his articles in the *Saturday Review*? or Mr. R. H. Hutton by his contributions to the *Spectator*? In all these cases the work bears the impress of the master's genius, but the form is of transitory interest. No doubt, Pascal's most celebrated work was thrown into the form of fugitive letters; and Swift was practically a journalist; and Junius is reputed a classic; and Courier's *Letters to the Censeur* are not easily distinguishable from his other works. Each case has to be examined separately. Pascal put the argument for secular society against churchmen in general, for the inflexible law against moral casuistry, into a form that made it intelligible to the fashionable and popular reader. Whether modern journalism could tolerate so much abstruse controversy is questionable; but at any rate Pascal's genius was exceptional, and much of the *Letters* preserves its vitality from being still applicable to Continental Catholicism. Of Junius, I confess to thinking that he has been extravagantly overrated. He had the good fortune to come at a time when the art of trenchant writing had suffered temporary eclipse, and to espouse popular views against the Court; but Macaulay's casual remark that he was "a most unequal writer,"[1] and De Rémusat's verdict, that he had "more cleverness than inspiration," pretty well reduce him to his proper level.[2] On the whole Swift and Courier seem to be the best instances of transcendent journalism. Now Swift, who is undoubtedly the greatest name in English literature between Milton and Burke, did much more bad work than good when he wrote for the moment. Out of thirty-two articles which he contributed to the *Examiner*, the one comparing Marlborough to Crassus is the only one that lives and is most remembered. No one but a scholar now reads the pamphlet on the *Conduct of the Allies*, or that on the *Barrier Treaty*. The really successful work Swift did as a journalist in the modern sense was in his *Drapier's Letters*; and even these, and some of the pamphlets on Irish matters, owe their real importance to the fact that the author, almost unconsciously, transcended his own purpose, and advocated the more permanent interests of his country, self-government, and an administration that should be regardful of the poor. Even so Swift owes his place among the immortals to the *Tale of a Tub* and to *Gulliver's Travels*, rather than to his attacks on the policy of his own day. We may say equally of Courier—in spite of his own admirable defence of the pamphlet—that he is always best when he handles an adequate theme; and that his *Letters to the Censeur* would not have been preserved

---

[1] *Essay on Warren Hastings.*
[2] De Rémusat, *L'Angleterre au Dix-huitième Siècle*, tome ii. p. 191.

if he had not written the *Pamphlet des Pamphlets* and the *Réponse aux Lettres Anonymes*. Now Courier was a very remarkable and very rare combination. Delécluze tells us that his real passion was to turn a phrase in the happiest possible style; and that he was not so much a fanatical politican as a Rabelaisian critic of whatever seemed extravagant and grotesque in administration. Courier therefore is an exceptional instance of the best conceivable man for newspaper work; a man who is not so much concerned with the thought itself as with the way of putting it before the world. It is surely not unreasonable to think that, as a rule, men who write with the sense that they will not be remembered, and that only the immediate impression is of importance, will differ from those who "speak to time and to eternity," as the moulder in wax differs from the artist in marble or in bronze.[1]

The influence of deep religious feeling and the influence of exalted intellectual energy have been of such incomparable importance in moulding individual character hitherto, that if we assume them to be powerfully reduced it is difficult to see what can take their place. The love of country or reverence for the State which seems likely to supersede both Church organisation and the tradition of family life, is hardly a principle that will strengthen initiative or self-reliance. Now and again, no doubt, in some great time of crisis the State may have to appeal to the self-devotion and fertility of resource of its citizens, but that great times of crisis—wars and social convulsions—will become less and less frequent, more and more temporary in their

---

[1] M. Cousin has developed this idea very forcibly in the preface to *Jacqueline Pascal* (pp. 5-7), "Un homme sérieux n'écrit que par nécessité, et parcequ'autrement il ne peut atteindre son but."

duration, and increasingly mild in the changes they cause, seems a consummation as probable as it is desirable. There remains, however, the question, just worth notice, whether a change in the physical conditions of human life may not affect character for the better. Science has done a great deal, and is constantly holding out the hope of more. Let us assume its anticipations realised—preventible sickness, which includes every form of epidemic, eliminated; the science of healing enormously improved; the average of life prolonged by ten or twenty years; and all this consolidated by the State Socialism which insists upon healthy homes and provides adequate wages. It is no great stretch of imagination to look forward to the day when there shall be a reasonable expectation of life for every child born, when the sorrow of premature bereavement shall be rarely felt, and when even the population of large towns, from which we cannot expect an exuberant vitality, may have such an average of wiry strength and capacity to work and enjoy as will at least render life tolerable. Should these anticipations be realised, it would seem that society ought to gain as it has gained in past years by the political improvements that have made life and property secure, or by the inventions and engineering works that have reduced the frequency of famines. To take exceptional instances, times like the breaking up of the Roman Empire in Europe, the rise of Mahratta power in India, or the Tae-Ping revolt in China, were times that demoralised the imagination and paralysed industry. Even the ploughman and the shepherd very often renounced toil which seemed profitless and turned themselves to plunder or vagabondage, but much more was the higher commerce extinguished and the educated professions died out. At present war is the only great source of ruin that seems likely to be permanent, and even wars are less frequent and shorter and more humane, and lead to less violent change where conquest is absolute. Of political convulsions like the French Revolution we may probably say that they also are likely to be mitigated by the ghastly recollection of the ruin they cause, and by the remedy for social unrest which the spread of liberal institutions offers. The worst effects of floods and droughts are now obviated by the great facilities for international traffic. Therefore, if we can conceive cholera, typhus, and all such diseases extirpated by sanitary science, the diseases that scourge immorality disappearing before a rigid police, and cures, such as are even now anticipated, actually discovered for consumption and cancer, perhaps even for diseases of the liver and kidneys, it will not be too much to say that the present expectation of life under healthy conditions would be more than doubled. Tennyson has alluded to the great stimulus hope would derive if we were

> In lieu of many mortal flies, a race
> Of giants, living each a thousand years.

It does not seem possible that we should ever attain to the thousand years, but there is perhaps nothing palpably unreasonable in assuming that ninety may be for some coming generation what seventy is in our own days; that the death-rate of children, which is one-third in Victoria for the very young of what it is for Austria, Italy, and Spain,[1] may be reduced very far below the healthiest average at present; and that for the ordinary

---

[1] For children under five in Victoria it is 38·6; for the same age in Spain, 106·2; in Italy, 110; and in Austria, 111·7.—Hayter's *Victorian Year-Book* for 1889-90, § 630, and Mulhall's *Dictionary of Statistics*, p. 127.

adult illnesses may come to be so manageable as to be hardly taken into account in the scheme of life. In this case it would seem that the generation would be far more able than now to "see its own work out," and that self-confidence, which is an efficient spring of energy, would be proportionately increased. To take a single instance from literature, Gibbon was only fifty-one when he completed the great work which is an epoch in historical literature. It had taken him twenty-seven years to perfect, and his expectation of life, as he himself tells us, allowed him only about fifteen years more.[1] He seems to have decided that, after taking the rest which was his just due, it would be too late for him to attempt any new task. Yet had his expectation of life been of thirty years instead of fifteen, his decision might have been different, and the world, had his life actually been prolonged, might have been the richer by a work showing Gibbon's ripest learning and maturest thought.

Against this consideration we must perhaps set the fact that a world in which the term of life is sensibly prolonged will be predominantly a world of old people. Unless we can assume, what is most unlikely, that the struggle for existence will become less and less severe as numbers multiply and the earth fills up, we must suppose that countries in the Temperate Zone at least will gradually approximate more and more to the stationary state. Society will accommodate itself to this by late marriages or by conjugal agreements to limit the number of children; and while the proportion of men and women over fifty is now, let us say, one in eight, it may easily come to be one in six. At this

---

[1] "The laws of probability . . . still allow about fifteen years."— *Memoirs of my Life and Writings*, by Gibbon, p. 127.

moment the proportion of persons over sixty-five in France, the capital instance of a civilised country that is stationary, is nearly double what it is England and more than double the proportion in America or Australia, not because the average of life is higher, for it is rather lower, but because the proportion of children born is so incomparably smaller.[1] Now, it may be admitted that none of the evils which Swift depicted as incident to the condition of the Struldbrugs would be likely to arise where the duration of life was still limited, and where physical strength was continued as now till within a short time of decay and death. What we have to suppose is that men with the admirable vitality of Newman, Gladstone, Radetsky, Moltke, Bismarck, Littré, Chevreuil, and Lesseps will become increasingly common, and that, as, in cases where the exact reason is more required than quick insight and promptitude of action or alacrity of eye and ear, the best work is very often done by the old, we may get an increasing average of the best work. We may even conjecture that the predominance of experienced and reflective men in a population—for those between forty-five and ninety might easily come to be more numerous than those between twenty and forty-five—would be an important conservative force balancing the democratic tendency to impulsive change. Increased stability of political order, increased efficiency of exact thought, are possible advantages that cannot be disregarded.

Yet in some respects they would perhaps be dearly purchased. A restriction of the birth-rate means a diminution of family life with its consecrating cares and

---

[1] 810 in the 10,000 in France against 458 in England and Wales, 350 in the United States, and from 119 to 254 in Australia.—Hayter's *Year-Book*, 1889-90, § 140.

pleasures. The protraction of life means that a woman shall outgrow motherhood by forty or fifty instead of by twenty years, and that she and her husband shall relapse practically into the conditions of single life without its liberty or its hopes. The general retarding of marriages will mean the blotting-out of a page of romance which, if often foolish, was almost always bright and animate. That children should be comparatively an infrequent presence will rob life of its most appreciable consolation. But the most visible effect to the world will probably be the decay of energy. If youth is the season of unrest, when change is welcomed for its own sake and when orderly growth is despised, it is also the brooding-time of speculation, the maturing-time of adventure. Old men are probably best fitted for carrying on the mechanical and routine work of the world, but the artists, the poets, the explorers, the propagators of new ideas are habitually to be found among the young. Of two great changes that have powerfully influenced modern society, it may probably be said that both the Reformation and the Revolution owed their impetus to the generation under forty. Wherever war has depended more upon promptitude and insight than upon scientific combinations—that is to say, where it was not imperative to handle great masses and arrange for long distances—the army commanded by a young general—a Condé, a Hoche, or a Napoleon—is apt to triumph over age and military lore. Therefore, if we assume men of middle and of mature age to add the influence of numbers to that which they already get from seniority, it is difficult to suppose that the history of the world will not be a great deal tamer in the future than it has been in the past. That life should be essentially sadder and grayer than it has been may mean very little; that it should be less capable of energy and reform, more prone to entrench itself in an established order, will undoubtedly mean that it is passing into its old age, and that those whom the present does not satisfy will have nothing to hope from what is to come.

It has seemed desirable to dwell minutely upon these conditions of character and action, because if religious conviction is replaced by sentimental morality, if imagination and fancy are circumscribed, finding no worlds to occupy, and if the prolongation of physical existence tends to make society as a whole less energetic and confident of its own powers, it is difficult to suppose that any external motives can take the place of faith, intellect, and hope. Nevertheless, it is easy to see that such external motives as the love of power, the love of money, and the love of fame are likely to become less and less powerful as the world becomes more settled and larger. It will always be an object of ambition to be the first man or among the first men in the community. In the past, however, the great man, whether he were the successful soldier, a Caesar or a Napoleon, or the organising statesman, an Augustus Caesar, a Richelieu, or a Chatham, was a man who had a policy of his own, which he was prepared to carry out single-handed. Such men were necessities of an imperfect civilisation. It needed two men of such different, yet sympathetic genius, as Julius and Augustus Caesar to rescue Roman administration and the fortunes of the whole civilised world from the violence and rapacity of the patrician order. Only a dictator could have crushed the nobles, established French unity, and inaugurated a new and national policy as Richelieu did. Only Chatham's will and insight could have given

England an empire; and only a soldier, wielding the whole military force of the country, could have rescued France from anarchy. To take the example most easily comprehended, can any one imagine a Pitt in these later times dominating a subservient senate, staking the whole fortunes of England upon wars of only half-comprehended importance, and, in order to conciliate the king, maintaining a vast army in Germany, though if the nation had one settled conviction it was to avoid Hanoverian entanglements. When Lord Palmerston, one of the most powerful and popular ministers of his time, meditated an intervention in favour of Denmark, he was met with a private remonstrance from a strong section of his supporters, and found that to carry out his policy he would have to rely upon the votes of his opponents. No doubt what is true of England and America is not yet true, to the same extent, of any Continental State. The most that even a hopeful observer can say is that religious wars are less likely to break out than they were, that States are approximating more and more to their natural limits, and that there is a growing disposition to form alliances that may prevent war from taking place, and that may restrict the acquisitions a conqueror makes. Beyond this, however, we may perhaps hope, without being oversanguine, that as the influence of the masses increases, and those masses are educated, they will throw their weight more and more into the scale of peace. Universal conscription has at least had this advantage, that it forces every household in a nation to realise the inconveniences of military service, and to dread the horrors of war. Every improvement that makes civic life more tolerable will tend to the same result. It is probably safe to say that a Cromwell is already impossible in England or the United States, and that a Napoleon is becoming impossible in France. The statesmen of this generation are not the originators of a policy, but the adaptors of innovations endorsed by public opinion. That the change tends incomparably to the advantage of society is probable, but it undoubtedly dwarfs the individual. Of the various attributes which Gray ascribed to power, the statesman in a civilised country retains only one in its completeness. He can command "the applause of listening senates"; but he is only the exponent of his party if he "scatters plenty," and happily he is no longer permitted to "shut the gates of mercy on mankind."

It is conceivable that the statesman's importance may be circumscribed in another and most desirable way. That change will ever cease to be needful cannot be anticipated. Rather as the sphere of State action is enlarged, the obligation ceaselessly to adjust an enlarged legislation to new wants will come to be more sensitively felt. Still it seems possible to suppose that the most momentous changes are already accomplished. The subordination of Church to State, the abolition of forced labour, the suppression of privilege, the right to express opinions with perfect fearlessness, the humanising of the penal code, have been reforms of such transcendent significance that we can hardly conceive any changes in the future that will renew society to the same extent. If women were to receive the suffrage in any great country, the experiment would excite a good deal of noisy feeling on both sides; but it is difficult to suppose that it could have the importance which the first Reform Bill had for its own generation in England.

A measure to buy back the lands of a country from their owners, such as has been contemplated in New Zealand, would be as important as the seizure of Church lands in England, or as the confiscations of the French Revolution; but it would in all likelihood be carried out more temperately and equitably, and it would not involve the same tremendous consequences—a change of faith or a sudden transformation of the whole social structure. Moreover, something depends on the more or less sensational manner in which a change is effected. Negro emancipation still impresses the imagination as a very memorable fact. In one sense its importance can hardly be exaggerated, for, by recognising the obligation to free even a half-brutal race, England practically accepted an enhanced duty towards the higher forms of labour. Nevertheless, looking back on it, one can see that the actual expectations entertained of lifting a degraded race to a higher level have been absolutely futile. On the other hand, the reforms of the criminal law, which have abolished pressing to death, burning, torture, and promiscuous hangings for almost every kind of fraud and larceny, have been so gradual that they have passed almost unobserved. It is only if we look back and sum them up that we can estimate their full importance, and we mostly forget the names of the men who carried them. It is probable that change in the future will generally be of the same tentative and orderly kind, giving no great popularity or power to the statesman who has the good fortune to associate himself with some of the details.

Swift, in a characteristic passage, declares that the names of those who have rendered the greatest services to their country are to be found upon no record, except a few of them whom history has represented as the vilest rogues and traitors.[1] As even Swift passionately admired half a dozen great men of antiquity, we must allow for some exaggeration in his trenchant aphorism. It is probably truer to say that the public estimate of notable men has always been capricious, and determined by such conditions as personal magnetism or the popularity of the causes they were connected with. To take one conspicuous instance, no one would seriously doubt at the present day that Sir Robert Peel was an incomparably greater man than Canning or Lord Althorp or Palmerston; but it is certain that he was more steadily reviled and depreciated than any of these, or than all three together. Fonblanque wrote of him as the Joseph Surface or Tartufe of politics;[2] Disraeli taunted him before an applauding house with "sublime mediocrity."[3] The facts are, that with every private virtue he was a cold ungenial man in mixed society, and his singular fortune impelled him to carry out two distasteful reforms—Catholic Emancipation and Free Trade—which he had for years tried to avert. Still, even in a case of this kind we can see that the circumstances of modern society are incomparably more just to a reputation than those of the ancient world were. Peel as a Roman of the Empire would have come down to us in the pages of a Suetonius or a Tacitus, as the aristocratic clique loved to speak of him; his greatness would have been toned down by epigrammatic sentences, such as we now know to be unjust, and in all likelihood his memory would have been charged with some scandals of which he was

[1] *Voyage to Laputa*, chap. viii.
[2] Fonblanque's *England under Seven Administrations*, vol. iii. pp. 182, 183.
[3] M'Carthy's *History of our own Times*, vol. ii. p. 214.

wholly innocent. As it is, the worst that has happened
has been that Peel never enjoyed during his lifetime
the harvest of reputation that was his due, and that
the honour we now pay him is as cold and unmeaning
as an epitaph. Still the votary of fame, "that last
infirmity of noble minds," must lay his account for
forfeiting immediate recognition if he wishes to do the
purest work in any capacity. Shelley never lived to
see his works read,[1] and Wordsworth and Browning
were only honoured when they were old. Peel frankly
admitted that to Cobden rather than himself should
have belonged the honour of passing Free Trade into
law; and Cobden was impossible. There is therefore
a chance in these matters which is never likely to be
eliminated. Beyond this, while the great names of
the past are luminous from being few, the prominent
men of modern times are jostled in an almost indistinguishable crowd. One of the few of this generation
in England, whose reputation in the higher mathematics
was more than insular, used to speak regretfully of
the chances by which real distinction of intellect was
enabled to forge to the front in days when the whole
civilised world was scarcely more populous than Scotland
and London together are now.[2]

Napoleon is said to have inquired what the lifetime
of a great picture was, and being told that in the nature
of things it could only last some centuries, to have ejacu-
lated contemptuously, "Quelle belle immortalité!" It
is more than conceivable that, as new nations spring into
prominence, as the record of past time is extended, as
the occupations in which men take interest multiply,

---

[1] With the single exception of the *Cenci*, which went through two editions in his lifetime.
[2] The late Professor Henry J. S. Smith.

fame will become less and less durable, though celebrity will be more and more cheaply purchased. An educated man in Shakespeare's time needed only to burden his memory with a few names, and of those mentioned casually in Montaigne's *Essays* the larger number are now obscure except to professed scholars. It is probably not too much to say that every great epoch to some extent obliterates one that has gone before it. If Wellington's victories had not been won, Marlborough would still be treasured with pride and familiarly known to Englishmen, and it is noticeable that the memory of the War of Independence has become fainter in the United States since the War of Liberation was fought with results equally momentous and with battles upon an incomparably grander scale. War, however, from its tragical circumstances and far-reaching effects, is the surest passport to immortality. Homer is comparatively forgotten, but Alexander is still a name of glory over great part of the world. Courier, indeed, has argued that some one else would have gained the battle of Rocroi if Condé had not been present, but that no one except Molière could have written the *Misanthrope*; and draws the inference that literary fame is of more intrinsic worth than military.[1] Against this, however, we have to set the fact that literary fame is circumscribed by the duration of the phase of the language to which it belongs. To a Frenchman of the present day Molière is only a little archaic, and for civilised men generally French is still one of the languages of society which no one dares disregard; but it cannot be fanciful to anticipate a time when Molière will only be read with a sense of strangeness by Frenchmen and as a classic, and when some new literature, such as Russian, will be dividing

[1] *Conversations chez la Comtesse d'Albany.*

the attention of highly-educated men. Nevertheless, the old dramatists are always likely to retain the advantage of being unsurpassable in a style that modern times will not care seriously to imitate. What, however, are we to say of lyrical poets, of essayists, of the vast multitude who will compete for distinction in such new forms as the coming age will tolerate, and who will be like the sand of the sea for number? It is surely impossible to suppose that the fame of many thousand men contesting recognition on fairly even terms, and producing fairly even work, will be so individual and distinct as to be a measurable incentive to action. Now, the argument that is good of literature will apply to every field of human activity. As chemists, engineers, physicians, lawyers, politicians, and soldiers multiply, it will be difficult, in the language of an old proverb, to see the trees for the wood.

The love of money is perhaps more likely to survive the changes of modern society than either the lust of power or the passion for fame. Even if we assume the State to encroach more and more upon the domain of private industry, and to undermine large properties with taxes and succession-duties, human nature will still remain with its inextinguishable cravings for whatever gold can purchase, and with a fertility of resource for acquiring wealth that will defy legislation. The experience of the United States, though there has been no modifying cause there like State Socialism, is very instructive up to a certain point. Gold in the United States does not purchase political power, and to some extent disqualifies for it. For a long time it did not even give social distinction, and the class that possessed it was unable to enjoy field-sports or costly pictures, and was limited in its private life by the trouble attending large households in a new country. Nevertheless, men went on speculating and accumulating with far more avidity than in Europe, and were very often content to find their reward in the lace and jewels which their wives wore.[1] There was the desire to achieve success against competitors, and there was perhaps a feeling that if wealth was acquired the science of enjoying wealth would gradually be learned. With a few there was the honourable wish to connect their names with great public benefits—to found a Girard College or a Cornell University. It is conceivable that State Socialism, while it reduces the chances of money-making, will even increase its desirability. If we assume industry and property to pass more and more under the control of the State, we are almost bound to assume a large body of State functionaries, none of whom the democratic temper will permit to be very highly paid. A system that turned physicians into public officers salaried by the State, as vaccinators now are in some countries, would almost certainly make no important distinction between the highest and the lowest talent. Unless, therefore, private practice were forbidden, the ablest men would entrench themselves in this, and would probably make larger incomes than they at present do, as they would refer all pauper patients to the State medical men. Again, though it is possible to conceive the State monopolising all the land and all the mines, it is difficult to think that it could set itself to monopolise production and distribution. It may conceivably limit the occupation of land so as to

---

[1] Mrs. Kemble (Butler) gives some instructive instances of this in a note beginning, "I have nowhere seen extravagance to compare with that of American women."—*Further Records*, vol. ii. p. 48.

prevent the building up of large leaseholds, but it can hardly forbid the purchase of corn and cotton on the most extensive scale. Neither can it prevent a particular mine from turning out fabulously rich and giving enormous dividends to its lessees. Even the expedient of taxes designed to break up large properties can only be cautiously applied, as it is certain to be met by evasions and corruption of State officials. Therefore, in the most extreme and hypothetical case that seems at present possible, when the State has taken to itself all land, railways, steamers, canals, tramways, waterworks, gasworks, telegraphs, and telephones, has salaried the professions, and has even invaded finance with a State bank, there will still remain infinite possibilities for speculation and for the amassing of great fortunes. The distance between wealth and competence will indeed be more sharply accentuated than it is at present, for large professional incomes and inherited fortunes will be comparatively rare, and these it is which at present fill up the interval between the small ordinary stipends of clerical work and the great gains of the speculator.

That the passion for wealth will be a little changed in one respect is perhaps conceivable. Hitherto it has generally been associated with the desire to found a family. If, however, we conceive the family ties weakened, and it has been argued that many changes are conspiring to this result, and an active interposition of the State to prevent the transmission of property in great sums, wealth will come to be valued especially with a view to present consideration and enjoyment. The type of the old-fashioned miser is already obsolete except among the uneducated, and if these changes in social structure come to pass it will rapidly be discarded everywhere. The ideal of men with the money-grasping intelligence will be to realise the capacities of a Monte Cristo, not of course for a steady purpose of revenge, but for opportunities of magnificent ostentation.

Summing up, then, we seem to find that we are slowly but demonstrably approaching what we may regard as the age of reason or of a sublimated humanity; and that this will give us a great deal that we are expecting from it—well-ordered polities, security to labour, education, freedom from gross superstitions, improved health and longer life, the destruction of privilege in society and of caprice in family life, better guarantees for the peace of the world, and enhanced regard for life and property when war unfortunately breaks out. It is possible to conceive the administration of the most advanced states so equitable and efficient that no one will even desire seriously to disturb it. On the other hand, it seems reasonable to assume that religion will gradually pass into a recognition of ethical precepts and a graceful habit of morality; that the mind will occupy itself less and less with works of genius, and more and more with trivial results and ephemeral discussions; that husband and wife, parents and children, will come to mean less to one another; and that romantic feeling will die out in consequence; that the old will increase upon the young; that two great incentives to effort, the desire to use power for noble ends, and the desire to be highly esteemed, will come to promise less to capable men as the field of human energy is crowded; and generally that the world will be left without deep convictions or enthusiasm, without the regenerating influence of the ardour for political reform, and the fervour of pious faith which have quickened men for centuries past as nothing else has quickened them, with a passion purifying the soul. It would clearly be unreasonable to murmur at changes that express the realisation by the world of its highest thought, whether the issue be good or bad. The etiolated religion which it seems likely we shall subside upon; the complicated but on the whole satisfactory State mechanism, that will prescribe education, limit industry, and direct enjoyment, will become, when they are once arrived at, natural and satisfactory. The decline of the higher classes as an influence in society, the organisation of the inferior races in menacing forms throughout the Tropical Zone, are the natural result of principles that we cannot disown if we would. It would be impossible for a conservatively-minded monarch to reconstruct the nobility of the eighteenth century in the twentieth; and even now no practical statesman could dream of arresting Chinese power or Hindoo or negro expansion by wholesale massacres. The world is becoming too fibreless, too weak, and too good to contemplate or to carry out great changes which imply lamentable suffering. It trusts more and more to experience; less and less to insight and will.

The Medea of Corneille, face to face with supreme misfortune, was able to say that there at least remained to her herself.[1] But that which is the saving hope of a strong character is the denial of hope to a generation of weak men. What is a society that has no purpose beyond supplying the day's needs, and amusing the day's vacuity, to do with the terrible burden of personality? It is doomed to live on into the ages, with all that the best ordered polity can secure it, with all inherited

[1] "Dans un si grand revers que vous reste-t-il?" "Moi. Moi, dis-j', et c'est assez." *Médée*, Acte ii. Scène 5.

treasures of beauty, with a faith in science that is perpetually mocked by weaker and weaker results, and with no spiritual sense to understand what surrounds it, with the mind's vision growing dim, with the apprehension of art dwarfed to taking comfort in bric-à-brac, with no hope or suggestion of sight beyond the grave. In the old age of the plant the roots continue to thicken out and deepen down, when there is neither blossom nor fruit. The spectacle of an old man with his intellect keen, with his experience bitter, with his appetites unsatiated, with the memory of past enjoyment stinging him, and deprived of the physical power to enjoy, is so familiar that we accept it as one of the commonplaces of life. Scarcely any one remembers that he will in turn live on into such an old age, if he does not sacrifice daily to the invisible powers; and even less does any of us assume that the world may easily put on this form of decrepitude:

> The consummation coming past escape,
> When we shall live most, and yet least enjoy.

Our morality will then be the emasculate tenderness of those who shrink from violence, not because it is a transgression of order, but because it is noisy and coarse; and having outlived strong passions, and the energy by which will translates itself into act, we shall plume ourselves on having abolished vice. Our intellectual discipline will be derived from the year-book and the review, and our intellectual pleasure from the French novel. Yet there seems no reason why men of this kind should not perpetuate the race, increasing and multiplying, till every rood of earth maintains its man, and the savour of vacant lives will go up to God from every home.

As an offset to these forebodings, it is undoubtedly well to remember that the world has passed through evil times before and has outlived them. It may even be admitted that wherever men have reflected enough to occupy themselves with forecasts of the future, their presentiments have been apt to take colour from their surroundings, and have sometimes been needlessly sombre. History tells us that the days upon which Gibbon afterwards looked back as the happiest humanity had known were days in which Christians and Jews were expecting the crash of the world, and in which the wisest of Roman Emperors gave it as a counsel of perfection, that the man who felt God within him should be ready for death as for a trumpet's call.[1] At a later time, which we now look back to as the golden season of romance and chivalry, England was covered with religious foundations created avowedly, as the charter of one of them states, because all things were tending visibly to extinction.[2] In the first of these cases the depression of thoughtful men was greater than the actual state of the world warranted; in the second, than facts later on justified; and yet if Marcus Aurelius could have seen the state of the world in the fifth, sixth, and seventh centuries, or if the pessimists of the thirteenth and fourteenth centuries had lived on into the fifteenth, when Pecock was able to say that "ever more the world decreaseth in people,"[3] they might have found abundant warrant for their despondency. On the other hand, history reminds us

---

[1] "περιμένων τὸ ἀνακλητικὸν ἐκ τοῦ βίου εὔλυτος."—Marc. Aurel. Antonin. lib. iii. p. 38.

[2] "Quia omnia tendunt visibiliter ad non esse."—*Statutes of Oriel College.*

[3] Pecock's *Repressor of overmuch blaming of the Clergy*, part iii. chap. v.

also that there have been two ages in which the world was hopeful and sanguinely self-confident. The first was the period when printing had conquered back a lost territory for the mind, and when the discovery of America offered a new world to Christendom in exchange for the lost East. These dreams of enlightenment and prosperity were the prelude to bloody religious wars extending over more than a century. The second time, of which those who shared its delirium have said, as one great contemporary said of the first, that merely to live in it was a joy, was the period that preceded the French Revolution—a time when men were dreaming that all which philosophy recommended could be inaugurated without bloodshed by decrees and mutual embraces and the planting of trees of liberty. There was some disenchantment from those dreams also. On the whole, neither our despondency nor our cheerful expectation can be assumed to correspond with any real forecast of the future. For a man to argue that he will recover from senile decay because he has outlived fever and a fall from his horse, would clearly be irrational. Neither do we, in fact, attach much importance to arguments of this sort. They are stimulating for a man or a nation in difficulties, but they lack the proportion necessary for comparison when we come to deal with the system of the Universe. What we mostly trust to, perhaps, is the sentiment expressed by Tennyson, that " somehow good will be the final goal of ill," and we either assume that we shall go on to all time vindicating the Creator's purpose by the mellowing perfection of our lives, or at least that we shall be allowed some centuries during which we may mature and sweeten in a world where incalculable terms of life seem already to have been allotted to the lower types. This man argues that we shall last as long as the coal-measures, and this other that there is no reason why the race should die out till the earth itself shall have begun to cool down into a skeleton of rock without atmosphere or central heat. Assume this protracted existence, and it seems natural to suppose that we are at present only in the infancy of man, and to anticipate that our remote descendants may be as far superior to ourselves in polity and intelligence as we are to the tribes of the lake period.

It is natural and perhaps good to indulge in these dreams, which encourage us to continued effort; but it is impossible not to remember that they derive no warrant from the analogies of nature, so far as we can be said to understand the natural world. If the recent surmises of geologists are correct, man has already been an inhabitant of the earth for some very long period, whether we measure it by tens of thousands or hundreds of thousands of years, and has only had a history worth recording for some forty centuries at most. Even during historical times, so-called, the world has mostly been peopled by races, either like the negro very little raised above the level of brutes, or at best, like the lower-caste Hindoo and the Chinaman, of such secondary intelligence as to have added nothing permanent to our stock of ideas. At this moment, though the civilised and progressive races have till quite recently been increasing upon the inferior types, and though the lowest forms of all are being exterminated, there seems, as we have seen, good warrant for assuming that the advantage has already passed to the lower forms of humanity, and indeed it appears to be a well-ascertained law that the races which care little for comfort and decency are bound to tide over bad times better than their superiors, and that the classes which reach the highest standard are proportionally short-lived. Nay, so profusely is life given in excess of what we can account the efficient use made of it, so many purposeless generations seem to pass away before humanity is in travail of a prophet or a thinker, that some inquirers have actually defined the method of creation as a law of waste. "To work in vain," said the author of *The Plurality of Worlds*, "is so far from being contrary to the usual proceedings of nature that it is an operation which is constantly going on in every part of nature." Of the weeds we trample down every one represents a wealth of wasted germs; of the fish that people the deep not one but is the fortunate survivor where, it may be, a million possible existences have perished before birth, and these again, if we go further back, represent other and often higher types that were animate and are extinct. Above us the infinite distances of space are studded with orbs, of almost all of which we can say more or less certainly that if they admit life at all it is not our life. Have we any warrant for assuming that man, the creature of a moment in time, the inhabitant of a speck in space, is really the heir of all the ages, or anything more than a sublimated form of terrestrial life, which will have its youth, its maturity, and its decay like everything else hitherto created. Science, with its record of glacial epochs and its forecast of vanishing heat; religion, with its warning that "the earth and the works that are therein shall be burned up," do not speak of life, but of death.

Happily, what the distant future of the world may be is a matter that does not much concern us, and about which we may rejoice to know nothing. It is quite possible that if the noblest Greeks and Romans had foreseen how short-lived the supremacy of Athens was to be, or at what cost of national character the empire of the world was to be achieved by Rome, they would have folded their arms, or have set sail, as Sertorius thought of doing, in quest of the Fortunate Isles,[1] where life was nothing more than lotos-eating. We are able to see that though the aspirations of patriotism have been defeated, the greater world of humanity has been the richer for what these men ventured and thought. Should it so be that something like what the Norsemen conceived as "the twilight of the gods" is coming upon the earth, and that there will be a temporary eclipse of the higher powers, we may at least prepare for it in the spirit of the Norsemen, who, as the *Ynglinga Saga* tells us, deemed that whether God gave them victory or called them home to himself either award was good.[2] We are so accustomed to the fierce rapture of struggle and victory, to that rough training of necessity by which the weak are destroyed, to revolutions of the political order, transferences of power and wealth, and discoveries in science, that we can hardly conceive a quiet old age of humanity, in which it may care only for sunshine and food and quiet, and expect nothing great from the toil of hand or thought. Knowing something of the limitations and very little of the capabilities of our moral nature, it is perhaps natural we should shrink from the prospect that the classes which have been the depository of refinement and breeding will be submerged below the level of democracy, that dis-

---

[1] "Sertorius . . . conceived a strong desire to fix himself in those islands, where he might live in perfect tranquillity at a distance from the evils of tyranny and war."—Plutarch's *Life of Sertorius*.

[2] *Ynglinga Saga*, chap. x.

tinctions of rank and fortune, of character and intellect, will become unimportant, that the family with its consecrated memories and duties will be transformed into a genial partnership of independent wills, that fancy and imagination will find no expression in literature, and that the faiths for which men have lived and died in times past will only survive as topics of meditation or as the discipline of ethical practice. When the gods of Greece passed away with the great Pan, nature lost its divinity, but society was overshadowed by a holier presence. When Christianity itself began to appear grotesque and incredible, men reconciled themselves to the change by belief in an age of reason, of enlightment, of progress. It is now more than probable that our science, our civilisation, our great and real advance in the practice of government are only bringing us nearer to the day when the lower races will predominate in the world, when the higher races will lose their noblest elements, when we shall ask nothing from the day but to live, nor from the future but that we may not deteriorate. Even so, there will still remain to us ourselves. Simply to do our work in life, and to abide the issue, if we stand erect before the eternal calm as cheerfully as our fathers faced the eternal unrest, may be nobler training for our souls than the faith in progress.

APPENDIX A

PROPORTIONS OF RACES IN TROPICAL AMERICA

Country.	Whites.	Indians.	Mixed.	Negroes.
Mexico (1882)	1,909,000	3,765,044	4,785,940	...
Guatemala (1889)	184,000 ?	876,000	400,000 ?	...
Honduras (1889)	82,000 ?	350,000		...
Salvador (1886)	10,000	654,000		...
Nicaragua	50,000 ?	330,000		...
Costa Rica	40,000 ?	3,500	160,000	...
British Honduras	15,000 ?	26,000	...	...
Colombia (1881)	450,000	1,800,000	1,500,000	120,000
Venezuela (1888)	480,000	326,000	1,200,000	50,000
Peru	474,390	1,832,000	650,000	50,000 Chinese
Ecuador	100,000	890,000	300,000	...
Bolivia	500,000	1,100,000	600,000	...
Brazil	3,787,289	386,955	3,801,787	1,954,452
Paraguay	66,000	130,000	264,000	...
	8,187,679	11,696,999	13,661,727	2,174,452

1,334,000 pure and mixed.

Of these numbers, taken merely from the *Statesman's Year-Book*, it may be observed—

1. That the number of pure whites allotted to Brazil seems extravagantly large. It probably includes all half-castes, except mulattoes.

2. In Guatemala, Honduras, Nicaragua, Costa Rica, and British Honduras, the number of whites is given conjecturally, or by collection, from all estimates. The estimate of whites for Colombia is taken from Lanier's *Amérique du Sud*, p. 372.

3. The last census of Venezuela shows a decisive increase of half-castes and diminution of pure Indians. Former censuses give the numbers as follows :—

	Whites.	Indians.	Half-castes.	Slaves.
1800	200,000	120,000	406,000	62,000
1810 (Alison) . . .	212,000	120,000	341,000	62,000
1839 (Wayle) . . .	260,000	222,000	414,000	50,000

We must take into account in considering Venezuela—(1) that in 1881 there were 34,916 foreign residents of white extraction; (2) that a great many wild Indians have been civilised after a fashion during the last half-century; and (3) that half-castes are bound to increase disproportionately, other things being equal.

4. If the numbers given above are approximately correct, the coloured races, pure and mixed, are as 28,000,000 or 29,000,000 to 8,000,000 or 9,000,000 of whites, or practically white. If, however, the whites are over-calculated for Brazil, as seems certain, the proportion of the coloured to the white races in these regions is probably as four to one. What are the chances that the white races will be reinforced by immigration so as to preserve its present ratio? and, if it is not so reinforced, must it not gradually be absorbed? Putting the Indians out of the question, the negroes alone, though now inferior in numbers to the whites, would easily increase in a century so as to swamp them if the two races multiply in the same proportions as the whites and coloured people of the Black Belt in the United States. It is not at present likely that the negroes will absorb Colombia, Venezuela, or Peru. It seems at least very possible that they will make Brazil practically a negro state with an influential white minority.

5. In the preceding calculation the negroes of the Black Belt in the United States have not been taken into account. It is obvious, however, that from 8,000,000 to 9,000,000 blacks, increasing at a rapid rate, and settling by preference in the warmer climates, are likely at no very distant time to reinforce the coloured population of Central and Southern America. They may contribute a yearly tide of immigrants by sea, simply because they want more space, or the legislation of the United States may be so framed as to dispose them to settle elsewhere. Central America at present would appear to offer them more inducements than Africa.[1]

---

[1] Bryce says of Mexico: "The population was in 1884, 10,460,703, of whom 20 per cent are stated to be pure whites, 43 per cent of mixed races, and the remaining 37 per cent Indians."—*American Commonwealth*, vol. iii. p. 260, note.

APPENDIX B

COMPARATIVE GROWTHS OF WHITE AND BLACK POPULATION IN THE UNITED STATES

	White Population.			
	1890.	1880.	1870.	1860.
Alabama	830,796	662,185	521,384	526,271
North Carolina	1,049,191	867,242	678,470	629,942
South Carolina	458,454	391,105	289,667	291,300
Florida	224,461	142,605	96,057	77,746
Georgia	973,462	816,906	638,926	591,550
Louisiana	554,712	454,954	362,065	357,456
Mississippi	539,703	479,398	382,896	353,899
	4,630,779	3,814,395	2,969,465	2,828,164

	Black Population.			
	1890.	1880.	1870.	1860.
Alabama	681,431	600,103	475,510	437,770
North Carolina	567,170	531,277	391,650	361,522
South Carolina	692,503	604,332	415,814	412,320
Florida	166,678	126,690	91,689	62,677
Georgia	863,716	725,133	545,142	465,698
Louisiana	562,893	483,655	364,210	350,373
Mississippi	747,720	650,291	444,201	437,404
	4,282,111	3,721,481	2,728,216	2,527,764

Of these statistics it may be remarked—

1. That the census of 1870 is regarded as inaccurate, and as erring on the side of imperfect enumeration.

2. The census authorities of the United States say that the increase of the white race in the South since 1830 has not been effected by the aid of immigration, except in Kansas and Missouri. As, however, the whites in the South have increased at the rate of 17 per cent, while the average rate, independent of immigration, has been 14 per cent, it seems as if immigration cannot be disregarded.

3. The great increase of railways in the Southern States since the war of 1862-66 has been accompanied by an increase of towns as distributing centres, and has therefore been favourable to the growth of the white population.

4. Taking the Union all round, the increase for the last ten years—exclusive of immigration—has been 13·90 for the blacks against 14 for the whites. It is claimed that the blacks increased faster only when they were recruited by the slave-trade; and that white immigration has completely turned the balance since then. On the other hand, the diminution of increase among the blacks from 34·82 in 1870-80 to 13·90 in 1880-90 is so vast, even if we allow the preceding census to have been incomplete, as to suggest a doubt whether the negro population has been completely numbered at the last census.

5. Assuming the facts of the last census to be unimpeachable, it seems to result that whites and blacks increase in nearly the same ratio, but that there is in the United States "a perceptible tendency southward of the coloured people." In this case the result will still be to make a belt of States predominantly negro.

6. If we reduce the increase of the whites in the Black Belt by 3 per cent so as to bring it to the normal American rate, their gain upon the negroes during the last ten years will appear to be very trifling.

INDEX

AFGHANISTAN not all mountains, 51
Africa, Central, colonisation of, by whites impossible, 38-41
Agassiz, early training of, 305
Ainos, 49
Albert, Archbishop, on the human heart, 208
Alcibiades charged with impiety, 262
Alexander's successors, effects of wars by, 90
Algeria, 44, 63, note; influence of, upon French society, 124
Almaden, mines of, 107
Amazon, Indians of, 52; whites of, 53
America, Central and Southern, not fitted for white men, 53
America, Southern, clergy control schools, 214
America, tropical, proportions of races in, Appendix A
America, U.S., white population in, 64; emigration to, 96; European heroism more than matched in, 218-220; experience of, about divorce, 245; displacement of office-bearers in, 279; not quite unreasonable, 280
American militia not very successful in War of Independence, and beaten in 1812, 115, 116
Anaxagoras charged with impiety, 262
Angola, 35
Anselm revives philosophy, 90; compassionate to animals, 218
Apaches untameable, 34
Araucanians untameable, 34
Argentine Republic, its circumstances exceptional, 58
Arminius, 89
Arnold, Matthew, failed as a lecturer, 164; jests on the Trinity, 201; responsible for a story about French schools, 223, 224; overpraises small men, 309
Asia, Central, capabilities of, 43, 44

Athens an instance of highly-developed city life, 148; under the best conditions, 156; in the Peloponnesian war, 181, 182; energy of its people, 263
Atrato, mouths of, pestilential, 57
Attila, 90
Australia the best inheritance of the higher races, 16; an instructive instance of new tendencies, 17, 18; peculiarly fitted for settlement, 42; emigration to, 96; urban population in, 142, 143; well-being of its people, 163; splendid chances in, 169; high schools in, 310
Australia, South, and progressive land-tax, 19
Austria gained by Solferino, 141
Austrian Parliament and Darwin, 267
Aztecs, 56; docile, 59

BACON, Roger, 13; pathetic fate of, 212
Balzac paints the French peasant, 169; and filial ingratitude, 297
Bankruptcy, national, examples of, 177, 178; consequences of, 178
Barrios, a half-caste, 56
Baylen, capitulation of, its character, 120
Beaconsfield, Lord, on critics, 307
Belgium, education in, 214
Bell, Graham, invents telephone, 102, note 1
Bell, Patrick, invents reaping-machine, 102, note 1
Beluchistan not all desert, 51, and note
Bert, Paul, revives Pascal's charges, 216
Bichat essentially a thinker, 151
Birkenhead, heroism of men of the, 139
Black Belt, States of the, 60, 62
Blucher's soldiers comparatively barbarous, 140
Boers, 36; occupy Natal, 36; defeat English at Majuba Hill, 114, 121, 122

Bolivia, Indians of, 52; a tropical Switzerland, 58
Booth's analysis of London population, 154
Borde on Englishmen, 99, note
Borneo, Chinese in, 47
Boudeuse, La, captain of, kills prisoners, 139, note
Bourrienne clothes French troops in England, 184, note
Boyle's estimate of Indian population, 54
Bradlaugh edits jest on the Trinity, 201
Brazil unfitted for Europeans, 53; largely negro, 59, 60
British North Borneo Company is stimulating immigration, 49
British rule, its tendencies in India, 51
Browne, Sir T., uncritical, 305
Browning, on the stage, 165; reflective, 167; only honoured when old, 331
Brunswick, Duke of, his invasion of France, 116-118
Bryce on laws restraining immigration, 15, note 2; on town population in America, 143, note 2; on the population of Mexico, 346, note
Buckle's success, 309
Buffon, fascinating style of, 312
Bukhara, 43, note
Bunyan, John, 274
Burke, predictions by, 2, 3; describes ravage of the Carnatic, 82; a worthy expression of English genius, 151
Burleigh's (Lord) view of marriage, 241, note 1
Bury as historian, 313
Bushmen worthless as slaves, 35; exterminated, 36.

CADE, sympathisers with, behead a bishop, 208
Caesar's (Julius) massacres in Gaul, 81: he saves Rome from the patricians, 326
Caesar, Augustus, 326
Calderon gives the primitive view of marriage, 234
California, chances in, 169
Calvin's rigorous discipline, 195
Cambodia, fine ruins in, 91, 92
Canada, consequences of its conquest, 5; mentioned, 44
Canning, prediction by, 3; knew English literature, 311
Canterbury, Archbishop of, opposes undenominational education, 215
Cape Colony, 35, 36
Carera, an Indian, 56
Carlyle approves Frederick II.'s political economy, 107; restricts his social intercourse, 157; only moderately successful as lecturer, 164

Carnatic ravaged, 82
Carnot organises the French army, 118
Cashmere not adapted for colonisation, 35
Castilla, 56
Catholicism parodied, 24
Cato the Younger lends his wife, 229, note 2
Cato the Censor blamed by Plutarch, 239, note 1
Cavaliers not disinterested, 191
Charles II. a rare exception, 190
Chateaubriand, 151
Chatham as orator, 313, 314; gave England an Empire, 326, 327
Chatham, Lord, an incapable general, 280
Chesterfield, Lord, predicts French Revolution, 5; his opinion of Chatham as orator, 313, 314, and note
Child on the Act of Uniformity, 193, note
China has little to dread from civilised nations, 34; her facilities for colonising Turkestan, 43, 44; certain to grow, 45-51; could support a larger population, 64-67; form its development will take, 95, 96; forced into civilisation, 111, 112
Chinamen, 31, 33; mortality of, in Nicaragua, 57; numbers of, in Siam, 66; have supplanted a higher race in Cambodia, 92; probable influence of their example upon Europeans, 123-126; supplant white labour, 125; have added nothing to thought, 341
Choiseul predicts loss of America to England, 5
Cholera, its effects in 1831-32, 153
Christianity copied Paganism, 24
Church has been very useful in the past, 192-194; its authority became intolerable, 194-196; inefficient against blasphemy and immorality, 196-198; could only succeed at the cost of liberty, 199-201; was less capable than the State is of enforcing purity, 201-203; was less capable of tolerance than the State is, 203-205; was inefficient in its dealing with pauperism, 205-209; and with slavery, 209-211; and has everywhere opposed a thorough system of national education, 211-216; has lost its hold on popular imagination, 216, 217; has a lower humanity than the State, 217-220; has evaded the recognition of divorce, 235; discourages critical examination, 264; distrusts the growing power of the State, 266
Cicero loathes life out of Rome, 148

Cid, story of, consistent with the times, 233
Clive a typical Englishman, 100 ; of a type disappearing, 263
Cobden the real author of Free Trade, 331
Cochin China, fine ruins in, 91
Coghill, Dr. M., approved corporal correction for a wife, 251
Coleridge, moderately successful as lecturer, 164 ; on Shakespeare, 307 ; as journalist, 318
Colley, Sir G., character of his defeat, 121, 122
Commin of Deuwick invents reaping-machine, 102, note 1
Comoy, John, demises his wife, 230, note 2
Congo, anticipations about the region of the, 31
Corneille modernises the story of the *Cid*, 233 ; his *Medea* quoted, 337
Cortez, 33, 34
Courier, 151 ; transformed by jealousy, 297 ; a transcendent journalist, 319, 320 ; on literary reputation, 332
Cousin on the source of inspiration in writers, 320
Cowley overrated by Johnson, 308
Criticism invaluable and fairly certain in science, 304-306 ; influenced by fashion and feeling in taste, 306, 307 ; apt to be too favourable, 307-309 ; likely to decline still further as the highest standards are disused, 310, 311
Cromwell, Puritan and Roman elements in, 275 ; adopts promotion by merit, 279 ; impossible in modern England or the United States, 327, 328

DALTON's discovery unsurpassable, 291
Dante perhaps a gainer by exile, 149 ; and by city life, 150 ; proscribed by Rome, 264
Darwin, Erasmus, dreams of, 290, and note
Darwin not a liver in cities, 157 ; proscribed by Rome, 264 ; belief in, 267 ; value of his discovery, 291, 303 ; admirable style of, 312 ; varied work by, 313
Davis, President, eulogised by Gladstone, 4
Death, Black, effects of, 153
Debts, national, often rightly incurred, 170, 171 ; or on plausible grounds, 171-173 ; may be dangerous, 173, 174 ; because (1) the State undertakes too much, 174, 175 ; and (2) then national integrity breaks down under the burden, 175-177

Decrès ou the term of service, 119
Democracy, real meaning of, 109, 261
Demosthenes, 315
Diaz, Porfirio, of mixed descent, 55
Dickens as lecturer, 164
Diocesan courts, 195, and note
Directory, French, issues orders denying quarter to Englishmen, 139
Disraeli on Peel, 330
Drake, 262
Dramatic poetry is dying out because passions are weaker, 296-298 ; and because topics have been exhausted, 298, 299
Dryden as a critic, 306, 307
Duff, Grant, on Indian reforms, 83 ; on effects of Thirty Years' War, 90, note
Dumas the younger, 167
Dutch at the Cape, 35, 36 ; in Natal, 36, 37 ; in Java, 42

ECCLESIASTICAL court, powers of, 196
Ecuador, Indians in, 52 ; whites in, 54 ; a tropical Switzerland, 58
Education, State, a necessity, 11
Edward III.,debts not yet paid, 177
Eliot, George, restricts her social intercourse, 157 ; was praised for inferior work, 309
Emancipation, slave, a sound bargain, 171
Emigration weakens national feeling, 257, 258
Emigrés, French, disloyal to their country, 190 ; well compensated, 191
England, treatment of children in, 246, and note ; is indebted to alien immigrants, 285
English debt being reduced, 171
English race, tendency of, to State Socialism, 96-98

FAME always capriciously given, 329-331 ; and likely to be more evenly distributed hereafter than now, 331-333
Family, unit of State, 228 ; powers of the paterfamilias anciently very great, 228-231 ; the blood-feud, 231-233 ; rights over life in, 233-235
Family feeling, advantages of, 253-256
Ferrar, Nicholas, 274
Finlay as historian, 313
Flemings, settlement of, in England, 283
Fletcher of Saltoun on Scotch pauperism, 208
Fleury a peace-loving minister, 137
Fonblanque on Peel, 330
Fortescue quoted, 96
Foy, General, on insurrectionary soldiers,

116; on reforms in French organisation, 117
Fox, predictions by, 3; knew the classics, 311
France, Reign of Terror in, 25, 26; increase of population in, 68, 74, 75; outstrips England in ironclads, 103; adaptable to the stationary state, 105; gained by defeat at Sedan, 141; education in, 215, 216; law and practice of marriage in, 231, 240-243
Francis, St., condemns intellect, 212; compassionates animals, 218
Frederick II., 46; his economical policy, 107; his ambition, 137
French army, size of, in 1740, 95, note 2
French princes, profligacy of, 198
French society broken up by the Second Empire, 158
Frobisher, 262
Froeschwiller, French cuirassiers at, 139
Future life, belief in, impaired, 271, 273

GALDOS paints Spanish villager, 169
Garibaldi worked as a soap-boiler, 286
Garrick made Shakespeare popular, 307
George IV. not reproved by the Church, 198
Germanic standard of chastity high, 239
Germany is driving out the Poles, 285
Gibbon, estimate by, of Roman subjects, 67; criticised by Maurice, 89, note; his excellent work, 303, 304; the best Church historian, 304, and note; his concision, 313; his expectation of life, 323; his estimate of the time of the Antonines, 339
Gilbert, admirable work of, 166
Gladstone, eulogy of President Davis by, 4
Gobelins, tapestry of, 107
Goethe on English inventiveness, 102, note 2; on progress, 203; on the beginnings of a science, 313; his literary articles, 318
Goldsmith predicts changes in France, Germany, Holland, and Sweden, 5, 6
Gray's view of the attributes of power, 328
Great men careless of gain, 288; their importance circumscribed in modern society, 326, 328
Greeks comparatively exterminated, 69; appreciated city life, 147
Grey Town pestilential, 57
Grote, Mrs., disapproves marriage for men of genius, 253
Guaranis, 56; docile, 59
Guardia, a half-caste, 56

Guatemala, few whites in, 33, 54
Guerillas of no real utility, 121

HALE, Sir M., uncritical, 305
Hamerton on French society, 202, notes; vindicates French schools, 224; on the effects of marriage, 253
Hamilton, predictions by, 6
Hare's theory popularised by newspaper discussion, 317
Hastings, Warren, not moral, by modern standards, 202; his type disappearing, 262
Hawthorne criticises Englishmen, 100
Heine predicts defeat of France by Germany, 7; criticises Englishmen, 100; his political articles, 318
Henry VIII., his aims 193, and note
Henry's (Patrick) oratory, 314, 315
Herschel on earthquakes, 141
Hindoos, 33, 34; increase of, 76; have added nothing to thought, 341
Holberg's estimate of Englishmen, 99-101
Holland, education denominational in, 214
Homer perhaps influenced by town life, 150; comparatively forgotten, 332
Honduras impossible for Europeans, 57
Horace on barbarian wives, 238, note 1
Hottentots, few, at Cape in 1795, 36
Howe improves sewing-machine, 102, note 1
Hugo, Victor, appreciates John Brown, 6, 7; his greatness as a dramatist, 167
Huguenots at the Cape, 35; in England, 283
Humaita, 33
Hutton's (R. H.) work as a journalist, 318
Hyder Ali ravages the Carnatic, 82

IBSEN partially appreciated, 167, 168
Ili, Chinese immigration into, 66; massacres in, 82; Mahommedanism stamped out in, 131
Immigration, alien rights of, everywhere restrained, 283-285; unfortunate consequences of this restraint, 285-287
India, its people too numerous to be exterminated, 34; character of reforms in, 83
Indians, 34; not dangerous in Argentine, 58; occupy fertile niches of Peru, etc., 58
Inkerman, English infantry at, 139
Ireland, population in, 68
Irishmen, increase of, 69, 70, 75, 76

Italy adaptable to the stationary state, 105; a gainer by war, 141

JAPANESE, 31, 32
Java, climate of, 42
Jemappes won by half-trained troops, 118
Jevons, Prof., on the coal-measures, 174, note
Jews in Russia, 76-80; capable of of agriculture, 77; causes of their increase, 78, 79; appear a danger to the Empire, 80
Johnson, Dr., a lover of town life, 147; social sphere of, 157; his estimate of Cowley and Shakespeare, 307; of Savage and Gray, 308
Juarez, 33, 55
Junius, a journalist, 318; overrated, 319
Juvenal praises city life, with a reservation, 148, 149; too vehement for modern times, 293

KAFFIRS take refuge under British rule, 36
Kanakas, some qualities of the, 32
Kant's estimate of Englishmen, 99; on patriotism, 183
Keble on a moral order, 268, 269
Kempis on predestination, 268; his view generally taken, 269
Kloster-Zeven, capitulation of, 122
Knowles, Sheridan, value of success of, 165

LABOUR, its regulation by law inevitable, 12
Lacordaire, why silenced, 194
Las Casas, 210
Laveleye on communal property, 106
Law, Mississippi scheme of, 177
Leibnitz, his doctrine of eternal life, 272
Lely on Englishmen, 99, note
Lesseps, M. de, vindicates climate of Nicaragua, 57
Lewis, Cornewall, predictions by, 4-6
Life may be prolonged by science, 321, 322; and this will be a gain to knowledge, 323; and to political order, 323-324; but will rob life of brightness and energy, 324-326
Local feeling dying out, 258
London, riotous meetings in, 281
Lords, House of, if abolished, 109
Louis XV., 190; censured by the Church, 197, 198
Lowell on patriotism, 183, 184
Loyola's conversion, 269
Luther's old name for the Turks, 133; perplexed by the liberty of the Reformation, 195; on temptations, 268
Lytton, Bulwer, success of, on the stage, 165

MACAULAY on Junius, 319
M'Cormick patents reaping-machine in America, 102, note 1
Machiavel uses uncritical materials, 305
Magyars crowded out in Hungary, 69
Mahommedanism a possible force in China, 131-133
Mahommedans of Yunnan, 34; of China, 132
Mahrattas, desolation caused by, 321
Maine's success, 309; work in journalism, 318
Maistre, De, paradox by, 141; on teaching religion, 216
Malaysia, capabilities of, 42, 43
Malthus, doctrines of, 142
Maories, 32
Marcus Aurelius, 89; his despondency, 339
Marlborough superseded by Wellington, 332
Marriage anciently indissoluble, 236-238; idea of purity imported into, 238-240; the marriage of suitability, 240-243; is being superseded by the marriage of inclination, which implies divorce, 243-245; and at least tends to weaken the marriage bond, 245-247; diminished importance of, favours individualism, 251-253
Mars-la-Tour, heroism of German infantry at, 139
Mashonaland, future of, 31
Matabeleland, future of, 31
Mauritius, decay of French in, 76
Meeting, public right of, everywhere restrained, 281, 282
Meissen, porcelain of, 107
Mejia, 33, 55
Mendez, 56
Merv, 43, note, 44
Meteren's estimate of Englishmen, 99
Mexico, Indians of, not exterminated, 33; whites can labour in, 33; population of, how composed, 54, 55; ruling class white, 56; use of guerillas revived in, 121
Michelet on French revolutionary levies, 116
Military education likely to be generalised, 136; in some respects advantageous to character, 138-141, 265
Mill condemns State labour, 107, 108; a master of style, 311, 312
Milton perhaps a gainer by solitude, 149
Milton a product of Puritan and Hellenic

influences, 273 ; his poetry compared with Burke's prose, 300-302
Mirabeau approves Frederick II.'s political economy, 107
Molière may become archaic, 332
Moltke's (Von) soldiers comparatively humane, 141
Monasteries and pauperism, 205, 206
Money, love of, likely to be a permanent force, 333-335 ; will be desired from more selfish motives than now, 335, 336
Montaigne's allusions to well-known names, 332
Morality not easily distinguished from religion, 265
Morazan, 56
More, Sir Thomas, his principles of action, 193 ; his doctrine of prayer, 170
Moreau, a civilian-made soldier, 118
Morocco, 44
Morris, his conception of a reformed England, 27
Mozambique, 35

NAPOLEON I., forecasts by, 7, 8 ; estimate of French revolutionary levies by, 117-119 ; his wars reduced French stature, 153 ; he regulates divorce, 238 ; adopts promotion by merit, 279 ; rescued France from anarchy, 326, 327 ; is becoming impossible in France, 328 ; his view of fame, 331
Napoleon, Louis, believed in by English society, 4 ; called a tyrant, 194 ; not reproved by the clergy, 198
Nasmyth, 101 ; his hammer first used in Creuzot, 102
Natal, example of, 36-38
Needle-gun tried and rejected by English officers, 103
Negroes, American, dangerous increase of, 10, 11, 59-63. Appendices A, B
Nelson would not be allowed to save the Empire, 202
Newman, J. H., avoids London, 157
Newspapers are superseding the pamphlet, the book of travel, and the philosophical argument, 315-317
Newton discovered the one great secret, 291 ; made it familiar, 303
Nicander Nucius on Englishmen, 99, note
Nicaragua, few whites in, 33 ; impossible for Europeans, 57 ; filibusters meant to work in, with slaves, 58
Nicholas I., 9
Nicias, timidity of, 263
Noblemen, English, die out rapidly, 70-73
Novel, the, cannot take the place of poetry, 301, 302

OGLE on the migration of population, 144, 155
Olmsted on comparative health of white and negro, 62
Ontario, education law in, 214
Orissa, famine in, 84
Orton's (Professor) views about Indians, 52 ; about whites in the Amazon, 53 ; finds an Indian governor, 56
Ovid loathes life out of Rome, 148

PAKENHAM beaten before New Orleans, 115
Palatines, settlement of, in England, 283
Palmerston controlled by his supporters, 327
Parents and children, legal relations of, 247-249 ; partly superseded by State control, 249-251
Paris like Athens and Rome, 149, 263
Pascal a Jansenist, 274 ; a Puritan of speculative genius, 275 ; a writer for the day's need, 318
Patriotism will become increasingly important, 181, 182 ; a virtue of a peculiar kind, 182-185 ; a very mixed virtue, 185-187 ; is gradually taking definite shape, 187, 188 ; and becoming more possible in its best form, 188-190 ; a higher feeling than loyalty, 190-192
Pauperism in England and Scotland, 208, 209
Pecock, Bishop, disgraced, 213 ; statement of, about population, 339
Peel knew English literature, 311 ; was steadily reviled, 330, 331
Pennsylvania, repudiation by, 176
Pepys, Samuel, 256
Pericles charged with impiety, 262
Persia, population of, 52 ; Shah of, 93
Peru, Indians of, not exterminated, 33 ; a tropical Switzerland, 58 ; early civilisation of, 91
Peter the Great, 8, 46 ; his treatment of his son, 229, 230
Peterborough a typical Englishman, 100
Philip II.'s treatment of his son, 229, 230
Philippe, Louis, a teacher, 284
Philoctetes, 148
Pitt attacked for purity of his life, 201
Pizarro, 33, 34
Plate, Lower, whites can labour in, 33
Plato's imperishable prose, 312
Pliny, social sphere of, 157
Poetry is dying out, except lyrical, 292-295 ; which is becoming richer and more various, 295, 296 ; but which may soon be exhausted, 300, 301. *See* Drama

INDEX

Police, how recruited in London, 154, note
Pompey, 239, note 1
Population, increase of, difficult to predict, 67, 68; methods to stint may be adopted, 130
Prayer, belief in, modified, 269-271
Protection likely to be adopted by the higher races, 128-130
Protestantism copied Catholicism, 24
Protestants, early outrages by, 200
Prussia a first-rate power, 110
Prussian army, size of, in 1740, 95, note 1
Ptolemais as described by Synesius, 182
Puritans favour Church interference, 196; awake to repress incontinence, 198; Puritan superstition, 268; the Puritan household, 275, 276

Ramus silenced, 213
Reformation, the work of men under forty, 325
Reichshoffen, French cuirassiers at, 139
Rémusat, De, on Junius, 319
Renaissance, the, excited great hopes, 340
Reuchlin attacked, 213
Revolution, French, the work of men under forty, 325; excited great hopes, 340
Revolutions likely to be less violent, 322, 329
Richelieu a dictator, 326
Rochambeau powerfully assists the Americans, 115
Rogers, Professor, on condition of working-class anciently, 127
Roland, Mdme., marriage of, 241, 242
Roman Empire under Trajan, 87, 88; causes of its decline, 88, 90; despondency attending its break-up, 321
Roman law of marriage, 236
Ross of Bladensburg beats American militia, 115
Rothschild smuggles gold, 184, note
Rousseau predicts Revolution, 5; unlike Voltaire, 150; his treatment of his children reprobated, 229; superstitious experiment by, 268, note 3
Rowe, 307
Russia and Turkestan, 43, 44; effects of conquest by, in Turkey in Asia, 63; capable of supporting a large population, 105; strong for aggression, 110; has aims on Persia, 111; gained by defeat in Crimea, 141; is oppressing Jews and Germans, 285; is largely indebted to foreigners, 285;
Russian army, size of, in 1740, 95 note 1

Saffi taught in Oxford, 286
Saint invents sewing-machine, 102 note 1
St. Aignan, 241.
St. Simon's view of marriage, 241, and note 1
Salvation Army, 156
Sand's (G.) views on marriage, 243-245
Sanguin, 241
San Sebastian, surrender of, 139; atrocities at, 140, note
Saragossa, defences of, their character, 120, 121
Sardou, 167
Science not reconcilable with faith, 288-290; is ceasing to impress the imagination, 290-292
Scotland, increase of population in, 75
Scotchmen frugal, 169
Scott, Sir W., did admirable work, 301; yet may be superseded, 302
Senegambia, 35
Sepoy outrages, 82
Sertorius thought of sailing for the Fortunate Isles, 343
Servants, changed relations of, to employers, 256, 257
Sèvres, porcelain of, 107
Sewell on the typical vertebra, 305
Shaftesbury, Lord, legislation by, 154
Shakespeare on the stage, 165; his songs, 168; his tragedy of *Lear*, 297
Shelburne, Lord, prediction by, 2
Shelley on the stage, 165; ostracised, 286, 302; not read in his lifetime, 331
Sheridan's oratory, 313, 314
Shirley on English pedigrees, 71
Shrewsbury, 210
Sidgwick (Prof. H.) on patriotism, 183
Smith, Adam, on mortality, 153, 154
Smith (H. J. S., Prof.) on constructive chemistry, 291; on the crowding-out of talent, 331
Smith, 210
Socialism, State, its essential aims in land laws, 20; how it may be introduced, 103-105; what influences will modify it, 122, 123; it may tend to promote health, 321
Socrates charged with impiety, 262
Spain, possessions of, under Philip II., 92, 93; praised for policy, 93; capable of supporting a large population, 105
Spaniards, greatness of, 93
Staël, Auguste de, advised by Napoleon, 286
Staël, Mdme. de, why she loved Paris, 149

State activity, increase of, 18-22 ; value of, to the modern citizen, 224-226
Stationary state, its good and evil, 336-338 ; arguments against it; 339-341 ; invalid, 341, 342
Statistical Bureau of U.S., estimate by, 61
Strafford, a traitor, 190
Straits Settlement, Chinese in, 46, 47, and note
Straw, Jack, confession of, 208, note
Sweden, increase of population in, 70
Swift's view of servants, 256 ; a transcendent journalist, 319 ; on the ill-fate of great men, 329, 330
Swinburne on the stage, 165 ; sometimes irreverent, 201
Szechuen, fluctations of population in, 65

TACITUS praises the Germans, 89 ; social sphere of, 157 ; on German marriages, 235 ; compared with Virgil, 302
Tae-Pings, character of their revolt, 34 ; how put down, 83 ; its effect on society, 34
Taine on English family life, 246, note 1
Talleyrand praises Hamilton, 6 ; his sagacity, 8, and note
Tara, Hill of, meeting at, forbidden, 281
Tarragona, storm of, 140
Tartufe, a representative of the religious man of his day, 274
Temper of European nations likely to change, 130, 131
Tennyson on the stage, 165 ; has changed the Arthurian legend for the worse, 296 ; his view of longevity, 322 ; his optimism, 340
Texas, whites can labour in, 33 ; its precedent, 59
Thackeray as lecturer, 164
Thirty Years' War, 81 ; its effect, 90
Thomas buys patent of sewing-machine, 102, note 1
Ticknor, M., prognostications by, 135, 170
Tocqueville, De, predictions by, 6, 8 ; statement about French society by, 151 ; re-cast a portion of modern history, 303 ; not exhaustive, 304
Towns increasing upon the country, 142, 143 ; partly because of improved communication, 143-145 ; partly because education makes men social and ambitious, 145-147 ; partly because city life stimulates talent, 147-150 ; though no fixed law can be laid down as to this, 150-152. But city life is unhealthy, 152-154 ; though much is being done to improve it, 154, 155 ; and the town population is only kept vigorous by country immigrants, 155, 156. The old cities were open to country influences, and with a manageable society, 156-158. The tendency is for the individual to dwindle in town-life, 158-160. Family feeling withers up in town, 160-162 ; nor can improved conditions of policy altogether remedy this, 162, 163. On the other hand, towns offer women relief from ennui, 163, 164 ; though the intellectual interests stimulated are not the highest, 164-166 ; as the drama is dying, 166-168 ; the music-hall vulgar, 168. It seems accidental that avarice is less a passion in towns than in the country, 168, 169
Towton, battle of, 132
Transylvania, movement of population in, 69
Trevisano, Andrea, on Englishmen, 99, note
Trinidad, the marshes of, pestilential, 57
Tripoli, 44
Tunis, 44
Tschernischevski, dreams of, 290, and note
Turkestan, Eastern, 43, note, 44
Turkestan, Western, Russia may colonise, 45
Turkish Empire, dissolution of, predicted, 8 ; inevitable, 45 ; greatness of, in 16th century, 93
Turks depress higher races, 68 ; moral character of, 94, 95 ; how called by Luther, 133
Tyler's followers behead an archbishop, 208

UNDERHILL, 210
United States filling up rapidly, 14, 15 ; the better for the War of Independence, 141 ; urban population in, 142, 143

VALERIUS, Maximus, on continence, 239
Valmy, a victory by half-trained troops, 118
Venezuela, described by Eastwick, 59
Verbrugghe, M., defends climate of Nicaragua, 57
Victoria and State landlordism, 19 ; State employees in, 21, 22 ; effects of Chinese labour in, 125 ; clergy of, oppose State education, 215 ; having failed to educate, 215 ; law of divorce in, 239 ; Medical Board of, refused to register a Chinese doctor, 283, 284 ; its teaching service a close one, 284 ; death-rate of children in, 322
Virginia, a mere breeding-place, 210

Voltaire on earthquakes, 141 ; his influence, 150 ; on Shakespeare, 307

WALPOLE, a peace-loving Minister, 137
War never likely to be replaced by arbitration, 136-138
Webster, 167
Wellington, predictions by, 3, 4 ; wrong forecast of, by Napoleon, 8 ; forbids English and French outposts to mingle, 140, note ; extenuates atrocities at San Sebastian, 141
Wieliczka, mine of, 107
Wiener's views about Indians in Peru, 52, 53 ; knows a half-caste priest, 56
Women, how affected by changes in society, 276-279

Wurtemberg, depopulation of, in Thirty Years' War, 81, 82

YNGLINGA SAGA, quoted, 343
York, Duke of, employed, though provedly incapable, 280
Young's (Arthur) sound estimate of the Revolution, 6
Yunnan, 34 ; massacres in, 82 ; Mahommedanism stamped out in, 131

ZAMBESI, anticipations about the region of the, 33
Zealand, New, and progressive land-tax, 19, 329
Zulus, 36, 37

THE END

www.ingramcontent.com/pod-product-compliance
Lightning Source LLC
Chambersburg PA
CBHW020233240426
43672CB00006B/507